AF323734

We live in unusual times, not just because of the pandemic or the serious economic crisis, which we unfortunately still have recent memories of. What is unprecedented is that the pandemic has generated a global reaction and the severe crisis stems from the deliberate decisions of governments to paralyze many sectors of the economy, all at the same time. No doubt, states were decisively managing multiple challenges. But how are we all going to get out of this situation? And what role will governments play from now on when dealing with market failures and bailouts that they themselves may have unwittingly caused? Lim Hwee Hua has extensive experience in business and public policy. The perspectives and the cases in this book will help us to better understand the world we live in.

Pedro Passos Coelho — Former Prime Minister, Portugal

"Government in Business: Leading or Lagging" is a comprehensive explanation of government's role in our complicated digital world. Lim Hwee Hua's knowledge of technology, innovation, politics and the relationship between public and private interests shines through in every chapter. Lim Hwee Hua's book is a well written and informative guide for those who regulate and for those regulated.

George Roberts, Co-Chairman/Co-CEO, Kohlberg Kravis & Roberts

Lim Hwee Hua is uniquely placed to share her observations and insights in her latest book "Government in Business: Leading or Lagging" as her rich experience straddles both the public and private sectors. Her book is not just an academic commentary but is based on extensive research into how governments around the world function to balance the interests of citizens and entrepreneurs/innovators to ensure that goods and services provided serve the overall interests of the public and not some vested parties. Her observations in the book are illustrated by 64 case studies drawn from around the world. It makes for a very interesting read for both the public policy makers and the business sector/entrepreneurs who would find it useful to know how governments operate.

Wong Kan Seng, Former Deputy Prime Minister, Singapore/
Chairman, UOB Bank

Lim Hwee Hua has enjoyed a scintillating career across the board. She was Singapore's first woman Cabinet minister. Prior to that and post retirement from politics, she has been actively engaged in financial services, especially private equity, and sat on the boards of a wide range of businesses. Hence, Lim Hwee Hua writes with authority on the forces that determine the survival, peace and prosperity of a national jurisdiction. Each nation has its own genius, which determines how it fares in an uncertain, and occasionally turbulent, world. Every nation has lessons, for better or worse, to offer the world. It is up to each country, both the public and private sector players, to determine how it may benefit from a close study of those lessons.

Joseph Y Pillay, Former Chairman, Council of Presidential Advisors/ Permanent Secretary/Chairman, Singapore Airlines

This book provides cogent and profound analysis on the perennial question of the role of government in business. It is singularly significant, however, in addressing head-on the complex nexus or convergence that informs governments and the business sectors, including rapid advances in technology; governance, politics and societal expectations; the environment and national security. What's more, it is replete with real-world examples that well illustrate some of the complex, and often times conflicting demands that governments must navigate and manage. All throughout, the challenges, and opportunities, posited by ever accelerating pace of change, remain a constant theme. An invaluable book.

Marty Natalegawa, Former Foreign Minister, Indonesia

This book is most opportune in addressing the recurring topic of Government in Business in fast changing times. Forty years ago, Ronald Reagan and Margaret Thatcher rolled back the role of Government in the economy and led a new era globally with liberalisation and a return to free enterprise and freer markets. Following the Global Financial Crisis and now the COVID pandemic plaguing the world, the policy direction for many if not most Governments has been reversing at this time. Besides having to intervene in unprecedented ways and scales in these crises to

chorus of both inspiring and disheartening cases supports the fundamental reflections on the tensions that exist and how to find the right balance.

Didier Cossin, Professor of Governance/Founder
and Director of IMD Global Board Center

Lim Hwee Hua has brought to the fore the challenges governments and regulators face in regulating businesses in the context of Today. This is also a guide to good governance as well as good business. The book is timely, thought-provoking in the context of public governance, market failure, social needs, political aspirations in this fast-changing, technologically-driven world, and in the midst of a pandemic. The amazing examples make the reading easy and yet provide in-depth insights into the challenges on both the public and private sector fronts. I am sure this book will be read and re-read for generations to come and will be a beacon of understanding of the intricacies of the government–business interface.

Muhammed Aziz Khan, Founder-Chairman,
Summit Group of Companies

Timeless yet timely, this book provides insights into the challenges faced by policy makers in navigating private sector innovation and the ever-changing landscape. Topics discussed span a wide range of issues with highly relevant case studies — from the Sharing Economy to the rise of Financial Technology and Cryptocurrency. Having served in the Singapore Cabinet, including as a minister in the Prime Minister's Office, and helmed several leadership roles in the private sector, Lim Hwee Hua provides a well-balanced view from both the public and private sectors. Recognition of the need for government involvement to maintain stability and equity is tempered with the foresight of the pitfalls of overregulation. Ultimately, this book provides good examples of effective public–private collaboration. An informative read, this book appeals to policy-makers, entrepreneurs and those seeking to understand the complexities of policy-making.

Eugene Zhu, Founder/CEO and Board Member,
Asia Pacific Exchange

GOVERNMENT IN BUSINESS
LEADING OR LAGGING?

Published by

World Scientific Publishing Co. Pte. Ltd.

5 Toh Tuck Link, Singapore 596224

USA office: 27 Warren Street, Suite 401-402, Hackensack, NJ 07601

UK office: 57 Shelton Street, Covent Garden, London WC2H 9HE

Library of Congress Cataloging-in-Publication Data
Names: Lim, Hwee Hua, author.
Title: Government in business : leading or lagging? / Hwee Hua Lim.
Description: New Jersey : World Scientific, [2021] | Earlier edition published 2013. |
    Includes bibliographical references and index.
Identifiers: LCCN 2020051965 | ISBN 9789811232367 (hardcover) |
    ISBN 9789811232473 (paperback) | ISBN 9789811232374 (ebook) |
    ISBN 9789811232381 (ebook other)
Subjects: LCSH: Industrial policy. | Business enterprises--Government policy. |
    Economic policy.
Classification: LCC HD3611 .L526 2021 | DDC 338.9--dc23
LC record available at https://lccn.loc.gov/2020051965

British Library Cataloguing-in-Publication Data
A catalogue record for this book is available from the British Library.

For any available supplementary material, please visit
https://www.worldscientific.com/worldscibooks/10.1142/12162#t=suppl

Desk Editors: Balamurugan Rajendran/Daniele Lee

Typeset by Stallion Press
Email: enquiries@stallionpress.com

GOVERNMENT IN BUSINESS
LEADING OR LAGGING?

LIM HWEE HUA

World Scientific

NEW JERSEY · LONDON · SINGAPORE · BEIJING · SHANGHAI · HONG KONG · TAIPEI · CHENNAI · TOKYO

Preface

When I began exploring and expanding on the various themes around the evergreen debate of government in business, never had I thought that I would witness the about-turn of long-held assertions all in the space of less than a year. Where it was fashionable not too long ago to incline towards a "less government, more market" economy, the Covid-19 pandemic has turned almost everything on its head. All at once, the government had to take control of everything — from the regulation of the procurement of surgical masks and personal protective equipment to oversight of both public and private healthcare facilities to the availability of test kits. On the economic front, some of the harshest, but deemed absolutely necessary, steps taken pertained to grounding all activity to a halt.

The pandemic's consequences are mind-boggling — all economies will remain severely dented for a while. Unemployment has spiked and households are crumbling from healthcare fears and joblessness. Very quickly, it has become virtually an "all government, no market" situation. Many governments have scrambled to mount a series of rescue or stimulus packages, all aimed at a combination of providing relief to the people from the ensuing hardship and stimulus to kick-start the economy. Their packages, which are far larger than anything in recent memory, would have a long debilitating effect on each country's financial wherewithal, some unfortunately, permanently. The financial woes do not stop here — many governments are duty-bound to bail out essential businesses. Given the global travel restrictions, airlines have crashed badly. Hitherto, many an airline company had already been struggling to balance its books. The pandemic has brought many airlines, including the well-run ones, to their knees and presented many governments, regardless of ownership, with bailout obligations. The list goes on.

Regardless of how long it will take for the global economy to recover from the pandemic, my expectation is that once normalcy is restored, albeit new normal, the same debate and themes would re-emerge. It would once again revolve around the various roles that government should play and the extent to which it should intervene, especially in newer areas of innovation.

Chapters 1 and 2 focus on the innovation-centred economic transformation. Innovation, enabled by technology, will continue to lead to a proliferation of services that straddle domains and geographies. The sharing economy, be it ride-sharing or accommodation-sharing, provides useful lessons on the inherent challenges encountered by both the private and public sectors. Likewise, fintech will continue to delight consumers while posing challenges to regulators. Where innovation encroaches onto a regulated domain, the state is forced to respond. Is the criticism of the government as a lagging regulator valid? Are there occasions when intervention may be justified?

Chapter 3 tracks the many aspirations that would require the government to partner the private sector so as to realise growth ambitions. This is all the more so post the pandemic, given the now empty public coffers in many countries. Yet, many Public–Private Partnerships have come to grief. What steps can governments take to minimise such risks?

Chapter 4 discusses government bailouts, which now take on greater prominence. With regard to the pandemic, there is no shortage of examples where a state bailout has been the only way out. This bailor-of-last-resort role, regrettably, will survive the pandemic. For as long as a country has too-big-to-fail national icons, especially banks and bloated state enterprises, there will always be the social pressure to mount a rescue for the economy's sake.

Chapter 5 dwells on an emerging widespread political reality. Populism, and the resulting short-termism, will continue to pose the greatest challenge to any planning for the long term or for sustainable growth. Some governments wilfully conflate their various roles towards political ends. Meanwhile, others encounter shifting expectations of the populace of the type of public goods and services required.

Chapter 6, taken together with Chapter 3, discusses the many instances of market failure that only the government is in a position to address. The more obvious undertakings pertain to infrastructural development. The longer term, and often ignored priorities include the unpopular economic restructuring and climate change responsibilities.

Chapter 7 examines the increasingly frequent use of the "national security or strategic" argument to reject a foreign investment which can smack of xenophobia. This is currently in full play, thanks to the pandemic, as geopolitical considerations dominate rather than whether there are truly risks to opening up certain key or sensitive sectors. Conversely, social services tend to be an area where many governments remain coy about active participation.

My conclusion after researching into the various examples and examining the public–private divide in many markets is that the degree of economic participation has to be dynamic, not least because innovation and technology move at an unforgiving pace. Governments these days do not have the luxury of public policy formulation and execution time like before. Neither will regulatory frameworks remain relevant forever. More than ever, close and active collaboration with the private and people sectors would be crucial to any government's stance, in a bid to avoid being branded as lagging.

Writing this book has been a great learning experience for me. As it was for my first book, I have been very fortunate to be able to receive the wise counsel and help with verification of cases from many friends. In particular, I wish to thank former Sri Lanka Prime Minister Ranil Wickremesinghe, Ali Qassim Jawad, Cheong Koon Hean, Hassan Abbas Abas, Muhammed Aziz Khan/Arun Sen, Pang Yee Ean, Seah Moon Ming, the Royal Golden Eagle team, Zhang Xumin and Steven Phan.

This book would not have been possible without the diligent eye and guidance of Chua Hong Koon and Daniele Lee, the witty illustrations by Nic Haliem, and the very able support of my researchers, Clara Tan, Chelsea Ong and Lau Wen Loong.

I remain indebted too to the many friends who have so kindly and patiently agreed to review the book, and provided invaluable advice — former Portugal Prime Minister Pedro Passos Coelho, my former Cabinet colleague Wong Kan Seng, George Roberts, Marty Natalegawa, Joseph Y Pillay, Hsieh Fu Hua, Andreas Sohmen-Pao, Ben Keswick, Didier Cossin, Muhammed Aziz Khan and Eugene Zhu.

Last but not least, I thank my husband Andy and the rest of my family members for their moral and emotional support. I hope you will find this book as helpful as I have had fun putting it all together.

Lim Hwee Hua
July 2020

SECURITY
BAILOUTS
NATIONAL
INTERESTS

About the Author

 **Lim Hwee Hua** enjoys a unique position of having straddled both the private and public sectors for extensive periods of time. She was first elected to Parliament in December 1996 and served till May 2011, last as Minister in the Prime Minister's Office, Singapore, and concurrently as Second Minister for Finance and for Transport. Between 2002 and 2004, she was Deputy Speaker of Parliament and Chairman of the Public Accounts Committee.

Prior to joining the Singapore Cabinet, Lim Hwee Hua enjoyed a varied career with international financial institutions. At Temasek Holdings, she oversaw divestments, sat on boards, restructured companies and established strategic relations with key foreign counterparts. Since 2011, she has been engaging in a wide range of domains, predominantly in financial services (private equity, banking) and global businesses. She is a Board Trustee of the International Valuation Standards Council and is a Distinguished Visiting Fellow of the National University of Singapore at both the Business School and the Lee Kuan Yew School of Public Policy.

Lim Hwee Hua graduated with a Master of Arts (Honours) in Mathematics/Engineering from the University of Cambridge in 1981. In 1989, she obtained a Master of Business Administration, major in Finance, from the Anderson School of Management, University of California, Los Angeles.

Lim Hwee Hua authored the publication *Government in Business — Friend or Foe* in 2014, which has been translated into Chinese, Portuguese and Spanish.

Contents

CHAPTER 1
LAGGING REGULATOR — CONVERGENCE OF DOMAINS

Chapter 1

Lagging Regulator —
Convergence of Domains

If one were to scan media coverage these days, one would encounter dissatisfaction with the government in a number of areas — from an apparent inability to regulate new services properly, to a lack of innovation bent, to an over-reaction tendency, essentially locking the stable door after the horse has bolted. In short, the government is often depicted as a lagging regulator, inept and incompetent.

Many have cited the sharing economy as an example of where the inability of the government to regulate satisfactorily and in a timely manner is most evident. From ride-sharing to bike-sharing to accommodation-sharing, regulation appears to be a series of reactive responses characteristic of a breathless regulator.

Equally challenging are instances where innovation straddles a few domains, leading to overlaps or convergence and which may include one or more regulated sectors. Such is the nature of innovation, exploiting the gaps in between. Any attempt by the state to integrate rules so as to accommodate more than one regulated sector then becomes a nightmare.

The criticism of the government exhibiting the semblance of a lagging regulator may however not be justified. It is in the nature of entrepreneurship and capitalism to constantly exploit new opportunities, including within lacunae in regulatory frameworks. The returns achieved by successful ventures would be huge enough to enable the private sector to attract and reward the necessary talent. Conversely, it is rare for any government to be able to attract its fair share of talent to be able to pre-empt trends and prescribe the necessary rules, be it for regulation of a strategic sector or for competition.

There are instances of innovation where state intervention has to occur for good social reasons, be it for health or increasingly data privacy for citizens.

In the same vein, the government may be forced to be proactive in responding to the challenges arising from the Covid-19 pandemic, even before it's done finalising the regulatory framework.

Breathless Pace of Change

Picture this — angry cab drivers thronging the streets in protest at the appearance of Uber drivers. They want their government to be fair and to impose the same tough regulations on Uber or Grab drivers, or better still, outlaw ride-sharing services. There is no way they would allow someone to eat their lunch so easily, if at all. They want the government to intervene, and to intervene now. This scene has repeated itself in many cities, from time to time, from London to Copenhagen to Bangkok to the Northern Territory of Australia and even within the United States, home of Uber.[1]

Investment is but only one necessary ingredient toward keeping the state abreast of changes or innovation. The harder challenge lies in ensuring that the regulatory framework remains relevant to the underlying scope for regulating. How does one regulate an activity or role that has not crystallised in full and for which the timing of occurrence is uncertain? Or worse still, how can one regulate an activity that is constantly morphing itself or straddles more than one domain or geography?

The world today is replete with real-life examples of the widespread frustration of business operators over the perceived inability of regulators to put the house, or rather their market, in order. What aggravates the challenge confronting the state or regulator is that very often, the public at large are net beneficiaries of the new services. All these stakeholder interests would make for a perfect cost–benefit analysis case study, if only it were that simple.

The different interest groups expect the government to be able to strike the right balance as and when the dilemma arises, and with every changing circumstance. This is of course an unreasonable expectation even of the most proactive or progressive of governments. However efficient and competent a government may be, it exists to design and prescribe rules for engagement in the "steady state", especially for regulated activity, ideally for the medium to long term. Certainty and consistency have hitherto been prized characteristics of competent governments. However, the reality is increasingly that these rules are only as good as they are relevant. The cycle of innovation, and hence the validity of any regulatory framework, is surely shortening, to the chagrin of lawmakers.

---

[1] https://www.telegraph.co.uk/travel/news/where-is-uber-banned/, 26 June 2018.

So what is a government to do? The pressure to update rules and regulations to re-level the playing field is relentless, unabatedly painful to the point of rendering the affected government department helpless, incompetent, or worse still, irrelevant. That "the regulator is always behind the curve or playing catch-up" is a widely held conclusion.

Inherent Difficulty of Regulating

Have a heart. Let's be fair.

Many innovative businesses are borne out of disrupting the norm and testing regulatory limits or lacunae, often beating the legal boundaries but in a legitimate fashion, around the argument of "what's not expressly disallowed is allowed". Think of successful online retailers like Amazon that cater to a borderless market in e-commerce, cloud computing, digital streaming, or Netflix, that sells content on a platform, essentially *sans frontières*. Or the ubiquitous WeChat Pay in China and elsewhere for all kinds of services, anchored by its ever-widening ecosystem of merchant-partners and powered by a user-friendly payment engine. It goes beyond plugging a lacuna. Innovation has enabled and will continue to empower such enterprises to serve markets never possible before and deliver services never dreamt of before. Giving an e-angpow to a favourite nephew in another continent is now possible, instantaneously and wherever he may be.

The cost of innovation, specifically of the brainpower behind the ever-growing pipeline of ideas, is far from trivial and it is the very basis for economic survival for many such enterprises. Back in 2017 when Amazon was looking to recruit some 17,000 software engineers for its second headquarters in the US, there were already nearly a quarter million job openings unfilled.[2] Other large companies like Salesforce and Cisco were also on the hunt for such talent, offering generous salaries.[3] The demand for talented developers continues to outstrip supply.

It is fair to assert that many dreams are built on the allure of future growth potential or how else can such operating losses, including the employment of armies of increasingly expensive technology experts, be sustained? This is the new brand of market or business economics.

---

[2] http://www.arcgis.com/apps/MapJournal/index.html?appid=b1c59eaadfd945a68a59724a59dbf7b1, 2017.

[3] https://venturebeat.com/2017/09/18/filling-amazons-50000-jobs-means-finding-new-ways-to-train-software-engineers-in-the-u-s/, 18 September 2017.

Unlike the seduction of unicorn potentials who would be funded to burn away cash while pursuing a gigantic big prize at the end, every government lives on real, often tightening revenues and will have to try to spend within its means. As it is, many are already running a deficit so they can scarcely hope to fund anticipatory efforts. To put it bluntly, it's asymmetrical — currently, there's no shortage of private funding for ideas to exploit regulatory lacunae but there's nobody to finance future regulatory initiatives.

In order for a government to be on top of the sum total of all changes in every sector of multiple players, known and unknown, the state would need to be proactive in identifying future trends in economic activity, consumption and technology and to be able to proactively prescribe the relevant changes to the regulatory framework where needed. To do this satisfactorily, a government will have to invest in the best brains, keep them happy, be able to review regulations across many domains and to act in a dynamic fashion. This means a new approach, encompassing perhaps more principles than rules and a ready willingness to ditch old practices and rules. The difficulty with the latter should not be underestimated.

What's the harsh reality? How many governments can ever do this and on a sustainable basis? Practically zilch.

Rightly or wrongly, this is fast becoming an established pattern, essentially forming a vicious cycle — a private sector operator offers an innovative service in an existing business domain; in fact, it frequently straddles more than one domain, often including regulated businesses. This will provoke existing operators into crying foul and urging the regulator to "act", a code word for getting rid of the new unregulated players. Meanwhile, the regulator reviews the regulatory or competition framework to see if complaints are legitimate. If so, the regulator either amends or layers on more rules or imposes penalties on "errant" new players, occasionally for purported antitrust behaviour. More uncertainty then creeps into the system as regulatory gaps, leading more private sector operators to join the fray with even more innovative, or new offerings not captured or governed by updated regulatory framework. And the vicious cycle continues.

This is fully fleshed out in the sharing economy, especially for the much welcome ride-sharing services across many jurisdictions, including Singapore. Depending on whose perspectives one takes, it can be a nightmare or sheer bliss.

Example 1.1: Ride-sharing — The Road Less Travelled

A confluence of factors is driving consumers away from car ownership to car-sharing or alternatives within the transportation domain. Many urban dwellers increasingly feel that a privately owned car is a wasted resource, as it spends most of its time parked in some garage and the rest of its time contributing to traffic congestion. Add to that the rising car prices, the uncertainty of energy costs, along with the pressure to increase energy efficiency and reduce carbon emissions. Enter ride-sharing — where online platforms connect drivers and vehicles with consumers who want rides on-demand and at an agreed price.

Boom in Ride-sharing Market

Valued at US$51 billion in 2018, the global ride-sharing market is estimated to more than quadruple to US$220 billion by 2025.[4] The services range from on-demand rides that one can book in advance by choosing the driver to real-time rides with taxis or with drivers that offer a private ride or a shared one for lower fares.

What was it like pre-ride-sharing days? In London, many people continue to have the utmost respect for the black cabbies. They are always friendly, professional and completely knowledgeable about the nooks and corners of the city. The only snag with riding a black cab was that one would frequently suffer a near heart attack — the meter would jump furiously whenever one got stuck in heavy traffic, which unfortunately was almost a certainty. Ensuring that there was enough cash to complete the ride became an unnecessary nightmare. When Addison Lee came onto the scene, it was such a boon. Over the years, commuters started having more choices — Uber, Bolt, Ola, and a growing list.[5] The flip side is: what about the future of the industrious black cabbies?

---

[4]"Ride Sharing Market to reach USD 220.5 billion with a CAGR of 20 by 2025", Orion Research [Press Release], 26 September 2019, https://www.marketwatch.com/press-release/at-cagr-20-ride-sharing-market-size-worth-usd-2205-billion-by-2025-analysis-including-growth-factors-market-segment-by-application-and-industry-forecast-study-2020-08-20.

[5]Heathman, A. "From Bolt to Ola: the next-generation of UK taxi apps to know", *Evening Standard*, 10 February 2020, https://www.standard.co.uk/tech/uber-app-alternatives-london-bolt-kapten-viavan-wheely-a4357906.html.

The story repeats itself in many cities, to varying degrees. The common theme running through is the healthy rivalry, if not deep animosity, between the traditional taxi operators and the ride-sharing upstarts. From cities in the US to Europe, Singapore to Jakarta, in China and even in Japan, these ride-sharing or cab-hailing services are now ubiquitous. That does not stop the taxi unions from continuing to protest against the unfair lack of regulation. This emerging appeal to personal mobility has been disruptive to existing markets. It will continue to face pushback from the taxi industry with claims that their counterparts have unfair advantages in terms of lighter regulatory compliance burden, ability to deliver lower prices and a more stable customer base, making it difficult for traditional cabbies to earn a living.

In many countries, while protesting, some taxi fleets have decided to jump onto the bandwagon, a case of "if you can't beat them, join them". Platforms like Gett and Kabbee, which offer taxis, are now part of the plethora of ride-sharing options in London.

Regulators' Efforts at Finding the Right Response

Against this backdrop, the emergence of ride-sharing giants Uber and Grab has prompted regulators in Singapore to rethink their approach to the vehicle-for-hire industry, making the necessary changes and revisions, occasionally over short periods.

Owing to the multitude of currently understood or potentially unknown risks associated with ride-sharing, the regulatory outlook for ride-sharing platforms has varied widely between different regions and cities. At one end of the spectrum, the global cheerleader of the ride-sharing industry Uber has reportedly been fighting a never-ending stream of lawsuits from Europe to North America.[6] Back in 2017, in countries such as Bulgaria and Hong Kong, e-hailing services were deemed illegal.[7] At one point, "unworkable" changes to rules requiring all cars to have fare meters and restrictions on car types proved too onerous for Uber in Denmark, which eventually suspended its service.[8] At the other end of the spectrum, some

---

[6]Henley, J. "Uber clashes with regulators in cities around the world", *The Guardian*, 29 September 2017, https://www.theguardian.com/business/2017/sep/29/uber-clashes-with-regulators-in-cities-around-the-world.

[7]Hao, K. "Map: All the places where Uber is partially or fully banned", *Quartz*, 23 September 2017, https://qz.com/1084981/map-all-the-places-where-uber-is-partially-or-fully-banned/.

[8]Henley, J. "Uber to shut down Denmark operation over new taxi laws", *The Guardian*, 28 March 2017, https://www.theguardian.com/technology/2017/mar/28/uber-to-shut-down-denmark-operation-over-new-taxi-laws.

cities have embraced ride-sharing platforms without any significant updates to the associated regulatory frameworks. The Saudi Arabian government, for example, invested US$3.5 billion in Uber's growth story.[9]

While the Boom Continues

Largely unfettered, China's market leader Didi Chuxing was serving more than 450 million registered users and handling an estimated number of 30 million rides daily across its platforms, including some 21 million drivers' licenced taxis and carpooling, as well as private car handling up to 2018.[10] It encountered a major hiccup in 2018 with the death of two passengers, raising safety concerns over rogue drivers. High receptivity to ride-hailing continued to power its user base to 550 million by the end of 2018. Didi, like Uber, made international forays into Brazil, Japan, Mexico and Australia.[11]

Calibrating the Right Amount of Regulation

Over in Singapore, regulators endeavoured to strike a balance: allowing firms to operate, while framing their development through specific regulations. Founded in San Francisco in 2010, Uber had established a global presence before entering the Singapore market in February 2013.[12] Shortly after, Malaysian-grown player Grab launched in October 2013 as a taxi-booking app and later extended its platform to private-hire cars.[13] Initially, both Uber and Grab were operating unfettered as their services did not fall neatly under the ambit of existing regulatory frameworks. In effect,

---

[9]Newcomer, E. "The inside story of how Uber got into business with the Saudi Arabian government", *Bloomberg*, 4 November 2018, https://www.bloomberg.com/news/articles/2018-11-03/the-inside-story-of-how-uber-got-into-business-with-the-saudi-arabian-government

[10]CNBC. "2018 Disrupter 50 Full Coverage", Updated 9 May 2019, https://www.cnbc.com/2018/05/22/didi-chuxing-2018-disruptor-50.html.

[11]Zhang, J. "Didi by the numbers: ride-hailing firm covered more miles in 2018 than 5 Earth-to-Neptune round-trips", *South China Morning Post*, 23 January 2019, https://www.scmp.com/tech/start-ups/article/2181542/didi-numbers-ride-hailing-firm-covered-more-miles-2018-5-earth.

[12]Ho, V. "Uber Comes To Asia, Starts Trials In Singapore", Tech Crunch, 31 January 2013, https://techcrunch.com/2013/01/30/uber-starts-trials-in-singapore/.

[13]Cosseboom, L. "GrabTaxi's journey to a billion-dollar startup (INFOGRAPHIC)", *Tech In Asia*, 4 June 2015, https://www.techinasia.com/history-unicorn-grabtaxi-infographic.

their private-hire car services were not subjected to any public standards or monitoring as only taxi operators and taxi booking services were regulated by the Land Transport Authority of Singapore (LTA) under the Road Traffic Act (RTA).

As third-party booking applications gained popularity, the regulatory landscape saw its first adjustment in November 2014, when LTA introduced a "basic regulatory framework" to be put into effect from the second quarter of 2015.[14] To give LTA more regulatory oversight so as to "safeguard commuter safety and interests", third-party platforms had to register their service with LTA and be certified before starting operations. In addition, operators had to meet certain disclosure requirements relating to fares before commuters accept the dispatched taxi.[15]

A Difficult Juggle

Despite the imposition of new regulations by the LTA, the local taxi operators, which jointly managed some 30,000 registered taxis, continued to view Uber and Grab as competition and called for a "level playing field" where they can compete on equal footing. In particular, they argued that it was unfair that the drivers of the private-hire car business were not subjected to the same regulations as taxis — such as a daily minimum mileage while simultaneously ensuring that 85% of a taxi company's fleet was available during peak periods.[16] In contrast, the Uber and Grab drivers being "private contractors" had no such obligations and were incentivised by the companies to drive more often during peak periods.[17]

Feelings of injustice were further exacerbated by the fact that taxi drivers have to pass a robust taxi driver vocational licence course conducted by the largest taxi operator in Singapore, ComfortDelGro. It requires taxi drivers to speak and read basic English, clear a medical check-up and undergo a driving refresher course every six years covering road safety, taxi

---

[14]Cheok, J. "Market players welcome LTA regulation of third-party taxi apps (Amended)", *Business Times*, 22 November 2014, https://www.businesstimes.com.sg/transport/market-players-welcome-lta-regulation-of-third-party-taxi-apps-amended.

[15]*Ibid.*

[16]Lin, P. "Here's why Khaw Boon Wan's attempt to level the playing field for taxi drivers will drive costs up", *Yahoo Finance*, 12 October 2015, https://sg.finance.yahoo.com/news/why-khaw-boon-wan-attempt-160000741.html.

[17]*Ibid.*

regulations, routes and service quality.[18] In comparison, private-hire car drivers were simply regulated by the tech company's guidelines, which were relatively new and less stringent. Background checks were not as thorough, vehicles less rigorously inspected and drivers not professionally trained or vocationally licenced. Some also questioned where the burden of responsibility and liability would fall should accidents happen, whereas commuters involved in a dispute with taxis can approach the LTA or operators for recourse.[19]

In addition to different licencing requirements, price competition became a major bone of contention with the taxi industry. Taxi drivers argued that ride-sharing platforms were unfairly allowed to set their own fares as they were not bound by the fare rules jointly imposed by the LTA and the Public Transport Council (PTC). As a result, fares offered by platforms were able to respond more readily to demand, including undercutting existing taxi fares. More controversially, Uber and Grab employed the use of "dynamic" or "surge" pricing — where fares can be raised in multiples of the normal rate during periods of high demand.

To forge "a fair solution", the Senior Minister of State for Transport led a public consultation in October 2015 with various industry stakeholders such as commuters, taxi drivers, private-hire car drivers, taxi companies, car rental companies, chauffeured services booking providers and the National Taxi Association (NTA) of Singapore.[20] Essentially, the NTA compiled feedback from over 300 taxi drivers, which *inter alia*, requested for "fair competition" through clear fare structures as well as for private-hire car drivers to go through the same checks as their taxi driver counterparts.[21] These demands are rather similar to those made by taxi unions in many other countries. When unmet, some unions have turned violent. Brazilian taxi drivers frequently threaten Uber drivers, Hong Kong

---

[18]"ComfortDelGro taxi: Vocational licence courses", https://www.cdgtaxi.com.sg/vocational-licence-courses.

[19]Lee, K. "Government to review private car-sharing apps such as Uber: Khaw Boon Wan", *The Straits Times*, 2 October 2015, https://www.straitstimes.com/singapore/transport/government-to-review-private-car-sharing-apps-such-as-uber-khaw-boon-wan.
[20]*Ibid.*

[21]Lim, A. "National taxi association submits list of recommendations for private-car hire services", *The Straits Times*, 16 November 2015, https://www.straitstimes.com/singapore/transport/national-taxi-association-submits-list-of-recommendations-for-private-car-hire.

taxi drivers staged an anti-Uber march and South Korean taxi drivers have set themselves on fire.[22]

Following the industry review, in April 2016, LTA announced the new Private Hire Car Driver Vocational Licence (PDVL) framework, stipulating that all private-hire cars are now required to obtain a vocational licence to operate and display a tamper-evident decal which indicates their PDVL status.[23] Alongside that came other regulations that are consistent with those governing taxi services. Drivers of the private-hire cars are required to similarly undergo a background check, participate in a training course and pass the necessary tests.[24]

Consolidation in a Small Market

After five years, Uber conceded defeat and bade Singapore farewell, round about the time Indonesia's ride-hailing Gojek made its foray into the city.[25] The multi-pronged fight between Gojek, Grab and the taxi companies for dominance will continue to spur greater efficiency in the use of transport assets, as part of the country's Sustainable Singapore Blueprint unveiled in 2015 to go car-lite.[26]

While the benefits from ride-sharing are largely spread over an entire body of existing and new passengers who welcome more price-competitive choices, the costs of these platforms have, till

---

[22] Premack, R. "South Korean taxi drivers are setting themselves on fire in protest of a proposed ride-sharing app", *Business Insider*, 10 January 2019, https://www.businessinsider.sg/south-korean-taxi-drivers-protest-kakao-ride-sharing-app-2019-1; Che, J. "9 countries that aren't giving Uber an inch", *Huffington Post*, 8 December 2015, https://www.huffpost.com/entry/uber-countries-governments-taxi-drivers_n_55bfa3a9e4b0d4f33a037a4b.

[23] LTA. "New regulations for private hire car drivers and vehicles to better protect commuter interests". *News Release*, April 12, 2016, https://www.lta.gov.sg/content/ltagov/en/newsroom/2016/4/2/new-regulations-for-private-hire-car-drivers-and-vehicles-to-better-protect-commuter-interests.html.

[24] *Ibid.*

[25] Ng, D. "How Uber, valued at billions, was sent packing by a start-up in Singapore", *CAN Insider*, 19 August 2018, https://www.channelnewsasia.com/news/cnainsider/uber-grab-singapore-ride-hailing-southeast-asia-private-hire-10630396.

[26] NUS, "A CAR-LITE FUTURE-YAY OR NAY?", April–June, 2018, http://www.nus.edu.sg/alumnet/thealumnus/issue-113/perspectives/forum/a-car-lite-future-yay-or-nay.

> *now, been disproportionately borne by the taxi companies and ride-sharing operators. Operators like Gojek and Grab should always seek to align themselves with LTA efforts to create a sustainable transportation ecosystem, so that they can co-exist with taxis. If one thing needs to be made clear, it is that ride-sharing operates in a very fluid environment and it might not look the same tomorrow as it does today. By the same token, however, challenging it may be, transport policies and regulations, including a constant review of the taxi business model, must keep pace with technology advancement and consumer preferences.*

For argument's sake, let's imagine a scenario where a regulatory framework is fluid and dynamic enough to accommodate any new features or circumstances. Even if one can be crafted, the consequential ambiguity would be useless when it comes to adopting a clear stand on, say competition issues. Ruling on antitrust disputes in minimally changing sectors is already challenging enough, let alone for fast-morphing ones. For the detractors of regulators who frown upon the supposed lethargy in reviews, it must be counterargued that an over-zealous regulator might on the contrary exact a higher societal cost, that of stifling innovation and denying the public potentially better services. The public will be none the wiser about what new inventive services have been outlawed before there's a chance to prove their worth. In practice, within the sharing space, there are numerous examples of how a fast-morphing landscape can trip up both the regulator and business operators.

Example 1.2: Cycling Towards a Cleaner Environment

Bike-sharing is essentially a city-wide experiment, a perfect complement to the first-and-last mile for public transportation and constitutes a significant effort at persuading car owners to ditch driving. But like all experiments, it is not without its imperfections. Many hopeful bike-sharing companies in Singapore bade a sad retreat owing to a lack of scale to offset huge start-up customer acquisition costs and an uncertain regulatory environment.

Genesis Borne Out of Good Intentions

On a hot summer's day in Amsterdam in 1965, a group of Dutch activists introduced the first raw form of bike-sharing. They were convinced that the idea, known as Witte Fietsenplan (white bicycle plan), was the answer to the perceived threats of air pollution, road congestion and modern-day traffic menace.[27] A small number of bicycles were painted white and left unlocked at various locations around the city, to be used by anyone in need of transport.

Though short-lived, that gem of an initiative had inspired many other similar projects. Since then, a multitude of bike-sharing systems have come and gone all over the world. Riding on shifting consumer preferences from owning to sharing, the North America e-bike-sharing market has been slated to witness a notable growth of 10% per year from 2019 to surpass US$10 billion by 2025.[28]

Unbridled Expansion

In the Asia-Pacific, the explosion in shared bicycles had been the most visible in China, with bike-share companies proliferating all over and readily flooding city streets with millions of brightly coloured rental bicycles. Investors were falling over themselves to pour serious money into dockless bike-sharing start-ups — the likes of Mobike and ofo, two of China's largest platforms, raised nearly US$2 billion in 2017 alone.[29]

With the fresh injection of capital, Mobike and ofo rolled into Singapore in early 2017 amidst great fanfare, marking the start-ups' first

---

[27] Van Der Zee, R. "Story of cities #30: how this Amsterdam inventor gave bike-sharing to the world", *The Guardian*, 26 April 2017, https://www.theguardian.com/cities/2016/apr/26/story-cities-amsterdam-bike-share-scheme.

[28] Global Market Insights, Inc. "Bike Sharing Market to surpass USD 10 Billion by 2025: Global Market Insights, Inc", 27 August 2019, https://www.globenewswire.com/news-release/2019/08/27/1906946/0/en/Bike-Sharing-Market-to-surpass-USD-10-Billion-by-2025-Global-Market-Insights-Inc.html.

[29] "Bike-sharing firms face pressure as sector undergoes contraction", *The Straits Times*, 20 July 2018, https://www.straitstimes.com/business/companies-markets/bike-sharing-firms-face-pressure-as-sector-undergoes-contraction.

expansion out of their home nation.[30] Within a few months, Mobike and ofo, along with local start-up oBike, flooded the city with nearly 30,000 bicycles that can be easily located and unblocked when parked anywhere on the street via a mobile application.[31] Upon reaching their destination, riders can simply park and lock the bicycles anywhere, paying a small fee based on ride distance or time of use. It's that convenient. But convenience has its price.

Disamenities Posed a Serious Problem

The ability to pick up and leave a bike anywhere should make bike-sharing effortless. Unfortunately, the real-world application of this business model had created unintended controversy, with many people complaining about thousands of bicycles cluttering city streets, particularly walkways which soon became a public nuisance. In no time, the situation escalated to alarming heights. People frequently reported pedestrian pathways obstructions, badly damaged bike-sharing bicycles and even bicycles being dumped into canals for no apparent reason other than mischief.[32] Bikes were also stripped for parts, some were missing number plates or QR codes and yet others had the company livery painted over.[33]

In Comes the Regulator

In March 2017, in an attempt to encourage more responsible behaviour, the LTA created new parking zones demarcated by bright yellow lines and announced that it was working with bicycle-sharing companies to "incentivise their users to park responsibly".[34] As part of a memorandum of

---

[30]Ng, K. "Chinese firm Mobike enters Singapore's bike-sharing market" Today, 22 March 2017, https://www.todayonline.com/singapore/chinese-firm-mobike-enters-spores-bike-sharing-market.

[31]"Bike blues: Shared bicycles turn up in strange places", *The Straits Times*, 22 January 2018, https://www.straitstimes.com/singapore/transport/bike-blues.

[32]Sivaram, V. "Man throws ofo bike into canal: 5 other cases of misuse of shared bicycles", *The Straits Times*, 16 June 2017, https://www.straitstimes.com/singapore/man-throws-ofo-bike-into-canal-5-other-cases-of-misuse-of-shared-bicycles.

[33]*Ibid.*

[34]Co, C. "Wheel woes: The rise and fall of Singapore's bike-sharing industry", *Channel News Asia*, 13 March 2019, https://www.channelnewsasia.com/news/singapore/wheel-woes-the-rise-and-fall-of-singapore-s-bike-sharing-11336200.

understanding (MOU) signed on October 2017 with LTA, the National Parks Board and 16 town councils, the five operators in Singapore pledged their commitment to remove errantly parked bicycles within half a day and implement geofencing technologies by the end of 2017, which would create a virtual boundary that would alert the company whenever a user failed to park a bike in a prescribed area.[35]

Despite these efforts, disamenities arising from bike-sharing services persisted and proved challenging to wipe out. In a bid to tackle the indiscriminate parking nuisance, the government enacted a new law in March 2019. The newly passed Parking Places (Amendment) Bill requires operators to formally apply for a licence from LTA, temporarily ban recalcitrant users who refuse to park in designated areas and adopt a QR code-based geo-fencing solution.[36] Companies will have their fleet size reviewed every six months. The amendments also require operators to remove faulty bicycles within half a day and provide public liability insurance for users.[37] Failure to comply with these rules could cost operators up to S$100,000 in fines, a reduction in fleet size, suspension, or revocation of their licences.[38]

Bidding a Hasty Retreat

As of 2018, there were 100,000 such shared bicycles, across six operators: oBike, Mobike, ofo, SG Bikes, GBikes and ShareBikeSG.[39] Shortly after the new regulations were in force, oBike abruptly exited in distress and was forced to liquidate, with court cases around alleged misappropriation of

---

[35] Abdullah, Z. "18 months of bike-sharing", *The Straits Times*, 27 June 2018, https://www.straitstimes.com/singapore/18-months-of-bike-sharing.

[36] Farhan, N. "QR code geo-fencing, new licensing regime to tackle indiscriminate parking of shared bicycles", *Channel News Asia*, 5 March 2018, https://www.channelnewsasia.com/news/singapore/bike-sharing-ofo-obike-mobike-qr-code-geofencing-10013984.

[37] Chua, A. "Collective ban, licensing regime for shared-bike users and operators in major bid to regulate industry", *Today*, 5 March 2018, https://www.todayonline.com/singapore/new-bill-tackle-indiscriminate-parking-shared-bikes-tabled.

[38] *Ibid.*

[39] Chua, A. "First phase of bike-sharing geo-fencing technology trials to conclude by 2019", *Today*, 7 March 2018, https://www.todayonline.com/singapore/authorities-looking-geo-fencing-technology-improve-tracking-indiscriminately-parked-bikes.

user deposits worth US$4.6 million.[40] Former bike giant ofo, which was on the verge of bankruptcy, had its operator's licence revoked after repeated failures to meet regulatory requirements. Both ShareBikeSG and GBikes ceased offering their bikes in quick succession in June and July of 2018. Following the protracted exits of oBike and ofo, in March 2019, Mobike, the last of the major players, eventually announced that it was pulling out of Singapore and surrendered its licence to operate 25,000 bikes in Singapore.[41] This left local firms SG Bike, Anywheel and Moov the only three remaining viable operations in Singapore.[42] Anywheel graduated from the LTA sandbox licence in April 2019, and along with Moov Technology, were granted licences to operate "dockless bicycle-sharing services".[43]

In particular, the demise of oBike heightened public scrutiny into the operations of shared bike companies, especially the accountability to users when businesses go south. Some also questioned the lack of safeguards to protect consumers when a service is suddenly made unavailable. They argued that evidently the regulators could not find a way to keep errant user behaviour in check, and the administrative levies implemented were unsustainable.

It Never Rains but It Pours

Barely had the dust settled than personal mobility devices (PMDs) exploded on the scene. One would have thought that the PMDs represent the perfect last-mile solution to a no-car policy. As a more viable alternative to bicycles, the insurgent PMDs in recent years have dented the provision of bike-sharing services. Unlike bicycles, PMDs allow users to travel at a

---

[40]"oBike liquidators urge affected users to submit deposit claims online", *Channel News Asia*, 12 July 2018, https://www.channelnewsasia.com/news/singapore/obike-liquidators-urge-users-submit-deposit-claims-online-10524154.

[41]Toh, T. "Mobike applies to LTA to withdraw from Singapore", *The Straits Times*, 12 March 2019, https://www.straitstimes.com/singapore/transport/mobike-applies-to-lta-to-withdraw-from-singapore.

[42]"LTA grants Moov Technology full licence to operate up to 10,000 bicycles", *CNA*, 14 October 2019, https://www.channelnewsasia.com/news/singapore/bike-sharing-operators-moov-technology-full-licence-11998346.

[43]Salim, Z. "Bike-sharing's not dead: anywheel wants to grow its fleet to 10,000 by end 2019", *Vulcan Post*, June 2019, https://vulcanpost.com/665789/anywheel-bike-sharing-singapore.

faster speed and offer portability as they are allowed on public buses and trains when folded.[44] However in practice, PMDs have proven to be dangerous, even deadly in the hands of an irresponsible user. From 2016 to 2017, Singapore witnessed a threefold increase in PMD-related accidents.[45] The uptrend over the past few years is a cause for worry, 213 people were treated at hospitals for accidents related to PMDs, including six deaths.[46]

Amid rising safety concerns, the LTA implemented a nationwide ban on all PMDs under the Active Mobility (Amendment) Bill, which took effect in March 2020.[47] Maximum penalties for key offences by both users and retailers of PMDs are also increased as part of these deterrent efforts.[48] Some have lamented that like bike-sharing, PMDs are getting choked out of existence by harsh regulations and the battle against errant use. The food delivery companies are especially aggrieved; the overnight ban on electric scooters left them scrambling. About a third of their 7,000 employees effectively were rendered jobless as a result of this.[49] As transitional assistance, S$7 million of trade-in grants were offered jointly by LTA and the operators.[50]

---

[44] Lim, A. "Up to 2,000 commuters taking personal mobility devices on trains during weekday peak hours", *The Straits Times*, 21 March 2017, https://www.straitstimes.com/singapore/up-to-2000-commuters-taking-pmds-on-trains.

[45] "Annals academy of medicine: electronic bicycles and scooters: convenience at the expense of danger?", April 2019, p. 1, http://www.annals.edu.sg/pdf/48VolNo4Apr2019/V48N4p125.pdf.

[46] Choo, C. "TTSH reports surge in accidents involving PMD riders over last 3 years, especially in 2019", *Today*, 21 October 2019, https://www.todayonline.com/singapore/ttsh-reports-surge-pmd-rider-related-accidents-over-last-3-years-especially-2019.

[47] Abdullah, Z. "E-scooter ban on footpaths to extend to all motorised PMDs under amendments to Active Mobility Act", *Channel News Asia*, 6 January 2020, https://www.channelnewsasia.com/news/singapore/e-scooter-ban-footpaths-extend-motorised-pmd-active-mobility-mot-12237050.

[48] *Ibid.*

[49] Phua, R. and Co, C. "MPs express concern over livelihoods of food delivery riders, jail terms for underage PMD users", *CNA*, 4 February 2020, https://www.channelnewsasia.com/news/singapore/pmd-ban-mps-food-delivery-riders-underage-active-mobility-bill-12391232.

[50] Abdullah, Z. "Almost 2,500 food delivery riders apply for e-scooter trade-in grant", *CNA*, 22 November 2019, https://www.channelnewsasia.com/news/singapore/2500-food-delivery-riders-apply-e-scooter-trade-in-grant-ban-pmd-12118118.

> *The seemingly chaotic journey of Singapore's bike-sharing sector is not unique. The Chinese market also encountered a similar trajectory, as bike graveyards and unused zombie bicycles have become the defining image of China's bike-sharing economy. Some have argued that the uncertain, oppressive regulatory environment has made the model untenable in Singapore. However, this is only one side of the coin. To truly enjoy the cost-efficiency and convenience offered by bike-sharing and PMDs, public awareness should be heightened of the potential perils in the absence of civic minded behaviour. The public should also appreciate the value of safety regulations and the compliance thereof. While regulators can enforce via more designated parking spaces or devise technological tools to deal with the abuse of bicycles, firms cannot ignore the social cost of their services. Ideally, to minimise negative externalities, regulators should always encourage firms to have in place the right set of incentives and disincentives to cultivate correct user behaviour.*

Not all innovation around a common theme, such as within the ambit of the sharing economy, should be dealt with in the same manner. The guiding principle must however be that the government will weigh the ensuing social implications against the various stakeholders' interests. Take home-sharing or accommodation-sharing services, the boon of backpackers or simply the bargain-hunter in every tourist but the bane of neighbours of the hosts.

Example 1.3: Putting a Temporary Roof over the Head

> *While ride-sharing has on balance positive net benefits, the same cannot be said for home or accommodation sharing. Airbnb is now world-renowned for its very successful accommodation-sharing platform, hugely popular with the below 40s. Apart from providing adventurous travellers with a wonderful assortment of accommodation choices, it also enables property owners to make extra income from spare rooms within their homes. This sounds like an excellent thing. Yet, there are detractors. What then are the detractors' unhappiness about? In a word, disamenities.*

Having served over 500 million guests since it was founded in 2008,[51] home-sharing platform Airbnb has evolved into a major player in the tourism sector, boasting an impressive valuation of more than US$35 billion achieved at the last fundraise in early 2019.[52] Airbnb's reach is truly global; connecting homeowners with tourists looking for authentic, off-the-beaten-track experiences in over 191 countries.[53] The rise of Airbnb has created twin benefits — a booming market that provides travellers with a complementary offering to the existing suite of hotel-based accommodation and supplementary income for those with an extra couch, spare room, or unused home. As a result, its proliferation has raised questions about its negative impact on local housing costs and erosion of neighbourhood social capital.

Runaway Success

Founded in August 2008 and based in San Francisco, California, Airbnb makes its revenue from charging guests and hosts a "service fee" for short-term rental stays in private homes or apartments booked through their online platform. It has three types of property listings: entire homes, private rooms and shared rooms. The largest and best-documented benefit of Airbnb is the increased supply and variety of accommodation, which makes travelling more affordable. It allows travellers to "live like a local", as those who rent out their homes on Airbnb share information about their neighbourhood's best restaurants, bars and attractions, including hole-in-the-wall spots that might not be found on traditional travel websites or guides.[54] Also, for many homeowners, the extra incomes earned can be sizeable. In fact, the New York State Attorney General reported the

---

[51] "Airbnb celebrates half a billion guest arrivals", Airbnb, 27 March 2019, https://press.airbnb.com/airbnb-celebrates-half-a-billion-guest-arrivals; Warren, K. "Meet Airbnb CEO Brian Chesky, who cofounded the company in 2008 to help pay his San Francisco rent and now may be taking his $18 billion business public", https://www.businessinsider.com/brian-chesky-airbnb-life-career-net-worth-relationship-philanthropy.

[52] Walsh, B. "Airbnb will go public next year as 'Unicorn' IPOs Continue", *Barrons*, 19 September 2019, https://www.barrons.com/articles/airbnb-will-go-public-2020-ipo-51568908485.

[53] Dickinson, G. "How the world is going to war with Airbnb", *The Telegraph*, 8 June 2018, https://www.telegraph.co.uk/travel/news/where-is-airbnb-banned-illegal/.

[54] Benner, K. "Airbnb wants travelers to 'live like a local' with its app", *The New York Times*, 19 April 2016, https://www.nytimes.com/2016/04/20/technology/airbnb-wants-travelers-to-live-like-a-local-with-its-app.html.

annual median earnings for an Airbnb host are $5,468 — money that may "escape local sales, hotel and unincorporated business tax".[55]

As part of their plans to crack the fast-growing Asia-Pacific markets, Airbnb set up its Asia headquarters in Singapore late 2012.[56] The platform was expectedly well received — in the 12 months leading up to August 2017, Airbnb rentals played host to 317,000 visitors in Singapore, with hosts raking in an average of S$5,300 per year.[57] While Singapore has been an early adopter of Airbnb, current regulations by policymakers — the Housing Development Board (HDB) and Urban Redevelopment Authority (URA) for public and private housing, respectively — in effect do not provide a blanket approval for homeowners to list their units on any home-sharing platform.

Public Housing Especially Tricky

Under the HDB Act, public housing owners can only rent out their entire HDB flats, with permission, for a minimum period of six consecutive months.[58] One- and two-room flats are excluded from rental. Private condominiums are subject to less stringent rules, where short-term rentals are allowed for a minimum shorter duration of three months under the Planning Act by URA.[59] However, units meant for such rental need at least 80% of the strata title holders of the development to grant approval, a vote to be renewed every two years. This can prove onerous.

In the context of the average duration of Airbnb rentals of 4.3 nights, both public and private homeowners are essentially crippled from using

---

[55] Dobbins, J. "Making a living with Airbnb", *The New York Times*, 7 April 2017, https://www.nytimes.com/2017/04/07/realestate/making-a-living-with-airbnb.html.

[56] Yeo, S. "Average Singapore Airbnb host 'makes about $5,000 a year'", *The Straits Times*, 6 December 2016, https://www.straitstimes.com/singapore/housing/average-singapore-airbnb-host-makes-about-5000-a-year.

[57] Agarwal, S., Foo, S. and Chia, L. "Commentary: Regulating Airbnb rentals not pressing until numbers grow", *CNA*, 4 November 2017, https://www.channelnewsasia.com/news/commentary/commentary-regulating-airbnb-rentals-not-pressing-until-numbers-9338538.

[58] Choy, D. "Lower income Singaporeans can benefit from Airbnb rentals, with a catch", *Today*, 25 April 2019, https://www.todayonline.com/commentary/lower-income-singaporeans-can-benefit-airbnb-rentals-catch.

[59] *Ibid.*

home-sharing platforms.[60] In April 2017, two Airbnb hosts were each dealt a hefty fine of S$60,000 over their breach of the rules of such rentals.[61]

Although several platform operators have appealed on the grounds that the rules were "overly restrictive" and had requested a lighter touch approach, local authorities have maintained the *status quo* on the illegality of short-term rentals in Singapore.[62] Following four years of consultations with a diverse group of stakeholders that ended on 31 May 2018, URA cited an "impasse" between the position of home-sharing platform operators and concerns from local communities, signalling the need for more time to study the issue.[63]

Disamenity Not to be Taken Lightly

Between 2015 and 2017, URA received more than 2,000 complaints of residential premises being illegally rented out. Of these, 1,808 were in private homes and 390 in HDB flats.[64] Based on a national survey commissioned by URA in the second half of 2018, the majority of respondents disapproved of short-term rentals as it was viewed as a major source of disamenity to their neighbourhoods.[65]

The complaints centred on privacy- and security-related concerns arising from the high turnover of transient guests in residential estates and developments. In particular, the majority believed that short-term rentals

---

[60] Statista, "Average number of nights per Airbnb booking in the United States and Europe from 2015 to 2018", 16 January 2019, https://www.statista.com/statistics/796534/average-number-of-nights-per-airbnb-booking-us-europe/.

[61] Lam, L. "Two Singapore hosts fined for illegal home sharing: Airbnb laws in various cities", *The Straits Times*, 6 December 2017, https://www.straitstimes.com/singapore/two-hosts-charged-over-illegal-home-sharing-airbnb-laws-in-various-cities.

[62] Leong, G. "Airbnb-style short-term home sharing still illegal, 3-month minimum period continues to apply for private homes: URA", *The Straits Times*, 8 May 2019, https://www.straitstimes.com/singapore/housing/3-month-minimum-stay-duration-will-continue-to-apply-for-private-accommodation-ura.

[63] *Ibid.*

[64] Au-Yong, R. "No rush to change laws on Airbnb: Lawrence Wong", *The Straits Times*, 12 July 2018, https://www.straitstimes.com/singapore/no-rush-to-change-laws-on-airbnb-lawrence-wong.

[65] Urban Redevelopment Authority, "Status quo for regulations on short-term accommodation in private residential properties", 8 May 2019, https://www.ura.gov.sg/Corporate/Media-Room/Media-Releases/pr19-21.

would result in misbehaviour, noise disturbances and damage to common facilities.[66] Since Airbnb does not conduct thorough background checks on guests, neighbouring residents would often feel unsafe in their own homes. Hosts are also often not on-site with their renters, so they may not factor the cost of these externalities into rental decisions.[67] Given the high-density nature of Singapore living, disamenities are definitely magnified.

Distortion to Subsidy for Public Housing

Unlike most cities where the housing market is largely private sector and therefore commercially driven, that in Singapore presents a unique dilemma. More than 80% of the population is housed in public flats developed and strictly regulated by HDB.[68] The HDB's primary mandate is essentially to provide "affordable homes of quality and value" to Singaporeans, in other words, at a heavily subsidised rate.

Without appropriate controls in place, HDB flat owners would be able to rent out their entire subsidised flat on Airbnb for potential income. This would be nothing less than an abuse of Singapore's public housing subsidies and a mockery of the underlying policy of providing affordable homes for the masses. Not only will it distort the concept of subsidised public housing but commercial operators snapping up properties primarily to profit from the platform could also price out genuine homebuyers in land-scarce Singapore. By the same token, regulators cannot allow the minority of private homeowners to let out their rooms willy-nilly on the home-sharing platforms either. Otherwise, there would be constant pressure on the government to allow HDB flat owners to do likewise.

Moreover, another key priority for HDB is to build cohesive communities. Since 1989, the racial quota in each Housing and Development Board (HDB) block and estate has been carefully calibrated to broadly reflect Singapore's racial proportion under the Ethnic Integration Policy

---

[66]Lin, M. "Rental law is key to Airbnb home-sharing", 12 June 2017, https://www.straitstimes.com/singapore/rental-law-is-key-to-airbnb-home-sharing.

[67]Bivens, J. "The economic costs and benefits of Airbnb", *Economic Policy Institute*, 30 January 2019, https://www.epi.org/publication/the-economic-costs-and-benefits-of-airbnb-no-reason-for-local-policymakers-to-let-airbnb-bypass-tax-or-regulatory-obligations/.

[68]"Estimated Singapore Resident Population in HDB Flats", 2 January 2020, https://data.gov.sg/dataset/estimated-resident-population-living-in-hdb-flats?resource_id=a7d9516f-b193-4f9b-8bbf-9c85a4c9b61b.

(EIP).[69] This objective would be jeopardised should home-sharing of HDB flats be allowed and units rented to foreigners for short-term stay.

Finally, it is onerous for regulators or homeowners to ensure that rentals are not used for illicit purposes. At the moment, URA can only urge property owners to regularly check on their tenants to ensure that they do not use their property to engage in unlawful activities, such as drugs or prostitution.[70] Private condominium managers have been tasked to tighten their security checks and report suspicious activities; however, they are still very much reliant on feedback from neighbours who may not be the most vigilant.[71]

Enforcement is Tricky

Evidently, regulating home-sharing is a tricky proposition. Some have decided to fine hosts, and others have placed caps on the days hosts can rent out their homes. Places like Mallorca in Spain have taken the hardest stance with an outright ban on Airbnb listings.[72] Moderate regulations are more widespread in cities such as Amsterdam, allowing residents to lease out their properties for a maximum of two months per year, for up to four persons each time.[73] In New York, it is illegal for homeowners to rent their rooms out for less than 30 days unless the permanent tenant is residing in the apartment at the same time.[74] Short-term rentals in Paris, one of the largest Airbnb markets in the world, are limited to 120 days a year.[75]

---

[69] Ng, K. "The policies that shaped a multiracial nation", TODAY, 8 August 2017, https://www.todayonline.com/singapore/policies-shaped-multiracial-nation.

[70] Co, C. "Illegal, short-term rentals in your condo? Tell us about it, say property managers" CNA, 1 March 2020. https://www.channelnewsasia.com/news/singapore/report-illegal-short-term-rentals-singapore-condo-airbnb-12455250.

[71] *Ibid.*

[72] Lagrave, K. "13 places cracking down on Airbnb", *CN Traveler*, 13 December 2018, https://www.cntraveler.com/galleries/2016-06-22/places-with-strict-airbnb-laws.

[73] Coldwell, W. "Airbnb's legal troubles: What are the issues?", *The Guardian*, 8 July 2014, https://www.theguardian.com/travel/2014/jul/08/airbnb-legal-troubles-what-are-the-issues.

[74] Greenberg, Z. "New York City looks to crack down on Airbnb amid housing crisis", *The New York Times*, 18 July 2018, https://www.nytimes.com/2018/07/18/nyregion/new-york-city-airbnb-crackdown.html.

[75] Sachs, A. "In France, Airbnb and others move to enforce rental caps", *The Washington Post*, 27 February 2019, https://www.washingtonpost.com/lifestyle/travel/

Where it is allowed, home-sharing platforms continue to do a roaring business. OYO in India prides itself as changing "the way people stay away from home" and allowing "a user to book a room in just three taps, or within five seconds". Boasting the most advanced hospitality technology, it chalked up an impressive US$380 million within five years of its founding in 2013, albeit still burning cash. Since then, OYO has attracted the attention of Yahoo Japan and penetrated the Japanese and Chinese markets. The downturn in its China operations and difficulties faced by its Japanese co-living arm have been exacerbated by the Covid-19 tourism woes.[76] Valuations are likely to settle at more sane levels going forward. Likewise, Airbnb has been hit by a spate of cancellations on the back of the Covid-19 epidemic.[77] Its IPO may be deferred, and its valuation potentially revised.

What the above accounts have illustrated is that the fortunes of these operators are vulnerable to economic and social developments. It points to the tentative nature of such activity. Nevertheless, the disamenities created can have lasting effects on the immediate neighbourhood, such as a lower property valuation or a perception of a less safe environment, or even crime.

The challenge is still there for the relevant authorities to strike a meaningful balance between being open to disruptive home-sharing technologies and safeguarding the interests of residents living in high-density districts. Unlike ride-sharing, it is not tenable to allow a more relaxed, reactive regulatory framework as the current negatives can be boundless, with few benefits to balance them out. Without significant net benefits, regulators may do well to adopt a more conservative stance and not allow any implementation of home-sharing activities lest they merely raise the expectations of the interested parties.

---

in-france-airbnb-and-others-move-to-enforce-rental-caps/2019/02/26/656b424e-36f0-11e9-a400-e481bf264fdc_story.html.

[76]Borko, S. and Schaal, D. "Oyo's post-coronavirus valuation could fall to around $6 Billion", *Skift*, 4 March 2020, https://skift.com/2020/03/04/oyos-post-coronavirus-valuation-could-fall-to-around-6-billion/.

[77]MacDougall, J. "Airbnb has a specific policy for coronavirus-related cancellations", *CNBC*, 5 March 2020, https://www.cnbc.com/2020/03/05/coronavirus-whats-airbnbs-cancellation-policy.html, 5 March 2020.

Unlike the proliferation of ride-sharing services which are completely embraced by an appreciative commuter public, the social implications of accommodation-sharing are not trivial. The disamenity arising from sharing public space at close proximity creates an unimaginable number of social issues especially in highly dense city living.

There's unfortunately no simple fix — every new innovation in sharing requires a whole new assessment by the state of all the stakeholders' interests. It is then incumbent on the government to strike that difficult balance.

Tackling Grey Areas

Where innovation straddles more than one domain, grey areas would emerge and present an array of issues. Increasingly, grey areas are widening in scope with no shortage of attempts at exploiting gaps in between regulatory frameworks. For such situations and for expediency when the government is compelled to act, the state may resort to throwing in the mother of all measures — a "strategic" oversight or for security reasons — as provided for in antitrust laws and extended to include protection of consumer rights.

Example 1.4: Leaving the Regulator Breathless

When the pace of innovation accelerates ahead of the relevant regulatory revisions or reform, the public at large would have to bear a whole range of consequences — from benefiting from new services, boosted by technology and never previously possible, to enjoying productivity enhancements of existing services, to being vulnerable to providers who hold consumers captive, by virtue of the large amount of private information collected by these providers. It is not surprising that in order to be able to respond appropriately, and to good effect, governments must have at their disposal an all-empowering piece of legislation that provides this "catch-all" safeguard.

For decades, most regulators have evolved their mandate coverage and authority along specific domain boundaries. The US Federal Trade

Commission (FTC) is no different. Still, where an express specific legislative mandate or clear administrative delegation is lacking, the agency will broaden its scope to allow the exercise of authority through enforcement proceedings, in areas such as data privacy. As threats arising from the unconstrained exploitation of private data usage by big tech companies become more sophisticated and pernicious, the FTC has accordingly evolved from a "bulwark against monopoly" into a "powerful consumer watchdog" or even "the most powerful technology cop". It derives its legal authority from Section 5 of the Federal Trade Commission Act, which allows the FTC to intervene against "unfair or deceptive business practices", a wide enough catch-all provision.[78]

Founded in 1914, the FTC is the oldest independent regulator in the United States. Since its establishment, the FTC has played a crucial role in maintaining market fairness and protecting consumers from deceptive acts and practices.[79] Hence, the antitrust regulation has been overwhelmingly focused on ensuring that consumers, not businesses, are not harmed by a lack of competition. Ironically, this paved the way for the rise of Google, Facebook, Apple and Amazon — which offered many valuable services to consumers for cheap or free, complicating any argument that businesses or industries are experiencing disruption.

Over the last two decades, these antitrust challenges remain. However, as the US lacks a single, comprehensive federal law that regulates the collection and use of personal information, the FTC faces significant pressure to rein in the power and footprint of the country's tech giants.[80] Notably, these companies have aggregated massive amounts of consumer data — market leader Google handles almost 90% of all desktop search queries,[81] and over

---

[78] Fung, B. "The FTC was built 100 years ago to fight monopolists. Now, it's Washington's most powerful technology cop", *Washington Post*, 25 September 2014, https://www.washingtonpost.com/news/the-switch/wp/2014/09/25/the-ftc-was-built-100-years-ago-to-fight-monopolists-now-its-washingtons-most-powerful-technology-cop/.

[79] Federal Trade Commission "About the FTC" https://www.ftc.gov/about-ftc/what-we-do.

[80] O'Connor, N. "Reforming the U.S. Approach to Data Protection and Privacy", *Council on Foreign Relations*, 30 January 2018, https://www.cfr.org/report/reforming-us-approach-data-protection.

[81] "Worldwide desktop market share of leading search engines from January 2010 to October 2019", *Statista*, https://www.statista.com/statistics/216573/worldwide-market-share-of-search-engines/.

93% of mobile search.[82] Google and Facebook control in aggregate, between 60% and 70% of the online advertising market share in the US, and about 99% of all new ad dollars.[83] With such scale and influence, the motivation to continue milking such growth is powerful. Developments frequently occur before regulations can be formulated from scratch or updated.

In the face of mounting concerns over the strong momentum behind big data innovation and the ensuing compromise of private data by these tech giants, the government turned to the FTC for enforcement. In recent years, the FTC has gone after the likes of Snapchat for their lax privacy features, which resulted in hackers exploiting a security weakness to compile a database of 4.6 million Snapchat usernames and phone numbers. Together with New York State, it slapped Google and YouTube with a US$170 million settlement for inappropriately tracking their young viewers' internet browsing habits for targeted advertising, sending a strong message to the marketplace that any company failing to protect consumer information would face greater legal risks than previously.[84]

Critics may argue that antitrust laws enacted over a century ago cannot keep up with the pace or nature of today's technological change, especially since privacy does not fit neatly into a business versus consumer folder. Some also worry that the agency lacks the financial resources and technical expertise to act as an efficient regulator of big tech. The agency manages on a budget of US$312 million in the Fiscal Year 2020[85] with around 1,140 full-time staffers and a puny team of 40 who are dedicated to privacy

---

[82] Number of explicit core search queries powered by search engines in the United States as of October 2019, *Statista*, https://www.statista.com/statistics/265796/us-search-engines-ranked-by-number-of-core-searches/.

[83] Heath, A. "Facebook and Google completely dominate the digital ad industry", 26 April 2017, https://www.businessinsider.sg/facebook-and-google-dominate-ad-industry-with-a-combined-99-of-growth-2017-4?r=US&IR=T.

[84] "Google and YouTube will pay record $170 Million for alleged violations of Children's Privacy Law", Federal Trade Commission [Press Release], 4 September 2019, https://www.ftc.gov/news-events/press-releases/2019/09/google-youtube-will-pay-record-170-million-alleged-violations.

[85] "Fiscal Year 2020: Congressional Budget Justification", *Federal Trade Commission*, 11 March 2019, https://www.ftc.gov/system/files/documents/reports/fy-2020-congressional-budget-justification/fy_2020_cbj.pdf.

enforcement.[86] That is dwarfed by Google's resources: a company valued at a trillion dollars and has nearly 90 employees for every one of the FTC's. To bolster their forces, the FTC announced in 2019 the creation of a dedicated task force to monitor the technology industry and subsequently launched a collective investigation into Alphabet, Amazon, Apple, Facebook and Microsoft's past mergers.[87]

In hindsight, the FTC's preceding approach has unwittingly been part of the "permissive" regulatory regime that has allowed US firms to be innovative leaders in the information technology industry.

Getting regulation right is always difficult, but it is all the more so when confronting evolving technology that operates along multiple dimensions. As the FTC takes centre stage to address concerns and conditions that confront online privacy, it should seek to balance any heavy-handed moves with encouraging the benefits of innovation, while providing greater clarity to consumers and regulated parties. Moreover, regulators must remember that internet-enabled communications and commerce are borderless, which means that policies aimed at protecting consumers should be crafted with a global lens.

Given the imbalance in resources directed at innovation, it is likely that most governments would continue to rely on an all-encompassing piece of legislation to counter any untoward innovation that seeks to gain at the expense of consumers. It is however incumbent upon every government when using such a powerful legal provision to do so judiciously, and perhaps sparingly, lest it stifles innovation or intervenes unnecessarily with free market forces.

A similar playbook was evidently in use in the US Justice Department's response to the proposed acquisition of Time Warner by AT&T. This is an example of overlapping domains, with strategic considerations revolving around competition and of course, undeniably, the politics of the day.

---

[86]Rich, J. "Give the F.T.C. some teeth to guard our privacy", *The New York Times*, 12 August 2019, https://www.nytimes.com/2019/08/12/opinion/ftc-privacy-congress.html.

[87]Feiner, L. "FTC will examine prior acquisitions by Alphabet, Amazon, Apple, Facebook and Microsoft", CNBC, 11 February 2020, https://www.cnbc.com/2020/02/11/ftc-will-examine-prior-acquisitions-by-big-tech-companies.html.

Example 1.5: Antitrust — Mission Impossible?

Throwing the antitrust book at supposed perpetrators might work well with a clearly defined industry structure and well-framed competition rules. Once domains start overlapping or merging, particularly with the advent of technology, the grey areas may dominate and make for an unwieldy definition of competition. This describes the media industry of today where hitherto, the value chain has been well defined. Even as consumers cheer at the increasing variety of entertainment options, the regulators are confronted with a throbbing headache.

Nearly 80 years ago, a landmark antitrust lawsuit changed the complexion of Hollywood, in terms how the whole entertainment business was to be conducted. That judgment — United States vs. Paramount Pictures — essentially demarcated clearly the different parts of the movie business, banning major movie studios from owning cinema chains because that gave them too much power.[88]

Fast-forward to 2017, the US Department of Justice (DOJ), once again in an attempt to preserve the delineation of the creation and distribution of programming, filed a lawsuit against AT&T to block the largest telecommunications operator from acquiring Time Warner Inc, the second-largest pay TV provider and owner of HBO, CNN, TNT, TBS, Cartoon Network and the Warner Bros. film and television studio.

AT&T and Time Warner had initially signed a deal in October 2016, but the merger was not consummated following the DOJ's suit. As the merger constituted a "vertical integration" given the minimal overlap between both companies, it was approved in June 2018 by U.S District Judge Richard Leon. The DOJ persisted in its efforts to prevent a concentration of power from the merger and filed an appeal in December 2018. During the trial, the DOJ presented an economic model to argue that the acquisition would create an entertainment giant, thereby threatening all sorts of competition and leading to a deleterious effect on consumer prices for television subscriptions. The DOJ alleged that, after the acquisition, AT&T could use its new market power to raise prices exorbitantly for cable and satellite operators that want to run Time Warner

---

[88] James, M. "U.S. faces tough battle proving AT&T would use Time Warner to squeeze competition", *LA Times*, 21 November 2017, https://www.latimes.com/business/la-fi-att-time-warner-20171121-story.html.

TV programmes.[89] The US$85 billion deal also solicited strong words from the then-presidential candidate Donald Trump, who opined that the merger would put "too much concentration of power in the hands of too few".[90]

Unfortunately, the DOJ's prognosis stood in stark contrast to what is happening across the fast-evolving media landscape today.

Who is the Real Competition?

In reality, AT&T's marriage with Time Warner was necessary for the telecom company to compete and survive in the cutthroat environment. Some are calling it the new golden age for the television industry, one increasingly disrupted by new integrated producer-distributors, new forms of content and new business models. A study by Nielsen in 2018 showed that cord-cutting, that is, people ditching their subscriptions to cable and satellite television, had grown by 48% over an eight-year period.[91] The long-term trend hit the various paid-TV service companies hard, with viewership losses across the board. Specifically, the five biggest US cable providers saw an aggregate loss of 3.8% or 3.2 million TV subscribers in 2018, which surpassed the 3.4% decline suffered in the year prior.

Pointing to the accelerating cord-cutting trend, AT&T argued that the merger will help strengthen the defence against digital rivals like Netflix, Hulu, Amazon, Apple, Facebook and YouTube, all of which have invested in original programming that they don't have to license to competitors. More importantly, AT&T noted that the merger would benefit consumers — by combining its troves of consumer data with Time Warner's expertise in media creation, they will be able to create

---

[89] Moore, S. "Why the AT&T-Time Warner Merger is a win for consumers", *The New York Times*, 31 June 2018, https://www.nytimes.com/2018/06/13/opinion/att-time-warner-merger-good-consumers-antitrust.html.

[90] Reiff, N. "AT&T and Time Warner Merger case: what you need to know", *Investopedia*, 7 December 2018, https://www.investopedia.com/investing/att-and-time-warner-merger-case-what-you-need-know/.

[91] The Nielsen Local Watch Report. "The evolving over-the-air-home", *Nielson Insights*, 14 January 2019, https://www.nielsen.com/us/en/insights/report/2019/nielsen-local-watch-report-the-evolving-ota-home/.

higher quality and more personalised content that better reflect consumer preferences.[92]

Unconvinced by the DOJ's argument that the transaction will "significantly lessen competition", the federal court rejected the appeal and upheld the strategic merger in February 2019. It was felt then that the DOJ's argument completely denied reality, largely because of their clinging onto a theoretical model which was rooted in a static media landscape.[93] More pertinently and somewhat ironically, the court's decision also strongly reaffirmed the DOJ's own view of antitrust law, unchanged since the publication of their Non-Horizontal Merger Guidelines in 1984, that vertical mergers between companies that don't compete pose little threat to consumers.[94]

With the benefit of hindsight, if not already evident then as the suit was panning out, the merger between AT&T and Time Warner can be justified as an attempt to defend their respective market positions, not a market domination plot. Given that globalised competition and the speed of technological change could yield unexpected challenges even for industry leaders, rigidly insisting on a clear separation of roles would seem antiquated.

Technology has often rendered traditional business models no longer viable, implying that companies are constantly under intense pressure to further evolve and modernise. Within the 17 months following the AT&T and Time Warner merger, their internet rivals Amazon won three Oscars, Hulu won the coveted Emmy for best drama and Netflix's market value surpassed Time Warner's.[95] It is abundantly clear that regulators have to maintain a dynamic stance when addressing a convergence of domains.

---

[92] Perez, S. "U.S cord cutters to reach 33 million this year, faster than expected", *TechCrunch*, 25 July 2018, https://techcrunch.com/2018/07/25/u-s-cord-cutters-to-reach-33-million-this-year-faster-than-expected/.

[93] Downes, L. "The AT&T ruling shows that U.S. regulators don't understand media's present — or future", *Harvard Business Review*, 13 June 2018, https://hbr.org/2018/06/the-att-ruling-shows-that-u-s-regulators-dont-understand-medias-present-or-future.

[94] Downes, L. "Why mergers like the AT&T-Time Warner deal should go through", *Harvard Business Review*, 16 November 2017, https://hbr.org/2017/11/why-mergers-like-the-att-time-warner-deal-should-go-through.

[95] Ip Greg, "Antitrust case against Merger of AT&T and time Warner feels stuck in the past", The Wall Street Journal, 1 March 2018, https://www.wsj.com/articles/

Managing Conflicting Interests

Many governments find themselves in a quandary when a new product solves one social problem but creates another in the process. Unlike the ruthless manner in which online retailing is displacing the brick-and-mortar shops at the mall, e-cigarettes are a different ballgame altogether. How should a government regulate e-cigarettes — by taking reference from an existing health challenge or as a potential social ill?

Example 1.6: E-Cigarettes — No Smoke without Fire

Are the ads on vaping enticing the young unwittingly or deliberately? Do they generate new demand which would otherwise not figure in a world of declining traditional smoking among the youth? Or are the benefits of electronic cigarettes towards smoking cessation under-stated and the risks of vaping exaggerated?

The debate around the benefits of vaping rages on. A recent World Health Organization (WHO) warning on vaping triggered a robust and immediate harsh response from public health experts in the UK.[96]

Let's take stock of where the debate is. The polarisation around the value of vaping could not be starker, with the WHO and the US at one end, opposing the very existence of e-cigarettes and the UK at the other, promoting the benefits of vaping to traditional cigarette smoking reduction, if not cessation.

Robust Arguments against Vaping

The Centers for Disease Control and Prevention (CDC) in the US and WHO not only cast doubt over the value of e-cigarettes to smoking cessation but also cited their health risks, such as a severe lung disease reportedly linked to THC[97]-containing e-cigarettes, and more importantly, the

---

antitrust-case-against-merger-of-at-t-and-time-warner-feels-stuck-in-the-past-1521647262.

[96]"WHO warning on vaping draws harsh response from U.K. researchers", https://www.sciencemag.org/news/2020/01/who-warning-vaping-draws-harsh-response-uk-researchers, 22 January 2020.

[97]THC or Tetrahydrocannabino is the principal psychoactive constituent of cannabis.

addictive property of vaping among the young. In the words of the Food and Drug Administration, "youth use of e-cigarettes has reached epidemic proportions". Moreover, there was apparently growing evidence that "youths who had used e-cigarettes had a 23% chance of starting to smoke, compared to only 7% chance without such use".

There is no let up. In November 2019, the New York state sued Juul, the largest US e-cigarette manufacturer for targeting its minors with its marketing campaigns, glamourising vaping through the use of colourful ads featuring young models and "misrepresenting its products as a safer alternative to traditional cigarettes".[98] There were reportedly some 3.6 million underage users of Juul and other e-cigarettes, a culmination of a surge in middle and high school students between 2011 and 2018.

The UK has an equally robust argument in favour of vaping, noting that fears of addiction were not backed by any evidence and that e-cigarettes indeed helped smokers quit. Some preliminary studies have also pointed to e-cigarettes as being more effective than nicotine replacement therapy for quitting smoking.

Regulating Tobacco Products

Governments elsewhere obviously are watching this raging debate with interest. The challenge is a multi-faceted one; how should e-cigarettes and therefore vaping be regarded as a matter of public health policy? What should then be the appropriate regulatory framework? E-cigarettes are deemed illegal in both Japan and Singapore. In the former, the ban on e-cigarettes containing nicotine since 2010 meant that product innovation has since begun focusing on heat-not-burn tobacco products. No regulation exists, at least for now, for non-nicotine e-cigarettes.

The ban in Singapore[99] is more wide-ranging — the Health Sciences Authority enforces the legislation[100] which prohibits the "importation, distribution, sale or offer for sale" anything that is designed to "resemble a tobacco product". In 2017, the ban was extended to cover purchase, use and

---

[98] "New York sues e-cigarette firm Juul for targeting youngsters", 20 November 2019, https://www.japantimes.co.jp/news/2019/11/20/business/new-york-sues-e-cigarette-firm-juul-targeting-youngsters/#.XiyCpy2Q01A.

[99] "Why Singapore bans e-cigarettes", https://www.todayonline.com/commentary/why-singapore-bans-e-cigarettes, 31 January 2019.

[100] Singapore legislation: Section 16 (1) of the Tobacco (Control of Advertisements and Sale) Act.

possession. Between a possible reduction in smoking incidence among hardcore smokers and generating unintended youth vaping addiction, the government has opted to be conservative. Unfortunately, there is no compromise or a middle-of-the-road solution.

Some other countries have also adopted an outright ban while others have left the regulatory lacuna intact through inadvertent inaction, mainly given the complexity of product definition. This promptly gets exploited by manufacturers of e-cigarettes.

Notwithstanding the ever-changing definition around specific substances like nicotine or types of tobacco or devices in use, the vaping conundrum is less of an issue with lagging regulations than with social considerations around demographics. For a country like Japan where smoking among its elderly population poses a real health issue, there is understandably the motivation towards reduction, if not cessation.

For countries with a younger population like India, the sense of urgency and factors for consideration might be more politically driven. Nip it in the bud before it becomes a major health scare. Or impose a prohibitively high tax on e-liquids like Indonesia or ban advertising like Denmark or restrict sales to a minimum age like Belgium.

The case with vaping, where polarisation of scientific views exists over a wide spectrum, presents a challenge to any government attempting to decide on how to regulate. Even if evidence is eventually clear on the benefits or risks to vaping, every government is already under pressure to respond dynamically to the fast-evolving landscape. The demographics are different across countries as is the stage of economic development or the maturity of the public healthcare system.

A government will therefore do well to establish the priorities by stakeholder groups, assess whatever evidence available and act on the least risky combination. Inaction, which will allow new product consumer patterns to take root, may prove to be more problematic in the medium term. Many situations will have no finality, another alternative to e-cigarettes would most surely emerge. Hence, waiting out as a lagging regulator is not an option.

Data Privacy Concerns Reign Supreme

Within the growing spectrum for updating regulations, one priority appears to be more critical than the rest that of data privacy. This takes on greater prominence as the business of data explodes. Many platforms are finding it lucrative to sell their databases, without sparing a thought for how these data might be used, including for insidious purposes.

Many regimes now have a version of legislation that ultimately seeks to protect data or information privacy of especially individuals. In the EU, there's the General Data Protection Regulation since 2018. Meanwhile the US has a myriad of sectoral laws towards information protection, and there is always the Federal Trade Commission Act fallback. Most Asian countries have promulgated similar laws. Most of such legislation prescribes the circumstances that allow information to be collected in the first place, be it by government departments or private operators.

Such attention is well justified considering how effortlessly information can be collected, stored and distributed without care, all in a nano-second. The dire consequences of a no-holds-barred regime are perhaps best illustrated in the Cambridge Analytica episode.

Example 1.7: "I know what you did"

Welcome to the 21st century, where we are confronting a data revolution. As the data universe keeps expanding, more and more of it falls outside the jurisdiction of the various specific privacy laws. Information about each of us is being generated faster than ever from our widespread use of internet-enabled searches, social media, e-commerce and smartphones. The changes in our hyper-networked world now come faster than legislation or regulatory rules can adapt to and have effectively erased the sectoral boundaries that have defined our privacy laws. Not surprisingly, many have viewed the government as a lagging regulator who is constantly playing catch-up, closing the stable doors after the horses have already bolted.

The Great Privacy Awakening

Today, Facebook is a global, publicly traded behemoth that functions as a digital directory, instant communications service, one-stop news source and marketplace. For millions of people, Facebook *is* the internet.[101] Evolving

---

[101] Mirani, L. "Millions of Facebook users have no idea they're using the internet", *Quartz*, 9 February 2015, https://qz.com/333313/milliions-of-facebook-users-have-no-idea-theyre-using-the-internet/.

over the past 16 years, it has accumulated a near-unfathomable amount of data from its base of more than 2 billion active users, many of whom freely share their entire lives.[102] While Facebook has been embroiled in data privacy issues since its launch in 2004, the company's most prolific scandal involved the now defunct Cambridge Analytica — a political consulting and data analytics firm purportedly behind the pro-Brexit Leave EU campaign, as well as Donald Trump's 2016 presidential campaign. Since then, Facebook has become the perfect poster child for how data, when placed in the wrong hands, can be dangerously misused.

The beginning of the end came when "whistle-blower" Christopher Wylie, a co-founder of Cambridge Analytica, revealed that the firm exploited Facebook to harvest data from 87 million profiles across the globe and used that data to develop "psychographic" profiles to deliver personalised pro-Trump material to them at the time of the 2016 US presidential election.[103] The idea was to map similar personality traits based on the users' behaviour and interaction on Facebook and then craft ads to precisely target small groups of voters. During the whole campaign, Cambridge Analytica failed to disclose information about their commercial or political profiling techniques. At its core, the underlying problem was a total lack of transparency, security and the rights of data subjects.

Prior to 2014, before Facebook tightened rules to limit access without gaining permission,[104] third-party developers were able to gain deep access to data from their users' friends, even though their friends may not have granted the app access.[105] Facebook could not proactively keep track of the data improperly acquired previously, including those of 300,000 people who responded to the "thisisyourdigitallife", a personality quiz.

Despite diligent efforts at pursuing Facebook, US Federal Trade Commission (FTC) officials sorely felt the lack of a national privacy law. It became very clear that regulating privacy was much harder than anyone originally expected. In 2019, Facebook was slapped on the wrist with a

---

[102] Gebel, M. "In 15 years Facebook has amassed 2.3 billion users — more than followers of Christianity", *Business Insider US*, 4 February 2019, https://www.businessinsider.sg/facebook-has-2-billion-plus-users-after-15-years-2019-2?r=US&IR=T.

[103] Meredith, S. "Facebook-Cambridge Analytica: A timeline of the data hijacking scandal", *CNBC*, 10 April 2018, https://www.cnbc.com/2018/04/10/facebook-cambridge-analytica-a-timeline-of-the-data-hijacking-scandal.html.

[104] *Ibid.*

[105] "Aleksandr Kogan: The psychologist at the centre of Facebook's data scandal", *The Straits Times*, 20 March 2018, https://www.straitstimes.com/world/europe/aleksandr-kogan-the-psychologist-at-the-centre-of-facebooks-data-scandal.

US$5 billion fine for the company's mishandling of user data following the giant Cambridge Analytica breach.[106] Aside from the multibillion-dollar penalty, the FTC imposed a new corporate governance regime including greater corporate accountability and more rigorous compliance monitoring.[107] Under the agency's order, which established oversight for the next 20 years, Facebook was mandated to create an independent privacy committee to "conduct a privacy review of every new or modified product, service, or practice before it is implemented, and document its decisions about user privacy".[108]

Similarly in the EU, more than 200,000 Italians have had their information gathered without their consent, moving Italy's privacy regulator to fine Facebook €1 million for the violation[109] — the largest fine against the social networking giant connected to that case. This came shortly before a £500,000 (US$644,000) fine sanctioned by the British privacy watchdog and a 6.6 million reais (US$1.6 million) fine in Brazil.[110] In addition, the announcement of the EU's General Data Protection Regulation (GDPR), a new set of strict regulations implemented on March 2019 to protect user data privacy, came hard on Facebook's heels.

In many ways, responses from the different jurisdictions are not surprising. Many of these social network technology companies are evolving at breakneck speed virtually in the absence of the kind of regulation we see in other industries. Besides, there is no established template on how to regulate. This is a by-product of how dynamic these technologies are and of the reality of the sheer time and effort needed to compose appropriate rules and regulations. Yet many businesses thrive in

---

[106] "FTC Imposes $5 Billion Penalty and Sweeping New Privacy Restrictions on Facebook", *Federal Trade Commission* [Press Release], 24 July 2019, https://www.ftc.gov/news-events/press-releases/2019/07/ftc-imposes-5-billion-penalty-sweeping-new-privacy-restrictions.

[107] *Ibid.*

[108] *Ibid.*

[109] Lomas, N. "Italy stings Facebook with $1.1M fine for Cambridge Analytica data misuse", *Tech Crunch*, 28 June 2019, https://techcrunch.com/2019/06/28/italy-stings-facebook-with-1-1m-fine-for-cambridge-analytica-data-misuse/.

[110] Olson, P. "Facebook agrees to pay U.K. fine over Cambridge analytica scandal", The Wall Street Journal, 30 October 2019, https://www.wsj.com/articles/facebook-agrees-to-pay-u-k-fine-over-cambridge-analytica-scandal-11572442488; Holt, K. "Facebook fined yet again over Cambridge Analytica Scandal", *Forbes*, 24 September 2019, https://www.forbes.com/sites/krisholt/2020/12/30/facebook-fined-yet-again-over-cambridge-analytica-scandal/#51602ea25f16.

this regulatory lag or lacuna — surging ahead with new technology, particularly those that straddle domains to produce unique solutions or services and exploiting the market opportunity first before being reined in, if at all.

> *In all fairness, when regulations are arbitrary or not enforced, the private sector would define their own boundaries and be prepared to run the risk of being punished for violating rules, often retrospectively. If an agency must regulate, it would be better to establish clear goals for how consumers interact with the firm and, where possible, establish operating principles as guidelines. Unless absolutely necessary from a risk contagion rationale, they should not regulate how businesses are organised or structured. Businesses, on the contrary, should establish their own sustainability strategy even in the absence of regulations — hat would be acceptable as sound business practices and governance issues, especially around data privacy and management. Moving forward, building privacy and security by design and as a default into companies' core business models will become increasingly critical.*

Reflections

The challenge confronting all regulators can be boiled down to the following hard truths.

Inherent Difficulty of Regulating — The market is replete with examples of new businesses and players who promise and deliver innovation and productivity, operate models across a few domains and create new business practices that leverage on fast-changing technology to gain that first-mover advantage. Certainty, from some form of finality, is thus an elusive if not impossible goal.

Diverging Definition of Domains — Where does banking or payment systems end and where does the provision of value-added non-financial services begin? Overlapping domains are increasingly the norm, frequently driven by an innovative mind, enabled by technology and motivated by the economies of scale to be secured.

Uneven Distribution of Talent — The private sector by design can better attract brains that are more innovative, seeking to disrupt or exploit legal lacunae for benefit or in short, embrace a DNA to "beat the system". In contrast, public sector regulators tend to be persons seeking to protect frameworks and ensure fair play and stability. Increasingly, regulators try to adopt a proactive or predictive perspective towards the formulation of rules, but to limited success. The harsh reality lies in the very different reward systems. This serves to aggravate the inherent difficulty of formulating relevant rules in a timely manner.

Social Considerations — Even as existing players may cry foul over the emergence of non-traditional players operating in grey domain overlaps, by and large, consumers have benefitted as evident in ride-sharing, payment systems and digital banking. Many such providers have exploded in size to such a scale that by the time the regulator acts, it runs the risk of offending a much larger public audience with any curbs on services. It's frequently a political toss-up between the demands of different groups of stakeholders.

Very often, we see that with innovation and technology driving changes in the market at a clip, a regulator inevitably ends up breathless. Some however can come up to speed a little faster than the average, but not always. Or when the Covid-19 pandemic presented itself, the resulting lockdown brought about substantial changes or adjustments to consumer behaviour, especially in the ride-sharing and food-delivery domains. For example, even before the Singapore government could settle on the most appropriate market- and innovation-friendly regulatory framework, it had to revise some stipulations to take into account these temporary but material changes in demand and supply trends. Taxi-drivers who were plying the streets empty have been allowed into delivery services.[111]

All said, post-Covid, where the need for the regulator to keep pace is most pressing is when technology innovation has been relentless. This is particularly evident in financial technology or fintech, including the once-seductive peer-to-peer lending or addictive gaming possibilities. The advent of drones elicits a mixed reaction as does the arrival of cryptocurrencies. Chapter 2 analyses the range of regulatory responses.

---

[111] https://www.channelnewsasia.com/news/singapore/covid-19-taxi-private-hire-car-drivers-home-deliveries-september-12763196, 23 May 2020.

CHAPTER 2
LAGGING REGULATOR — TECHNICAL INNOVATION

Chapter 2

Lagging Regulator — Technical Innovation

The plethora of payment systems, fintech offerings, cryptocurrencies and the promise of digital banking services can be mind-boggling. Consumers should be having a good time these days, availing themselves of plenty of choices at their fingertips, services which are readily accessible anywhere in the world. When does a good thing turn bad?

When social ills result from excessive or the wrong use of fintech innovations, real or anticipated, the regulator has no choice but to intervene. Depending on how serious the social impact is, occasionally, the regulator may have to slam the brakes hard, for example, on addictive gaming in youths.

Some technological innovations bring forth tremendous value. The arrival of drones heralds a wide range of possibilities never dreamt of before, from security surveillance to telemedicine to home delivery of goods ordered online. Conversely, when deployed inappropriately by hobbyists, drones can be a downright nuisance.

How does the regulator position itself against the fast-evolving technology? Even if it could, being proactive may not necessarily lead to the larger good, as innovation may be stifled before the potential value of new products and services can materialise.

Imagine if any government had imposed strict security demands on providers of video conferencing services. This would have created a serious hurdle to communications as the Covid-19 pandemic unfolded. The pandemic has triggered an explosion in the demand for telecommunications-related services and payment systems as transactions and interactions migrated online.

The challenge remains for financial services regulators to keep pace and engage industry innovators so that an appropriate response can always be formulated, come what may.

Pervasive Technology Disruption in Finance

Whenever innovation straddles two or more regulated domains, the tasks for the government will become inordinately complex. Add to this the disruption that technological advances bring.

One can see how new payment systems are giving a fresh meaning to, if not eclipsing past governmental efforts at achieving, a cashless society. Traditional brick-and-mortar banks cry foul at the arrival of new intermediaries, competition that is not subject to the same stringent rules that they are. The instinct is no different from that of the cab drivers — outlaw these disruptors, if not at least subject them to the same onerous regulatory compliance.

Or the pervasiveness of the digital bank — one which is giving the same traditional branch-style banking a run for the money. As it is, many Asian governments do not want to be accused of falling behind the curve and are inviting applications for digital banking licences. This opportunity to provide alternative banking services is not surprisingly attracting non-bank players. Think ride-sharing platforms, telcos, fintech and one gets the drift.

See the common enabler through the above examples which are taking the world by storm, in economies both big and small? Technology. Think technology, think *borderless*, think *scale*, think *connectivity*, think *relationships*, think *global order*, think *artificial intelligence*, think *big data*, or in summary, think *empowerment*. Sustained by continuous zealous and well-funded innovation, technology breaks down geographical and ideological barriers, challenges location-specific rules, renders redundant traditional definitions of industries and domains, births new businesses not previously possible and most significantly of all, is capable of exploiting regulatory lacunae.

The pace of transformation with the onslaught of technology is palpable especially for existing businesses. One needs to look no further than the advent of online retail or the transportation sector, be it in logistics or port management. To put in perspective, strong anecdotal evidence of national effort that is able to keep pace can be found in the massive sums being set aside by many governments to stay current, budgets which are often complemented by an overwhelmingly impressive stream of private capital, estimated to be in the ballpark figure of US$4 trillion.[1]

---

[1] "Tech spending will near $4 trillion this year. Here's where all the money is going and why", 8 April 2019, https://www.cnbc.com/2019/04/08/4-trillion-in-tech-spending-in-2019-heres-where-the-money-is-going.html.

We all get breathless just tracking technology disruption in every sphere of our lives, particularly when it can be effortlessly delivered via that small ubiquitous mobile device within constant reach. Nowhere is this more prominently felt for the layperson than in the payments space. As frequent Singaporean travellers to China can testify to, we often feel like a dinosaur who's struggling either with cash or some UnionPay account or WeChat payment QR code. Even so, it's no longer payments *per se*; one can avail oneself of fund transfers, payment of utilities bills, rail and flight bookings, ride-hailing services all in the palm of one's hand. Left to their own, there is very little incentive for current players, particularly dominant ones, to initiate a change. Once a government believes that a shift is in the larger public interest, it would have to act purposefully and clearly.

Fast forward to today, in many jurisdictions, many consumers, both banked and unbanked, are eagerly awaiting the arrival of digital banks which every other regulator is seeking to licence in double quick time.

Example 2.1: Living Around a Mobile Device

The galloping mobile penetration rate over the past decade is testimony to the vital role the once-innocent-looking device is now playing, beyond making simple phone calls and sending text messages. The owner's life, his daily habits, communication preferences and links to the external world now revolve around convenience via his mobile. Innovators are therefore scrambling to fulfil these needs, leap-frogging over expensive legacy systems once regarded as state-of-the-art but may now be the very impediment to business survival for their owners.

As a nation with an impressive 154% mobile penetration rate,[2] 186% wireless internet saturation rate, along with an impressive 96% of the population having a bank account, Singapore appears to be well-positioned to be at the forefront of payment innovation by all accounts.[3] Yet, six out of every

---

[2] Penetration rate tracks mobile subscriptions and can therefore exceed 100% of population, i.e. when people take up more than one subscription.

[3] Infocomm Media Development Authority (IMDA) "Statistic on Telecom Service for 2019 Jan–Jun", https://www.imda.gov.sg/infocomm-media-landscape/research-and-statistics/telecommunications/statistics-on-telecom-services/statistic-on-telecom-service-

ten transactions in Singapore were still settled via cash or cheque in 2016, pointing clearly to the Lion City's laggard position on the payment front.[4]

The undisputed leader is China, the world's biggest marketplace for cashless payments by virtue of its gargantuan population of over a billion consumers, thanks to the innovation-led growth of WeChat and Alipay. Although Singapore was an early adopter of e-payment solutions, the lack of interoperability between the proprietary systems created by commercial entities stymied the potential proliferation of contactless payments in Singapore, until the government intervened.

As part of his National Day Rally speech in 2017, Singapore's Prime Minister Lee Hsien Loong made a concerted push for Singapore to adopt e-payments as widely and as quickly as possible. He highlighted the irony in Singapore's unwillingness to go digital when it comes to payment, despite the digital-friendly façade.[5] He also appealed to the industry to "simplify and integrate" the vast number of payment options available in Singapore that was fast becoming an impediment.[6] This aspiration is of the same ilk as what the Swedish government has articulated. Over in Sweden, the government is leading the race to become the world's first almost cashless society by leveraging on its supportive legal framework and robust infrastructure. The cash in circulation as a percentage of gross domestic product (GDP) has dipped below the 2% mark, and this is expected to decline to less than half a percent by 2020, making it the envy of many governments.[7] In comparison, Singapore's cash in circulation stood at 10% as of 2018.[8]

---

for-2019-jan; Monetary Authority of Singapore (MAS) "KPMG: Singapore Payments Roadmap, Enabling the future of payments" August 2016. https://www.mas.gov.sg/-/media/MAS/News-and-Publications/Press-Releases/Singapore-Payments-Roadmap-Report--August-2016.pdf.

[4]Tham, I. "Can Singapore catch up in race to go cashless?", *The Straits Times*, 24 August 2017, https://www.straitstimes.com/opinion/can-singapore-catch-up-in-race-to-go-cashless.

[5]*Ibid.*

[6]*Ibid.*

[7]Browne, R. "People in Sweden barely use cash — and that's sounding alarm bells for the country's central bank", *CNBC*, 3 May 2018, https://www.cnbc.com/2018/05/03/sweden-cashless-future-sounds-alarm-bells-for-the-central-bank.html.

[8]"Cash and cheques still account for 40% of Singapore payments", *Singapore Business Review*, 21 February 2019, https://sbr.com.sg/financial-services/in-focus/cash-and-cheques-still-account-40-singapore-payments.

Earlier Efforts at Going Cashless

In fact, going digital and cashless is not a new or novel experience for the residents of Singapore. Over 30 years ago in 1986, Singapore pioneered one of the world's first nation-wide e-payment services known as the Network for Electronic Transfer Singapore (NETS).[9] Implemented by a consortium of five local banks comprising the Development Bank of Singapore (DBS), Oversea-Chinese Banking Corporation (OCBC), Overseas Union Bank (OUB), United Overseas Bank (UOB) and the Post Office Savings Bank (POSB), NETS was seen as a big step forward in Singapore's drive towards a cashless society.[10] The NETS card issued by local banks when a consumer opens an account has long served as an island-wide debit card and e-payment method at retailers, restaurants, entertainment venues and taxi services. This was followed by other digital payment innovations such as NETS Cashcard in 1995 — a pioneering form of stored digital cash for making small-value e-payments at car parks and Electronic Road Pricing (ERP) toll charges, where it held exclusive rights to the system.[11]

In between, the Land Authority of Singapore (LTA) launched another major e-payment system in 2001, a magnetic fare card known as EZ-link.[12] While NETS dominated the retail space, EZ-link quickly monopolised the public transit market.[13] It resulted in a cumbersome situation for commuters; one could only use either the NETS Cashcard at NETS-equipped retailers and car parks or the EZ-link card on buses and trains. The incompatibility of these two card issuers essentially fragmented the payment landscape as they operated on the basis of 'divide and conquer', giving rise to the

---

[9]History, S.G. "Network for electronic transfers is launched: 18 Jan 1986", *National Library Board*, https://eresources.nlb.gov.sg/history/events/9ea5aea3-d8ab-459c-9fcb-89b19a1ba53e.

[10]Fernandez, M. "Use your bank card to shop from June", *The Straits Times*, p. 23. 15 March 1985. Retrieved from NewspaperSG. https://eresources.nlb.gov.sg/newspapers/Digitised/Article/straitstimes19850315-1.2.45.3.

[11]Tham, I. "The ST Guide To…cashless payment systems in Singapore", *The Straits Times*, 9 September 2017, https://www.straitstimes.com/tech/cashless-payment-systems-in-singapore.

[12]Tham, I. "Pay for hawker centre meals with ez-link cards at Nets terminal from April", *The Straits Times*, 24 January 2018, https://www.straitstimes.com/singapore/pay-for-hawker-centre-meals-with-ez-link-cards-at-nets-terminals-from-april.

[13]*Ibid.*

problem of merchants accepting one payment option but not the other.[14] Cost was a consideration as both system providers had invested heavily in their existing infrastructure and established their own network of cards and card readers. Correspondingly, the banks, who are the consortium shareholders, fiercely protected the NETS system as a first mover and were reluctant to admit any other player into their system.

Entry of Yet More Players

The e-payments landscape was further fractured when the market evolved in recent years to include the likes of Apple Pay, Samsung Pay, Android Pay and multiple QR code payment solutions developed by banks to serve their own customers. Instead of helping consumers choose how they want to transact, the dizzying array of options presented even more inconvenience, if not confusion. Not only do customers have to carry multiple cards but also do businesses have to bear the cost of installing multiple readers. This is the eyesore that consumers frequently encounter at the cashier's desk. The real issue at hand was the obvious absence of an interoperable system which all payment modes can tap into.

Push Towards Common Interface

Eventually, the government made a concerted push to create a commercially viable and unified e-payment interface. In September 2018, The Monetary Authority of Singapore (MAS) and Information and Media Development Authority (IMDA) jointly led an industry task force to develop and roll out the Singapore Quick Response Code (SGQR), a single QR interface that combines 27 e-payment solutions. By adopting the SGQR, consumers no longer have to face the trouble of finding the right QR code to transact and merchants are saved the hassle of dealing with multiple e-payment providers. As of September 2019, more than 32,000 SGQR codes have been deployed, representing 20% of all retail point-of-sale transactions.

In the same year, NETS was appointed to implement an open access e-payment solution for food centres, including 200 coffee shops, 25 hawker

---

[14] Tan, W. "The Big Read: No more 'divide and conquer', as banks face up to e-payment disruption" TODAY, 1 September 2017. http://www.todayonline.com/business/big-read-no-more-divide-and-conquer-banks-face-e-payment-disruption?google_editors_picks=true.

centres and 20 industrial canteens over a period of 2 years. According to the MAS, 40% of dining in Singapore takes place at coffee shops, hawker centres or canteens where 70% of the transactions were made using cash.[15] The all-in-one terminal developed will be able to accept 20 cashless payment options, which ranges from QR codes to EZ-link fare cards.[16] To encourage merchants to make the switch, the government provided ample incentives by renting the terminals to merchants at no charge for the first three years.[17] Transaction fees, traditionally set at 2%–5%, were also significantly lowered to 0.5%, with the intention to bring it all the way down to nothing during the same period.[18]

Digital Banking — The Next Big Thing

Such is the pace of innovation — breathless and mostly scalable, in stark contrast to the pace of change — tardy and mostly reluctant, dragged down by legacy systems. Barely had the dust settled on the debate on a unified payments user interface when the digital banking concept presents itself, an amalgamation of payments and traditional financial services delivered on a technology platform.

Non-banks have been jostling to become licenced digital banks in Singapore, demonstrating a growing convergence between technology and traditional financial services in Southeast Asia. In June 2019, MAS sent a ripple through the ecosystem, announcing its intention to issue five digital bank licences, comprising two for digital full banks and three for digital wholesale banks. The former would be allowed to take retail deposits and be subject to a higher minimum paid-up capital of S$1.5 billion beyond the 1–2 years of operating under restrictions.[19]

A digital bank would offer the same type of traditional banking services, but at a lower cost as it operates entirely online without any physical

---

[15]Tham, I. "Is the cashless jigsaw complete?" *The Straits Times*, 20 September 2018, https://www.straitstimes.com/opinion/is-the-cashless-jigsaw-complete.

[16]Tham, I. "Nets to run unified e-payment system for hawker stalls", *The Straits Times*, 13 September 2018, https://www.straitstimes.com/singapore/nets-to-run-unified-e-payment-system-for-hawker-stalls.

[17]*Ibid.*

[18]*Ibid.*

[19]Seow, B. "MAS spells out criteria for new digital bank licences", *The Straits Times*, 30 August 2019, https://www.straitstimes.com/business/banking/mas-spells-out-criteria-for-new-digital-bank-licences.

presence unlike bank branches.[20] MAS will look at candidates' ability to offer a technology-driven differentiated value proposition prudently and sustainably, including servicing the domestically underbanked segments.

As of January 2020, 21 firms, several of whom are consortia, have reportedly applied for the five digital bank licences.[21] Companies that have expressed interest in formal applications include an interesting combination of non-bank businesses. They include Southeast Asian consumer internet company Sea Ltd., which owns the e-commerce platform Shopee, online gaming arm Garena and digital financial services provider SeaMoney, which Sea Ltd is counting on to serve millennials and SMEs well.[22] Others include a collaboration between ride-hailing firm Grab and telecommunications provider Singtel, and the gaming hardware firm Razer-led consortium. The list of aspirants makes for interesting reading.[23]

Countries in the European Union and elsewhere in Asia, such as China, Japan and South Korea, have already seen the establishment of digital-only banks.[24] In 2019, Malaysia announced too that the country's central bank intended to issue up to five digital bank licenses under a licensing framework to be finalised shortly.[25]

Chinese cities like Shanghai and Beijing have already entrenched their positions as kings of the cashless revolution. Hong Kong, which had already started the process in 2019, was witnessing the launch of the eight new online-only banks. ZA Bank, the first off the block of the new digital-only banks, heralded its arrival by offering a 6% interest rate, more than

---

[20] Lim, J. "Explainer: What's the big deal about digital banks?", *TODAY*, 1 September 2019, https://www.todayonline.com/singapore/explainer-whats-big-deal-about-digital-banks.

[21] *Ibid.*

[22] Yu, D. "Sea joins Singapore's digital banking race", *Tech in Asia*, 7 January 2020, https://www.techinasia.com/sea-joins-singapore-digital-bank-race/.

[23] Choudhury, S. "Singapore regulator says it received 21 applications for digital bank licenses", *CNBC*, 6 January 2020, https://www.cnbc.com/2020/01/07/singapore-regulator-says-it-received-21-applications-for-digital-bank-licenses.html.

[24] Choo, Y. "21 applications submitted for up to 5 Singapore digital bank licences: MAS", *The Straits Times*, 7 January 2020, https://www.straitstimes.com/business/banking/21-applications-submitted-for-5-singapore-digital-bank-licences.

[25] "Malaysia to issue up to 5 digital bank licences next year" CNA, 27 December 2019, https://www.channelnewsasia.com/news/business/malaysia-banking-sector-5-new-online-lenders-12215388.

3% points higher than that offered by traditional banks such as HSBC and Standard Chartered.[26]

The arrival of digital-only banking may signal a "rate" war, although it remains to be seen how sustainable this is. Digital banks are likely be able to complete only in the mass retail and SME space or offer basic products that do not require face-to-face interaction. A PwC study also found that digital banks are not expected to replace existing banking relationships for the majority of customers, with most likely to view their digital bank as a secondary account.[27] Two in five respondents in Singapore indicated that they would only consider opening a digital bank account if it is "popular and successful". At the same time, 67% of them will continue to use their existing account as their primary one where most transactions take place.[28]

> *Regardless of the customer shift and substitution patterns, the banking and payment landscape of the future will most certainly look radically different from what it does today. As countries forge ahead with making cashless payments a way of life for society across all segments of the economy, the potential downside risks must be recognised and prudently managed. An overly rapid transition could potentially create financial exclusion, where vulnerable and underserved citizens who are not accustomed to new technologies may face barriers integrating into the cashless arena.*
>
> *Sceptics have also raised concerns regarding data security as transactions are digitally recorded and can be vulnerable to theft, wilfully or otherwise. Nonetheless, without the active role of the Singapore regulator to spearhead standards setting and coordinate a common platform among the (disparate) payment providers, for the greater good for society, the journey towards a cashless society would not be possible. Intervention in this case is more than justified.*

---

[26] "Hong Kong's first digital bank offers 6% rate for deposits that dwarfs HSBC's", *The Straits Times*, 13 January 2020, https://www.straitstimes.com/business/banking/hong-kongs-first-digital-bank-offers-6-rate-for-deposits-that-dwarfs-hsbcs.

[27] Shiao, V. "2 in 5 will only consider 'popular and successful' digibanks in Singapore: PwC poll" *Business Times*, 10 February 2020, https://www.businesstimes.com.sg/banking-finance/2-in-5-will-only-consider-popular-and-successful-digibanks-in-singapore-pwc-poll.

[28] *Ibid.*

Tackling Convergence of Domains

How does one classify the business of Amazon? Or WeChat? Or Apple? Or Gojek? The reality, if not irony, is that the more successful they are as an aggregator or platform of sorts, the greater the value they bring to businesses and customers within their ecosystem but also the deeper the systemic risk they pose from not being directly regulated. Many central bank regulators are constantly stumped by the spate of emerging technologies and the attendant new fintech services or challenged by existing players to prescribe the necessary regulations to rein these new players in.

Where it straddles more than one regulated domain, how should regulators coordinate their response? Should both set of laws be revised simultaneously to avoid inconsistencies or gaps, or should new laws be introduced altogether to provide a more holistic approach? The answer, regrettably, isn't always clear but the pressure is definitely there.

Example 2.2: Race to be Payment Platforms

Gone are the days when a transaction needs to involve an exchange of cold hard cash or a transfer between the bank accounts of parties involved. Neither does a transaction have to be between parties in close proximity or with prior knowledge of each other. Two decades ago, when asked if instantaneous payments were possible on a mobile device, many would have considered this a pipe dream. Accessing services via such payment platforms would be regarded as pure fantasy. Yet these days, many Chinese citizens would shudder at the thought of losing access to the plethora of payment systems and services at their disposal.

While America spent the past decade upgrading its bank-based magnetic-striped cards with chips, China experienced a payment revolution. China is fast establishing itself as a truly progressive, cashless society, thanks largely to digital payment solutions operated by two Chinese tech juggernauts — Ant Financial and Tencent — whose brands now reverberate around the world. Ant is estimated to be worth US$200 billion as of the end of 2019,[29] marginally behind much older behemoths like HSBC, putting it among the world's most valuable financial firms. Tencent's financial

---

[29] Zhu, J., Wu, K., and Yan, Z. "Exclusive: China's Ant aims for $200 billion price tag in private share sales — sources", *Reuters*, 17 January 2020, https://www.reuters.com/article/us-ant-

services are wrapped inside Tencent Holdings, which has a US$470 billion market capitalisation.[30]

Unfettered Opportunities

Both companies have moved beyond payments into selling products like micro-loans and money-market funds — a complete suite of services to the end customer, the embodiment of a true one-stop solution. They will, unless checked by concerned regulators, grow much bigger. But the days of *laissez-faire* and easy growth are decidedly on the decline for FinTech firms in China as regulators catch up, as they should.

For more than a decade, Alibaba affiliate Ant Financial and gaming company Tencent, with its social media platform WeChat, have had free rein to innovate and run vast networks of new internet-enabled business models, taking advantage of the regulatory lacuna. According to data from the People's Bank of China (PBOC), the value of mobile payments in China hit almost RMB 280 trillion (US$41.5 billion) in 2018,[31] almost 7 times that reached in the United States.[32] Over 90% of that sum stemmed from Alipay and Tenpay, commanding the lion's share of the mobile payments market.[33] Systems such as Apple Pay and PayPal, popular elsewhere in the world, have been relegated to the "others" category. The user base numbers speak for themselves. Ant's digital wallet Alipay has reached 1.2 billion users from 50 markets worldwide, of which 900 million are active users from China.[34] Popular messaging application WeChat[35] is

---

financial-valuation-exclusive/exclusive-chinas-ant-aims-for-200-billion-price-tag-in-private-share-sales-sources-idUSKBN1ZG1C6.

[30] Tencent Holdings Market Cap, $472.1B as at 28 February 2020, https://www.forbes.com/companies/tencent-holdings/#2f122ea2158b.

[31] McSheaffrey, P., Robson, B., and Huang, A. "The rise of the tech giants", *KPMG*, September 2019, https://assets.kpmg/content/dam/kpmg/cn/pdf/en/2019/09/the-rise-of-the-tech-giants.pdf.

[32] "Chart of the Day: China's Mobile Payment Transaction Volume Hits $41.51 Trillion in 2018", *Caixin Global*, 22 March 2019, https://www.caixinglobal.com/2019-03-22/chart-of-the-day-chinas-mobile-payment-transaction-volume-hits-4151-trillion-in-2018-101395789.html.

[33] *Ibid*, p. 3.

[34] Choudhury, S. "China's Ant Financial has no timetable for a listing but targets 2 billion users in a decade", *CNBC*, 19 November 2019 https://www.cnbc.com/2019/11/19/ant-financial-no-ipo-timetable-but-plans-to-acquire-more-users-outside-china.html.

[35] WeChat Pay sits on the Tenpay platform in terms of licencing and settlement.

also deeply embedded in the daily lives of almost every Chinese individual who has a smartphone, with monthly active users exceeding the 1 billion mark.[36]

It is noteworthy to mention that China UnionPay, also known as CUP, originally dominated all payments in China. The company was effectively a state-backed monopoly due to its central bank mandate, making it impossible for any other firm to compete. Unlike the more agile tech companies, it was inactive and entered the lucrative mobile payments sector only at the end of 2017, whereas Alipay launched its mobile payments solution in 2009 and WeChat Pay followed suit in 2013.[37]

Apart from rapid expansion in the payment sector, the Alipay and Tenpay duopoly also extended their offering to other financial services such as wealth management. For instance, Ant Financial launched its own online wealth management platform, Yu'e Bao, which at its peak was managing nearly RMB $2 trillion (US$300 million) of assets as the world's largest money-market fund.[38] Since its inception in 2013, Yu'e Bao has attracted more than 600 million Chinese investors.[39] The credit loan service arm of Ant's private commercial bank also provided micro-loans to 16 million small businesses in China by 2019.[40]

Pitting itself against Ant Financial and Tencent, Didi Chuxing, China's ride-hailing giant, launched a suite of financial products including crowd-funding, insurance and personal loans in early 2019. Responsible for a giant 90% share of e-hailing trips in China, Didi is expected to benefit from a significant network effect from its base of 500 million users.

---

[36]"Number of monthly active WeChat users from 2nd quarter 2011 to 3rd quarter 2019", *Statista 2020*, https://www.statista.com/statistics/255778/number-of-active-wechat-messenger-accounts/.

[37]"UnionPay Attempts Mobile Payment Catch-up through Partnership with Internet Giant", *Caixin Global*, 18 August 2017, https://www.chinadaily.com.cn/business/tech/2017-09/28/content_32598336.htm.

[38]Yu, E., Yang, Y., Chen, L., and Sun, H., "World's No. 1 money-market fund shrinks by $120 Billion in China", *Bloomberg*, 6 September 2019, https://www.bloomberg.com/news/articles/2019-09-05/world-s-no-1-money-market-fund-shrinks-by-120-billion-in-china.

[39]*Ibid.*

[40]"Jack Ma's 2-trillion yuan loan machine is changing Chinese banking", *The Straits Times*, 29 July 2019, https://www.straitstimes.com/business/banking/jack-mas-2-trillion-yuan-loan-machine-is-changing-chinese-banking.

Genesis of Regulatory Concerns

Still, as an industry expands in a somewhat unbridled fashion, so too do its vulnerabilities. Concerns have mushroomed over the unlimited explosion of personal unsecured lending, growing at about 20% a year over the past decade.[41] Systemic risks related to such credit extension intensified as loans are known to have surpassed the RMB 1 trillion (US$151 billion) mark.[42] Security issues over the usage of QR code payments have also emerged. In the southern province of Guangzhou, a total of RMB 90 million (US$13 million) were stolen via QR code scams, where fraudsters replaced legitimate codes with fake ones to access the scanner's smartphone and steal personal bank account information.[43]

Worried that the collapse of Ant and other financial holding companies may pose a systemic risk to the financial system, the government sought to bring oversight up to speed by beginning to impose a series of curbs. In what's considered an attempt to prevent misuse of client money, the PBOC raised the payment platforms' reserve funds ratio from 20% to 50% on April 2018, and eventually to 100% the following year, effectively putting all the funds held in escrow under its own centralised management.[44] This move wipes out the billions of yuan in interest revenue previously earned by parking their customer deposits in commercial banks or other money-market funds. Tencent reportedly earned RMB 3.9 billion (US$560 million) in interest income in 2017 or 1.7% of total revenues.[45] What's more, in an attempt to rein in fraud and protect customers, PBOC enacted a cap on mobile spending via QR codes, which users can scan with Alipay or Tenpay

---

[41] Hamlin, K. "Mini-Loans Have Spurred a Business — And Debt — Boom in China", *Bloomberg*, 29 October 2019, https://www.bloomberg.com/graphics/2019-new-economy-drivers-and-disrupters/china.html.

[42] Xiao, L. "In China, unsecured short-term lending now a trillion-Yuan industry", Caixin Global, 21 November 2017, https://www.caixinglobal.com/2017-11-21/in-china-unsecured-short-term-lending-now-a-trillion-yuan-industry-101174258.html.

[43] Tao, L. "QR Code scams rise in China, putting e-payment security in spotlight", *The South China Morning Post*, 21 March 2017, https://www.scmp.com/business/china-business/article/2080841/rise-qr-code-scams-china-puts-online-payment-security.

[44] "China cbank to raise reserve funds ratio for payment firms to 100 pct", *Reuters*, 29 June 2018, https://www.reuters.com/article/china-pboc-payments/china-cbank-to-raise-reserve-funds-ratio-for-payment-firms-to-100-pct-idUSB9N1TE02O.

[45] WIldau, G. "Tencent and Alipay set to lose $1bn in revenue from payment rules", *Financial Times*, 16 July 2018, https://www.ft.com/content/b472f73c-859e-11e8-96dd-fa565ec55929.

to make purchases or order services. Based on security measures and user credentials, the regulations will cap individual QR code payments at RMB 500 (US$70), RMB 1000 (US$145), or RMB 5000 (US$715) per day.[46] These limits ultimately shaved revenue streams and curtailed their rapid pace of expansion.

> *By the time the regulators decided to act, in many regards, Ant Financial and Tenpay are already emblematic of companies considered "too big to fail". To mitigate the accumulated systemic risks while facilitating the healthy and sustainable development of internet finance, the Chinese authorities are now seeking to re-assert control with care. Too much new regulation could lead to potentially far-reaching consequences. Too light a touch may however leave risks unaddressed.*
>
> *Although Ant's financials may not look so propitious with the changing regulatory dynamics, its potential continues to be promising. Its continued innovation will not cease to pose a challenge to regulators, most likely in ways beyond the regulators' understanding. To balance supporting innovation with guarding against risks, regulators should make constant efforts in engaging such innovators, improving regulation efficiency and enhancing infrastructure while trying their level best at catching up with the genius behind these transformative financial innovations.*

Unlimited Access to Credit

Once unbridled, innovation can lead to unintended consequences where the authorities will have no choice but to intervene or even slam the brakes hard in some cases. This was a predicament that the Chinese authorities found themselves in with the explosion in peer-to-peer (P2P) lending and gaming.

The unfettered access to credit, outside of the tightly regulated formal banking sector, coined harmlessly as P2P lending, led to unsustainable, if not undesirable, consumption. This was more than the writing on the wall;

---

[46] WIldau, G. and Jia, Y. "China moves to impose order on mobile payments boom", *Financial Times*, 28 December 2017, https://www.ft.com/content/b7866e7c-eb8e-11e7-bd17-521324c81e23.

they threatened the very values that many societies, not just the Chinese, hold dearly around diligence and thrift and spending within one's means.

Example 2.3: The Ugly Side to P2P Lending

Online P2P lending was once touted as a way to transform finance. No one embraced it more than the people in China, which boasts the world's largest P2P lending sector. Amidst a massive boom in internet-enabled finance, P2P lending platforms took off in 2013 and quickly emerged as a valuable source of credit for consumers and small businesses who would otherwise not be able to access loans through the traditional banking system.

It can be said, with the benefit of hindsight, that while P2P lending creates enormous socio-economic benefits, it contains moral hazards and somewhat unwittingly presents itself as a channel for criminal activities. Stories of owners of failed platforms disappearing into thin air, misallocation of funds, mass criminal enterprises amidst desperate cries from investors for state assistance are sobering reminders of the dangers lurking behind new forms of unregulated, alternative finance. Many continue to question what more the already overburdened authorities could have done to protect investors, or why these platforms were allowed to get away with portraying themselves as government approved in the first place.

P2P lending, including the concept and model, first entered China around 2006. Unlike a bank — which pools deposits and on-lends these funds for a spread, and which has an obligation to payback depositors even if loans go bad — online P2P lending occurs whenever a match between a borrower in need and a lender with spare money occurs on the platform. These platforms have in the past attracted lenders with hooks such as "one-month rate at an annualized five percent".[47]

In China, rural residents and smaller entrepreneurs find it hard to access consumer credit owing to the lack of a national credit ratings system. Meanwhile, the emerging middle class is flush with liquidity but are hesitant about investing in the speculative property and volatile stock

---

[47]Cho, Y. "China's peer-to-peer lenders fight for survival", *Nikkei Asian Review*, 18 February 2019, https://asia.nikkei.com/Business/Business-trends/China-s-peer-to-peer-lenders-fight-for-survival2.

markets.[48] Enter the magical P2P lending platforms. At its peak in 2015, there were 2,595 lending platforms in the market; lending transactions reached 982.3 billion RMB (US$151 billion), up 288% from 2014.[49]

Some are Mere Ponzi Schemes

In the initial years of the P2P surge, regulators in China took a light, in fact hands-off approach. However, problems with fraud started to mount with the long period of regulatory vacuum. In 2015, one of the biggest and most brazen cases involved the Chinese P2P lending company, Ezubao. It was revealed as a record-breaking Ponzi scheme which had amassed over RMB 59.8 billion (US$8.5 billion) and scammed over 900,000 investors.[50] Ezubao had promised annual returns of between 9% and 14.6%, but as many as 95% of the projects listed on the company's website then were fabricated, according to a confession from an ex-employee.[51] In fact, statistics released in 2016 by the Chinese Banking Regulatory Commission showed that about 40% of P2P lending platforms were in fact outright Ponzi schemes.[52]

The Beginning of Regulation

Given the potential social unrest among investors, the authorities had no choice but to reverse their position on not regulating P2P lending. In August 2016, a host of Chinese financial regulators and government departments, led by the China Banking Regulatory Commission (CBRC), jointly promulgated the Interim Rules for the Administration of the Business Activities of Internet-Based Lending Information Intermediary Institutions

---

[48] Feng, E. "Chinese government faces peer-to-peer lending scandals dilemma", *Financial Times*, 12 November 2018, https://www.ft.com/content/c71eea4a-c198-11e8-84cd-9e601db069b8.

[49] Xinhua News, "China's online P2P lending almost quadrupled in 2015: report", 2 January 2016, http://www.china.org.cn/business/2016-01/02/content_37439668.htm.

[50] Reuters, "Leader of China's $9 billion Ezubao online scam gets life; 26 jailed", 12 September 2017, https://www.reuters.com/article/us-china-fraud/leader-of-chinas-9-billion-ezubao-online-scam-gets-life-26-jailed-idUSKCN1BN0J6.

[51] Macauley, R. "Nearly one million investors may have been fleeced in China's latest Ponzi scheme", *Yahoo News*, 1 February 2016, https://finance.yahoo.com/news/nearly-one-million-investors-may-035043402.html.

[52] https://www.finextra.com/blogposting/17107/the-rise-and-fall-of-p2p-lending-in-china.

("Interim Rules").[53] The Interim Rules clarified that P2P lending platforms were required to appoint a third-party custodian bank and were prohibited from providing guarantees in any form to lenders. P2P lenders were also not allowed to sell wealth management products nor issue asset-backed securities.

Again, in August 2017, the CBRC acted, releasing new market disciplines requiring P2P platforms to make timely disclosures of funding sources, the amount of outstanding loans, loans that are overdue for more than 90 days. At the same time, it delegated oversight to the local authorities.[54] Finance bureaus operating under these local government authorities in turn passed the work down to district bureaus, which relied heavily on P2P firms for data and disclosure.[55] Consequently, critical issues arose from this arrangement — local governments with limited expertise could not effectively oversee operations. Moreover, they faced a moral hazard when evaluating platforms that were extending credit to government-linked projects.[56]

The Beginning of the End

Even as the new rules were gradually implemented, the winds were shifting and lenders lost market confidence. Many P2P companies shut down rather than face tougher regulations or faced a liquidity crunch as banks drastically cut funding, prompting investors to withdraw their money quickly. Unlike banks, P2P companies did not need to maintain reserve capital. Such abrupt closures triggered street protests in major cities including

---

[53] Nemoto, N. Storey, D., and Huang, B. "Optimal Regulation of P2P lending for Small and Medium-Sized Enterprises", *Asian Development Bank Institute Working Paper Series*, January 2019, https://www.adb.org/sites/default/files/publication/478611/adbi-wp912.pdf.

[54] Cheng, L. "Quick Take: China to improve oversight of peer-to-peer lending", *Cai Xin Global*, 28 August 2017, https://www.caixinglobal.com/2017-08-28/quick-take-china-to-improve-oversight-of-peer-to-peer-lending-101136810.html.

[55] Tham, E. and Leng, C. "In China, P2P insiders say regulatory shortcomings have choked industry", *Reuters*, 6 September 2019, https://www.reuters.com/article/us-china-p2p-regulation-analysis/in-china-p2p-insiders-say-regulatory-shortcomings-have-choked-industry-idUSKCN1VR055.

[56] Chorzempa, M. "Massive P2P failures in China: Underground banks going under", Peterson Institute For International Economics, 21 August 2018, https://www.piie.com/blogs/china-economic-watch/massive-p2p-failures-china-underground-banks-going-under.

Beijing and Shanghai. In particular, thousands of investors affected by the closure of Tuandai.com gathered at the firm's headquarters in Guangzhou to demand the return of their money. The platform had about 220,000 lenders and borrowers at the time of its collapse and about 14.5 billion yuan (US$2.2 billion) had been pooled into the system by the time of its collapse.[57] This was a recurring ugly scene in many places. The growth of China's P2P lending sector had reversed as dramatically as it had ballooned only a few years before. Only 427 existing P2P firms were still operating by the last quarter of 2019, down from their peak in 2015.[58]

The breathless expansion and then quick collapse of China's P2P lending industry offers crucial lessons for regulators on how to handle emerging fintech innovation, especially when they cannot match the pace of development of a fast-changing industry, enough to properly protect retail investors. In reality, the technological innovation of P2P lending business models makes regulations and rules obsolete almost immediately.[59] While innovations like P2P lending can plug gaps left unserved by traditional banks, the risks these new business models bring can also be substantial and negate the benefits. Sudden or heavy regulation in response to a potentially large social problem could cause financial chaos among P2P companies, consequently putting them in crisis and ironically causing the very social unrest and panic that the regulations seek to address.

> *Regulators need to ensure that appropriate resources are deployed to address emerging issues and set regulatory boundaries so that as a new industry scales, companies are clear on the responsibilities to support good practice. At the same time, ideally, consumers can be insulated from the potentially negative consequences that may arise, such as scams, over-consumption of credit and bad actors using these innovations for nefarious purposes. Apart from specifying clear regulatory limits for P2P operators, there could*

---

[57] Mai, J. "Chinese city calls in riot police as angry investors protest outside P2P lender's headquarters", *Yahoo News*, 7 April 2019, https://sg.news.yahoo.com/chinese-city-calls-riot-police-103240373.html.

[58] Zhang, M. "Mainland investors say goodbye to double-digit returns as Beijing tightens regulations on online lending platforms", *South China Morning Post*, 11 June 2017, https://www.scmp.com/business/banking-finance/article/2097828/mainland-investors-say-goodbye-double-digit-returns-beijing.

[59] Douglas, W. A., Barberisd, J., and Buckleyr, R. P. "The evolution of Fintech: A new post-crisis paradigm?" 47 Georgetown, *Journal of International Law* 1271, 1318–19, 2016.

> *be public education too for investors on how to deal only with firms that follow sound business practices. This would be useful to keep P2P lending in line with the major attribute of sharing economy — the leverage of idle capacity.*

Another Form of Addiction

Like P2P lending, online gaming's genesis initially appeared harmless enough, but over time, the adverse social impact has become increasingly glaring and worrying. Prior to 2018, the lack of a regulatory framework for a catapulting addiction to gaming caused, and continues to generate, great concern over a social ill with grave consequences.

Example 2.4: Gaming isn't All Fun

When a government is presented with a dilemma — of a burgeoning industry while securing the top global market position and social ills with unquantifiable long-term consequences, how should it react? China found itself having to address both the success and addiction ills associated with a rapidly expanding gaming industry.

Remember the cute chomping *Pac-Man*? Or *Jumpman* aka *Mario* of Nintendo's *Donkey Kong*? From hand-held devices like Game Boy, video games were offered on desktop personal computers or consoles through the 1990s.[60] The race towards producing winning video games unfortunately inspired many to resort to gore and violence. By the 2000s, games took on reality show elements, and thanks to the internet, enabled virtual communities to be formed across borders. Advanced graphics and seamless online play fast became the characteristics of successful games. Soon, millions across the globe found themselves increasingly addicted and would while away hours on new platforms over social media or smartphone apps. Not all games had undesirable outcomes — even the Army adopted games as a means of addressing policy and management issues.

---

[60] https://www.museumofplay.org/about/icheg/video-game-history/timeline, accessed 5 February 2020.

Size of the Fast-Growing Pie

Accelerating past the long-time gaming giants US, Japan and the UK, growth in China's revenue in the gaming industry has roots dating back to 2009.[61] Owing to a big domestic market, China quickly rose and maintained its position as the world's biggest game market, with more than 500 million users and an estimated US$38 billion in revenue,[62] while Tencent, a Shenzhen-based company, is now the biggest game company in the world.

Gaming Addiction Classified as Disease

Internet addiction has received fresh scrutiny after the World Health Organization added gaming disorder to its international classification of diseases in 2018, 10 years after China first classified it as a public health threat.[63] Video game companies have also been accused of deliberately making their games more addictive, with *Fortnite* developer Epic Games recently accused of hiring psychologists to "make it as addictive as possible".[64]

A national vision report in 2015 said around 500 million Chinese — nearly half the population above five years old — suffer visual impairment.[65] Fearing the social ills, health risks and rising levels of near-sightedness among minors, the Chinese authorities announced the establishment of a gaming regulator — the State Administration of Press and Publications (SAPP) which is under the direct control of the Central Committee of the Communist Party of China (CCP) in 2018. SAPP has

---

[61] Xu, K. "The role of China in gaming industry regulations", *Kontinentalist*, 17 June 2019, https://kontinentalist.com/stories/the-role-of-china-in-gaming-industry-regulations.

[62] Cho, Y. "China's 500m gamers drive growth at Tencent and other IT giants", *Nikkei Asian Review*, 2 December 2019, https://asia.nikkei.com/Business/Media-Entertainment/China-s-500m-gamers-drive-growth-at-Tencent-and-other-IT-giants.

[63] Chen, C. "Inside China's battle to keep internet addiction in check", *South China Morning Post*, 27 June 2019, https://www.scmp.com/tech/policy/article/3016183/inside-chinas-battle-keep-internet-addiction-under-check.

[64] Cuthbertson, A. "Fortnite lawsuit: epic game hired psychologists to make game 'Very, Very Addictive'", *The Independent UK*, 7 October 2019, https://www.independent.co.uk/life-style/gadgets-and-tech/gaming/fortnite-lawsuit-gaming-addiction-epic-games-a9146486.html.

[65] AFP "China to restrict digital games over myopia concerns", https://www.straitstimes.com/world/china-to-restrict-digital-games-over-myopia-concerns.

vowed to place aggressive curbs such as limiting the approval of new games, restricting playing time and developing an age restriction system.

The same year, the approval process of games entering the China market faced a major overhaul. China enacted a halt on approvals for new video games, which lasted nine months, dealing a significant blow to the lucrative industry. All games were required to obtain approvals and licences before being allowed to be published and distributed in China, resulting in a huge backlog of games seeking approval. Companies making games for Chinese audiences have reported more than $1 billion in foregone sales due to the halt in approvals.[66] Among the 52 listed companies in China's gaming industry, 38 companies saw a 20% slump in their stock price. More specifically, Tencent's share price dropped by 14% and suffered 1,100 billion yuan (US$160 billion) loss in market capitalisation in 2018.[67] Against a count of more than 8,500 games which were awarded licences in 2017, the number of games set to receive licences in 2019 was estimated to be only a fraction, around 2,000.[68]

Ethics as a Consideration

In conjunction with the freshly minted gaming regulator SAPP, an online game ethics committee was created to introduce stricter content policies, targeting content depicting "sexual explicitness, goriness, violence and gambling".[69] Before the committee was set up, online games only had to pass administrative evaluation. As of end 2018, gaming machines and devices having gambling functions, such as maximising returns with small wagers by setting betting odds, including Poker and Mahjong games, were no longer approved. These digital forms of traditional leisure activities are

---

[66] Webb, K. "China is cracking down on new video games entering the country and it's costing publishing giants billions in profit", *Business Insider*, 25 October 2018, https://www.businessinsider.sg/china-video-games-crackdown-costing-billions-2018-10/.

[67] Wong, F. "China's New Gaming Regulations: What it Means for Investors", *China Briefing*, 27 September 2018, https://www.china-briefing.com/news/chinas-new-gaming-regulations-impact-foreign-investors/.

[68] "China's state administration of press and publication releases new notice on preventing addiction among minors in online games", Niko Partners, 6 November 2019, https://nikopartners.com/chinas-state-administration-of-press-and-publication-releases-new-notice-on-preventing-addiction-among-minors-in-online-games.

[69] Zialcita, P. "China introduces restrictions on games for minors", *NPR*, 6 November 2019, https://www.npr.org/2019/11/06/776840260/china-introduces-restrictions-on-video-games-for-minors.

immensely popular for studios because they are relatively cheap to make and bear lucrative fruit.

Likewise, games that contain images of corpses and blood were also rejected. Developers previously modified blood colour to green to circumvent restrictions, but the renewed guidelines have effectively ruled out any colour variations of blood.[70] Certain games inspired by the imperial past over concerns of "obscene contents and political metaphors" were similarly disallowed.[71] These new rules essentially call on game makers and publishers to respect the traditional values of Chinese culture. This includes adhering to core socialist values and developing games that offer independent intellectual property.

Regulator Further Flexes Muscle

In 2019, SAPP announced further drastic curfew measures and published a new set of restrictions on playing video games including spending limits. The new measures specifically target youth online gaming. Under the new rules, those identified as minors (under 18) will be restricted to gaming an hour and a half per day on weekdays, or three hours per day on weekends and public holidays. They will also not be able to play during the hours of 10 pm and 8 am[72] A similar law exists in video game powerhouse South Korea — banning minors under 16 from playing online games between midnight and 6 am since 2011.[73] Additionally, the new guidelines place restrictions on the amount of money minors can transfer to their online gaming accounts. Those from ages eight to 16 can spend a maximum of 200 RMB a month and RMB 50 on a single transaction, and ages 16 to 18 will be limited to 400 RMB per month.[74]

---

[70] Liao, R. "China's new gaming rules to ban poker, blood and imperial schemes", *TechCrunch*, 22 April 2019, https://techcrunch.com/2019/04/21/chinas-new-gaming-rules-to-ban-poker-blood-and-imperial-schemes/.

[71] Ahmad, D. Senior analyst at Nikos Partners, suggested to TechCrunch.

[72] Cuthbertson, A. "China bans children playing video games for more than 90 minutes a day or at night", 7 November 2019, https://www.independent.co.uk/life-style/gadgets-and-tech/gaming/china-gaming-ban-video-game-addiction-a9188806.html.

[73] Huang, Z. "China's games industry at a turning point amid regulatory crackdown, with Korea offering a vision of its own future", *South China Morning Post*, 11 September 2018, https://www.scmp.com/tech/policy/article/2163595/chinas-games-industry-turning-point-amid-regulatory-crackdown-korea.

[74] *Ibid.*

> *In order to navigate a complicated bureaucracy and increasingly overbearing market regulator, smaller game studios and publishers are frantically searching for a way out, mid-tier developers are laying off employees to cover losses, while larger firms like Tencent have shed hundreds of billions of dollars in market value amid warnings of much slower growth[75]. Although some Chinese game developers may be quick to devise methods to circumvent requirements, it may only work out for companies armed with sufficient developing capabilities and resources to counter the new policies. At the end of the day, while China's authoritarian control may seem extreme or even draconian, the industry, and in fact the public at large, should pay heed to the need for intensifying regulation to ward off social ills.*

Advent of Drones — Blessing or Curse

Quite often, an innovation begins on a good note, to fulfil an honourable objective. Cutting both ways can have no better illustration than in the evolution of drones or, more generally, unmanned aircraft. The scope for deploying drones for everyday activity is limitless. The likes of JD.com and Alibaba can now serve an even larger spread of consumers, bringing to them a wider variety of goods than previously possible, right to their doorstep.

Example 2.5: Drones — Flying High

When drones appear on the scene, the last-mile solution for the online customer living out in the boondocks became a possibility. It feels like an equalisation of sorts — rural residents are no longer deprived of access to goods found in swanky malls. It is as convenient as swiping one's phone. What are the implications for both online and brick-and-mortar retailers?

---

[75] Wang, Y. "As China's regulatory freeze drags on, its gaming industry searches for an answer", *Forbes*, December 2018, https://www.forbes.com/sites/ywang/2018/12/10/as-chinas-regulatory-freeze-drags-on-its-gaming-industry-searches-for-an-answer/#3d1f56b3653c.

With revenue estimates topping US$1.9 trillion in 2019 alone, China's e-commerce market is the largest in the world,[76] propelling Asia-Pacific's ascent as a digital powerhouse. In line with the rise of e-commerce, China's courier and "last-mile" delivery has exploded over the last few years. A vast geography with different levels of maturity in logistics across different cities, coupled with a consumer that is weaned on same-day delivery promises, form some of the biggest challenges for e-commerce. No matter how impressive the buying experience, delivery leaves lasting impressions on today's most demanding, advanced and innovation-hungry digital shoppers. In addition, the lack of technological development in rural Chinese areas is holding back e-commerce companies from reaching their full potential. To solve the expensive "last-mile" problem for couriers, companies around the world are racing to develop unmanned aerial drones and investing heavily in building up logistics infrastructure to make online and offline delivery as "seamless" and accessible as possible.

From Amazon to Domino's Pizza, technology giants and e-commerce retailers have been dreaming of drone deliveries for years. Chinese e-commerce giant, JD.com ("JD"), was the first to make it a full-fledged reality. JD, or 京东, as the company is known in Chinese, is China's second-largest e-commerce company. While Alibaba still commands a big market share of e-commerce in China, JD.com has gained ground in recent years. Unlike Alibaba, which began as a platform upon which third parties bought and sold goods, JD.com began as a full-service e-commerce platform, building up its own inventory, supported by its in-house logistics system and offered shoppers same-day delivery on orders placed before 11 am.

Advent of Drones for Last Mile

In October 2015, to deliver goods to otherwise inaccessible areas, JD started developing its own delivery drones via its JDX innovation lab.[77] The following June, they began trialling flights to deliver small packages to shoppers in the four pilot regions: Beijing, Sichuan, Shaanxi and Jiangsu.[78] Within three years, the company developed seven types of delivery drones

---

[76] Gupta, R. "Just how far ahead is Alibaba in China's e-commerce market?", *Market Realist*, 17 July 2019, https://marketrealist.com/2019/07/just-how-far-ahead-is-alibaba-in-chinas-e-commerce-market/.

[77] JD.com Corporate Blog, Drone Factsheet (2018), https://jdcorporateblog.com/wp-content/uploads/2018/03/JD-Drone-factsheet-201805.pdf.

[78] *Ibid.*

which clocked in more than 300,000 minutes of flight time over 100 routes, according to a fact sheet posted by the company in May 2018.[79] The acclaimed drones are known to fly up to 100 km per hour, delivering packages weighing from 5 kg to 30 kg. Intense research efforts are directed at developing drones that can carry as much as one ton.[80]

For JD, drone delivery solves a critical problem and provides a winning strategy to exploit the ample retail opportunities in China's underdeveloped rural areas, where it competes fiercely with Alibaba. Delivery costs in Chinese cities are fairly inexpensive, as order volumes are high and labour costs manageable. On the contrary, the lack of robust roads, underdeveloped cellular infrastructure, together with dismal rural logistics network, have combined to make it inefficient and costly to deliver goods to the 564 million living in rural areas. According to JD's CEO Richard Liu, the usage of drones can deliver cost savings of more than 70% than delivering by truck and at a fraction of the time.[81]

Having secured the first state-level approval in 2018 from the Civil Aviation Administration of China (CAAC) to operate in selected regions, JD announced plans to build 150 drone launch facilities in southwestern Sichuan province for unmanned aerial vehicle (UAV) parcel delivery.[82] It has since also launched its own logistics arm, JD Logistics, employing almost 85,000 delivery personnel and several thousand hubs.[83]

In 2019, Alibaba deepened its logistics play by investing an additional RMB 23 billion (US$3.3 billion) in their logistics affiliate, Cainiao.[84] Alibaba, which traditionally favours an asset-light approach, planned to ramp up their efforts in building a smart logistics network of cutting-edge

---

[79] *Ibid.*

[80] Meredith, S. and Kharpal, A. "Chinese e-commerce giant JD.com is developing a drone that can deliver packages weighing as much as one ton", CNBC, 10 June 2017, https://www.cnbc.com/2017/06/08/e-commerce-jdcom-alibaba-amazon-drone-delivery-china-asia-technology.html.

[81] Handley, L. "This Chinese retail giant is building 150 drone launch centers for people in the countryside", *CNBC*, 13 April 2017, https://www.cnbc.com/2017/04/11/this-chinese-retailer-is-building-150-drone-delivery-launch-centers.html.

[82] *Ibid.*

[83] "How Alibaba, JD.Com and Jumia are revolutionizing the ecommerce supply chain", *Elementum*, 27 Ua, https://www.elementum.com/chain-reaction/the-ecommerce-revolution-how-alibaba-jd.com-and-jumia-are-changing-how-people-shop.

[84] "China's Alibaba invests $3.3 billion to raise stake in logistics unit Cainiao", *Reuters*, 8 November 2019, https://www.reuters.com/article/us-alibaba-cainiao/chinas-alibaba-invests-3-3-billion-to-raise-stake-in-logistics-unit-cainiao-idUSKBN1XI0YR.

technologies. The additional investment came right after Cainiao entered into an agreement with Beihang Unmanned Aircraft System Technology, to build an unmanned aerial system (UAS). The 3.6-ton super drone is expected to support a 565-cubic foot cabin large enough to fit nine people and fly autonomously for 1,500 km, with a payload of one to 1.5 metric tons, the equivalent of a sports car.[85] Cainaio and Beihang hope to start test flights in 2020 and begin mass deployment in 2025.[86]

Regulatory Stance Important

While Amazon has also revealed ambitions for delivery by drone, it seems as if JD has also beaten Amazon to the punch due to China's more inviting regulatory environment. In fact, Jeff Bezos, CEO of Amazon announced his plan for an automated-drone delivery system way back in December of 2013.[87] The concept, Amazon Prime Air, would allow 86% of the items Amazon ships to be delivered to customers in as short a period of time as 30 minutes.[88] It was an instant theoretical hit, but progress proved slow due to regulatory red tape at the Federal Aviation Authority (FAA). Specifically, the FAA reportedly took so long to approve Amazon's requests to test-fly the unmanned drones that by the time the licence was granted in 2015, the prototype models they developed became obsolete.[89]

As the overall geographic coverage of the e-commerce market expands, the ability to offer reliable and consistent services and delivery will be the major point of differentiation for companies. The Chinese regulators' light-touch approach has enabled JD.com, the Amazon-like Chinese counterpart, to soar past its American rival in terms of a more

---

[85] Deng, I. and Soo, Z. "Chinese companies are testing civilian drones that can carry a tonne of cargo", *South China Morning Post*, 1 June 2018, https://www.scmp.com/tech/china-tech/article/2148692/chinese-companies-are-testing-civilian-drones-can-carry-tonne-cargo.

[86] Zhao, L. "Biggest civilian drone designed for couriers", *China Daily*, 31 May 2018, https://www.chinadaily.com.cn/a/201805/31/WS5b0f32f0a31001b82571d482.html.

[87] "Amazon unveils futuristic plan: Delivery by drone", *CBS News*, 1 December 2013, https://www.cbsnews.com/news/amazon-unveils-futuristic-plan-delivery-by-drone/.

[88] Bennett-Smith, M. "Amazon can now test its drone delivery system in the US — for real, this time", *Quartz*, 12 April 2015, https://qz.com/381546/amazon-can-now-test-its-drone-delivery-system-in-the-us-for-real-this-time/.

[89] Nicas, J. "Amazon says FAA approval to test delivery drones already obsolete", *The Wall Street Journal*, 24 March 2015, https://www.wsj.com/articles/amazon-says-its-approval-to-test-delivery-drones-already-obsolete-1427219327.

comprehensive coverage. The Covid-19 outbreak at the beginning of 2020 also led to a deeper appreciation of the usefulness of drones in times of crisis. During this time when China was virtually shut down, JD was able to adapt and mobilise their drones for "contactless" delivery to households.[90] The burgeoning Chinese effort in drone technologies points to a future that will change not just for sales and delivery not only inside China but also abroad, as many of the key companies expand their global presence. In fact, JD announced in 2019 the completion of Indonesia's first government-approved drone flight — a breakthrough for drone delivery in Southeast Asia.[91]

> *Drone technology has obviously disrupted last-mile delivery to the rural areas and is certainly a boon to online retailers and hitherto under-served customers alike. The technology is now ready and ripe for large-scale commercialisation — but in the absence of an appropriate regulatory framework to provide guidelines around safety, security and privacy, deployment at scale will not be feasible.*

All's good when drones are deployed for perfectly sound purposes, like fulfilling the last mile of a retailer's supply chain. The possibilities for drone applications are limitless — telemedicine can now be truly fulfilled to the last mile. Likewise, the precise distribution of fertilisers over large plots of agricultural land amounts to a real boon in cost and quality control for farmers. While the pace of change leaves one breathless and the scale of implementation removes impediments for smaller operators, the regulator is often confronted by what to regulate and the extent to doing so. Take delivery of hitherto prescribed medication under telemedicine for example. How does one ensure that the right medication is properly dispensed and delivered via drones to the correct patient? Enforcement will be a real challenge — something that regulators would have to consider.

---

[90] Rexaline, S. "JD.com makes drone deliveries in China as Covid-19 virus paralyzes country" *Yahoo! News*, 12 February 2020, https://finance.yahoo.com/news/jd-com-makes-drone-deliveries-145406667.html.

[91] Russell, J. "China's JD.com tests drone delivery in Indonesia in first overseas pilot", *TechCrunch*, 22 January 2019, https://techcrunch.com/2019/01/22/jd-drone-indonesia/.

On the contrary, spraying fertilisers over fields of crop seems innocuous enough and will be readily accepted as a productivity tool.

All's fine until the hobby of flying drones for leisure or even nefarious motives take them into restricted airfields or private real estate. They then transform themselves quickly into a nuisance that must be restricted for sound safety reasons. The rise in incursions around commercial airports has obviously heightened concerns over safety and security.

Example 2.6: Flying into Turbulence

Drones are generally a good thing. However, like all new technologies, when operating in an unregulated or yet-to-be regulated environment, they may unwittingly create problems. Or worse still, in the wrong hands, they may be deployed for sinister ends. Airfields and key security installations are obviously areas hobbyist drones should never drift into.

An unmanned aircraft sweeps through a neighbourhood taking photographs that showcase the exterior and interior of a home listed for sale. Another hovers over a 10-acre field of soybeans to sprinkle pesticide. A third buzzes overhead to deliver units of blood and medicine to remote clinics in mountainous Rwanda. While this may sound like a sci-fi movie scene set in the future — it's not. The real-world application of this robotic technology today, also known as drones, is poised to register as a US$100 billion market by 2020.[92] While its benefits extend well across many industries, like a double-edged sword, drones have gained infamy for causing air traffic disruption. Events that have unfolded in recent years reflect urgency in addressing the conundrum, leaving authorities with the imminent task of reacting to and enforcing regulation on a technology that is still rapidly growing and developing.

At Singapore Changi Airport

This point was driven home when several unauthorised drones intruded into the restricted airspace around Singapore's Changi Airport and disrupted its operations over two nights in June 2019. As the world's seventh

---

[92]"Drones: Reporting for Work", *Goldman Sachs Insights*, March 2016, https://www.goldmansachs.com/insights/technology-driving-innovation/drones/.

busiest airport for international traffic and a major transit hub, Changi, which handled a record 68.3 million passengers in 2019, simply could not afford any major operational hiccups.[93] The drone incursion resulted in the delay of more than 50 flights, diversion of at least 7 flights and intermittent closure of one or two runways at the airport — demonstrating how disruptive drones can be in the hands of those intent on causing havoc.[94]

At Gatwick and Newark Airports

What happened in Singapore is not new. A surge in the availability of drones has become an increasing security concern for airports around the world, including Gatwick Airport in the United Kingdom. In December 2018, the UK's second largest airport had to suspend all flights for five days after airport staff sighted several drones flying close to the airfield during the peak of holiday travel. Gatwick had to make an executive decision to cancel or delay over 1,000 flights, leaving 140,000 passengers stranded and frustrated. This particular incident cost Gatwick Airport £1.4m, and airlines had to bear the brunt of cost with compensation bills and revenue losses adding up to a hefty sum of £15m.[95] A similar drone incursion around the Newark Liberty Airport at New Jersey in the US caused the same inconvenience, albeit for a shorter period of time in January 2019.[96]

Regulators' Variety of Response

Following the slew of drone menace, authorities responded by tightening rules. The Civil Aviation Authority of Singapore (CAAS) released guidelines stipulating that the flying of drones without a permit is banned if they are flown within 5 km of airports or military airbases or at altitudes above

---

[93]Changi Airport Group, "Changi airport handled 68.3 million passengers in 2019", 31 January 2020, https://www.changiairport.com/corporate/media-centre/newsroom. html#/pressreleases/changi-airport-handled-68-dot-3-million-passengers-in-2019-2966486?utm_source=rss&utm_medium=rss&utm_campaign=Subscription&utm_content=pressrelease.

[94]"Get tough on irresponsible drone use", *The Straits Times*, 4 July 2019, https://www.straitstimes.com/opinion/st-editorial/get-tough-on-irresponsible-drone-use.

[95]Topham, G. "Gatwick drone disruption cost airport just £1.4m", *The Guardian*, 18 June 2019, https://www.theguardian.com/uk-news/2019/jun/18/gatwick-drone-disruption-cost-airport-just-14m.

[96]"Drone sightings temporarily halt flights at US airport", *Reuters*, 24 January 2019, https://www.straitstimes.com/asia/drone-sightings-temporarily-halt-flights-at-us-airport.

61 m. Furthermore, in order to better identify potential perpetrators, all drones operating in Singapore were required to be registered by the end of 2019. Errant drone users will also face severe penalties, such as a jail term of up to 12 months or a fine of up to S\$20,000.[97]

Similarly, London Heathrow Airport enforced new rules to widen the drone no-fly zone around airports to 5 km and installed a system to detect and identify unauthorised drones.[98] In addition to detection capabilities, the system will be able to locate the drone pilots who will face a penalty of up to 5 years in prison.[99] It was equally crucial to both authorities to beef up their capabilities so as to be able to detect and disable malicious drones, nab and then severely deal with errant operators.

Given such incursions, one might be tempted to ask: Why not just ban drones, especially those used for recreation? Some countries, such as Saudi Arabia and Morocco, have taken the decision to issue a blanket ban on the private ownership and civilian drone use everywhere in the country. Security concerns — specifically, potential terrorist attacks — were cited for the ban.[100] Others such as Cuba and Côte d'Ivoire do not allow drones through the airport, and recreational drone use is only permitted for indoor use in Madagascar. It seems like the easy way out, at least for now. An outright ban on drones is neither feasible nor possible to enforce. It would most likely be just kicking the can further down the road as drone usage is likely to intensify and towards meaningful social and economics ends.

The near misses with aircraft and the closure of airports due to drone incursions are testimonies to how authorities can be illequipped to regulate this new technology. As with any technology,

---

[97] Mahmud Hazid, A. "Mandatory registration for drones by year-end as police investigate recent incursions", *Channel News Asia*, 8 July 2019, https://www.channelnewsasia.com/news/singapore/drones-compulsory-registration-december-changi-airport-11700904.

[98] Mason, R. "Drone no-fly zone to be widened at airports after Gatwick chaos", *The Guardian*, 20 February 2019, https://www.theguardian.com/uk-news/2019/feb/20/drone-no-fly-zone-to-be-widened-at-airports-after-gatwick-chaos.

[99] Wright, M. "Heathrow Airport deploys new drone-catching system to prevent Gatwick-style shutdown", *The Telegraph*, 15 January 2020, https://www.telegraph.co.uk/news/2020/01/15/heathrow-airport-deploys-new-drone-catching-system-prevent-gatwick/.

[100] "Morocco Bans Import of Drones, Remotely-Controlled Devices", *Morocco World News*, 1 March 2015, *https*://www.moroccoworldnews.com/2015/03/152836/morocco-bans-import-drones-remotely-controlled-devices/.

> *it comes with accountability. On the one hand, policymakers need to up the ante to prevent these accidents from happening. On the other hand, placing a one-size-fits-all set of strict rules will not leave room for entrepreneurs and hobbyists to realize opportunities. How much the new world gets to realize and reap the benefits from this new technology will depend on regulators' ability to draw the fine-line between restriction owing to nuisance value and benefits for the larger good.*

Drone use for leisure purposes is understandably a new hobby for which some kind of regulation is in order, particularly in high-density or built-up areas. However, not all incursions into airfields or strategic premises are innocent. Some have sinister intentions as was seen by the drone attacks on two major oil facilities run by state-owned Aramco, shutting down around half of its oil output.[101] The response to such vicious attacks is usually, and not surprisingly, of the same magnitude of severity as the damage wrought.

Very often, there is no clear-cut regulatory framework with which a government can readily roll out to supervise a new activity. Or it could simply take time to devise an effective framework. To its credit, the CAAS was relatively quick to get off the mark in prescribing the regulatory framework in 2015 for "Unmanned Aircraft Systems", which include radio-controlled aircraft, drones and remote-controlled kites.[102] The framework, which was subsequently updated in November 2019, aims to prescribe the scope of regulation governing, *inter alia*, safety of operation and areas where they can be operated in, regardless of purpose, be it recreation, research or purely business. Meanwhile, the Republic of Singapore Air Force (RSAF) will continue to track developments in drone technology.

The reality is that new gadgets falling outside this definition of *Unmanned Aircraft Systems* under the jurisdiction of the CAAS are entirely possible, in terms of potential invention or innovation. In practice,

---

[101] "Saudi Arabia oil facilities ablaze after drone strikes", *BBC News*, 14 September 2019.
[102] "Unmanned Aircraft" https://www.caas.gov.sg/public-passengers/unmanned-aircraft, 26 February 2020.

they could simply be regarded as grey areas for which the regulator would exercise judgment over, depending on the severity of problems created.

Buzz Around Innovation

Credit should be given to the efforts that some governments make by keeping pace with a changing business environment, especially when they are dealing with entirely new constructs. A good example would be fintech, one that captures the imagination of all fresh undergraduates who are inspired by the amount of innovation that goes into the creation of new financial products and services. Of course, it doesn't hurt to have some participation in a potential unicorn. After all, how many young millionaires, let alone billionaires, can one encounter these days in the traditional fields?

Talk cryptocurrency and eyes will lit up for you. But to the central bankers around the world, this is a nightmare as can be seen in the reaction towards Facebook's Libra, a permissioned blockchain digital currency.

Example 2.7: Spellbound by Cryptocurrencies

Digital payments have taken the world by storm. Markets lap up new versions as soon as they are launched as they represent an ideal supplement to if not replacement for cold, hard cash. Not only that, they and other new technologies inspire an entire spectrum of possibilities of financial services or what is referred to as fintech. Not surprisingly, when cryptocurrencies come into the picture, the idea of a global, digital form of currency becomes a seductive one. But who will regulate them and supervise such transactions?

Genesis of Cryptocurrencies

Crises like the 2008 housing bubble's collapse and failing currencies in economies like Venezuela and Zimbabwe saw people scrambling for alternatives to traditional banking and financial systems. Along comes cryptocurrency and the creation of a digital "trust-less" cash system. Bitcoin, the first manifestation of a peer-to-peer, distributed ledger currency, was introduced in 2009. Unlike traditional fiat currencies, Bitcoin and similar cryptocurrencies such as Ether do not require a centralised authority to issue the new currency or confirm payment activities; instead, the network as a whole is involved in authorising transactions and generating new currency. Furthermore, the individuals trading the cryptocurrency may be anonymous (or at least "pseudonymous", in that real-life identities are not disclosed). As of October 2019, there are approximately 2,957 cryptocurrencies being traded with a total market capitalisation of $221 billion.[103]

Although cryptocurrencies have been around for a decade, it was only as recently as three or four years ago that regulators began to feel intense pressure to act. Before then, monetary authorities regarded these digital assets as something belonging to a different world that they thought would never collide with theirs. However, as cryptocurrencies started to gain popularity and invade capital markets, widespread cryptocurrency transactions have led to concerns regarding money laundering, financing of criminal activities and consumer protection. Aggravated by the breathless pace of cryptocurrencies' evolution, the clamour around regulation has been intensifying around pertinent questions like: what is the optimal policy position? Is a ban altogether potentially more effective than regulation?

The Dark Side

In November 2019, Russian authorities came out against cryptocurrencies, like Bitcoin, announcing that only the ruble was legal tender. They cited significant risks of cryptocurrencies as the "laundering of money obtained through crime, as well as financing terrorism". This negative sentiment is shared by several other regulatory regimes.[104]

Not surprisingly for a currency which was designed with anonymity and lack of concentrated control in mind, Bitcoin has proven to be an attractive and lucrative target for use by criminals. Between 2013 and 2018, two men sold steroids and other drugs across the US via their website "NextDayGear" and on the dark web. They sold over 10,000 packages and accepted payments in cryptocurrency and Western Union payments, which

---

[103] Bagshaw, R. "Top 10 cryptocurrencies by market capitalisation" Yahoo, 8 October 2019. https://finance.yahoo.com/news/top-10-cryptocurrencies-market-capitalisation-160046487.html.

[104] "Russian Central Bank comes out against Bitcoin, would support a ban", 1 December 2019, https://beincrypto.com/russian-central-bank-comes-out-against-bitcoin-would-support-a-ban/.

they laundered and converted into cash.[105] Even as global authorities have shut down two of the biggest illegal online drug markets Wall Street Market and Valhalla, the amount of cryptocurrency spend on so-called dark web markets where stolen credit card information and a wide array of illegal drugs can be purchased with Bitcoin continued booming to reach a new high of US$601 million in the last quarter of 2019 itself.[106]

Hamas, the militant Palestinian group, designated a terrorist organisation by Western governments, has developed an increasingly sophisticated campaign to raise money using Bitcoin in 2019. Having been locked out of the traditional financial system, the group began reaching out to online followers, explaining the origins of Bitcoin and declaring it permissible to use it for charitable donations.[107] The success of Bitcoin-fuelled illegal activity points to the struggles that regulators have been facing in containing the bad behaviour that cryptocurrencies have enabled or perpetuated.

In addition to the use of cryptocurrencies for illicit purposes, there was increasing scope to make money through coordinated price manipulation of these virtual currencies; for example, through classic "pump and dump" and fraudulent mis-selling schemes. The reality is that the price of Bitcoin, under normal market conditions, would probably never have rocketed from a low of below $968 to a high of nearly $20,000 in 2017 were not for external actors manipulating its price.[108]

Enter a Somewhat Legit User

Many more have grown aware of cryptocurrencies since the world's largest social media network Facebook announced its own cryptocurrency called Libra in June 2019 with the goal of 'helping the world's unbanked enter the

---

[105] Sterling, B. "A cryptocurrency money laundering conviction", *Wired*, 24 April 2019.

[106] Popper, N. "Bitcoin has lost steam. but criminals still love it", *The New York Times*, 28 January 2020, https://www.nytimes.com/2020/01/28/technology/bitcoin-black-market.html.

[107] Popper, N. "Terrorists turn to Bitcoin for funding, and they're learning fast", *The New York Times*, 18 August 2019, https://www.nytimes.com/2019/08/18/technology/terrorists-bitcoin.html.

[108] Rooney, K. "Much of bitcoin's 2017 boom was market manipulation, research says", *CNBC*, 13 June 2018,, https://www.cnbc.com/2018/06/13/much-of-bitcoins-2017-boom-was-market-manipulation-researcher-says.html.

financial system'.[109] Libra was meant to be launched some time in 2020 but has cut no ice with many lawmakers who have been quick to criticise it. Many have demanded that Libra and other cryptocurrencies be regulated, with some even calling for it to be banned. Data protection officials in the US, EU, UK, Australia and Canada have united to raise concerns over the "privacy risks", urging the Libra group to offer more information on how users will be profiled and whether any of their data will be shared among Facebook and Libra's 27 other founding partners including venture capital firms, credit card companies and tech giants.[110]

In particular, the EU finance ministers have agreed to a *de facto* ban on the launch in the region until the bloc has a common approach to regulation that can mitigate the risks posed by the technology.[111] As a result, the Libra project was dealt major blows by the speedy departure of seven of the 28 original founder members from the vehicle set up to steer the initiative, as giants including Visa, MasterCard, PayPal, Stripe and eBay apparently took flight after the regulatory backlash.[112] Interacting with large projects like Libra has proved challenging for governments aiming to protect their populations from the risks of unsavoury use of technology without restricting the innovations that are offered. Although Libra is very much like all the cryptocurrencies before it that exist entirely in digital form, its blockchain will be managed by the founding members in the early stages but will evolve into a fully open system in the future. Another distinction lies in the design of Libra — it was meant to be anchored to a basket of assets which purportedly would include the likes of deposits and government securities denominated in stable currencies. Despite the design differences, it looks like gaining acceptance in its own home and EU markets would be a tall order especially when privacy protection reigns supreme.

---

[109]"Here's what you need to know about Facebook's controversial cryptocurrency", 24 October 2019, https://www.cnet.com/news/heres-what-you-need-to-know-about-facebooks-controversial-libra-cryptocurrency/.

[110]Murphy, H. "Facebook cryptocurrency raises privacy questions, say regulators", *Financial Times*, 6 August 2019, https://www.ft.com/content/9194df7a-b796-11e9-8a88-aa6628ac896c.

[111]Guarascio, F. "EU agrees tough line on digital currencies like Facebook's Libra", *Reuters*, 5 December 2019, https://www.reuters.com/article/us-eu-ecofin-cryptocurrencies/eu-agrees-tough-line-on-digital-currencies-like-facebooks-libra-idUSKBN1Y91E4.

[112]Lomas, N. "No Libra-style digital currencies without rules, say EU finance ministers", *Tech Crunch*, 6 December 2019, https://techcrunch.com/2019/12/06/no-libra-style-digital-currencies-without-rules-say-eu-finance-ministers/.

All said and done, there are counterbalances to the dark side above. Positive signs include many cryptocurrency companies that intend to comply with regulations. That includes Facebook as well, with CEO Mark Zuckerberg stating that "…even though the Libra association is independent … Facebook will not be a part of launching the Libra payment system anywhere in the world, even outside the US, until the US regulators approve".[113]

There are also jurisdictions that have strived to be forward-looking and to embrace blockchain technology and cryptocurrencies, even as they continue to ensure that consumers are protected. These include Singapore with the recent commencement of the Payment Services Act on 28 January 2020[114]; Switzerland which has granted two companies banking licenses, allowing them to deal in the area of digital assets,[115] as well as Wyoming which has put forward significant changes to its laws in a bid to attract technologists and companies in this field.[116]

Many smaller companies have also submitted applications for the requisite licences in their respective jurisdictions, mostly in the jurisdictions that have at least remained neutral about such technology. For instance, Propine Technologies is entering the Monetary Authority of Singapore's Sandbox.[117]

While runaway technological inventions present regulators the world over with nightmares, the message for governments and regulators is clear — step up your game or you will lose either the opportunity to grow with new markets or the ability to regulate meaningfully, especially when your counterparts are already

---

[113] Abbruzzese, J. and Kent, J.L. "Facebook's Zuckerberg says Libra won't launch without U.S. approval", *CNC News*, 23 October 2019, https://www.nbcnews.com/tech/tech-news/facebook-s-zuckerberg-says-libra-won-t-launch-without-u-n1070561.

[114] "Singapore's payment services act expands MAS' scope to regulate crypto payments", 28 January 2020, https://fintechnews.sg/36201/mobilepayments/singapores-payment-services-act-comes-into-force/.

[115] Lim, K. "Tokenisation startups Sygnum, SEBA clinch conditional Swiss banking, securities license", *Garage by The Business Times*, 26 August 2019, https://www.businesstimes.com.sg/garage/tokenisation-startups-sygnum-seba-clinch-conditional-swiss-banking-securities-licences.

[116] Long, C. "What do Wyoming's 13 new blockchain laws mean?", *Forbes*, 4 March 2019, https://www.forbes.com/sites/caitlinlong/2019/03/04/what-do-wyomings-new-blockchain-laws-mean/.

[117] MAS Sandbox, https://www.mas.gov.sg/development/fintech/sandbox.

doing so. Indisputably, tighter regulations are essential to disrupting financial flows to criminal and terrorist groups online, with further measures such as disclosure of identities being taken to bring digital currencies in line with existing Anti-Money Laundering and Counter-Terrorism Financing legislations.

Regulators also need to keep in mind that timing is everything and that there is no perfect solution. Actions may therefore take on an incremental fashion. Outlawing cryptocurrency altogether till there's a common, satisfactory approach to regulations may eliminate positive spillover benefits to other fields. From improving access to financial services to providing businesses a competitive advantage, admittedly there are potential upsides to cryptocurrency. Without an appropriate light touch, regulators that approach such technology in a binary manner may unwittingly do more of a disservice to the very consumers they are seeking to protect.

Response of Central Banks

What is a financial regulator to do about all this wave after wave of fintech innovations? Particularly under pressure are regulators of leading financial hubs like London, Tokyo, Hong Kong and Singapore who would have to defend their respective market positions while watching out for potential systemic risks. Likewise, regulators of the larger economies like the US or China are very much alive to potential financial or social risks that fintech innovations carry, along with the bountiful benefits.

Example 2.8: Playing in the Sandbox

The world is in the grip of a financial revolution, specifically a FinTech boom. Should it stir up excitement in the form of new, innovative applications that consumers can avail themselves of? Or are they no more than nightmares that leave financial regulators breathless? Regardless of how regulators truly feel, the reality is that FinTech cannot be locked out of a system for too long, if at all. So how should regulators deal with the onslaught of fintech innovations?

Financial technology (FinTech) is a global phenomenon that has seen extraordinary growth — valued at about US$128 billion in 2018, the industry is expected to leap forth by almost 25% annually through 2022 to reach US$310 billion.[118] Against this backdrop, as the applications of these new financial technologies are becoming more sophisticated, there is "growing uncertainty over whether the innovation complies with existing legal and regulatory requirements".[119]

Unless clear guidelines are provided or a means for running controlled experiments can be allowed, some financial institutions (FIs) or start-ups may err on the side of caution and choose not to implement their innovation. This outcome is undesirable as promising technologies may be discouraged, resulting in missed opportunities. Conversely, regulators may not be prepared to give full rein to innovative new services that appear to border on compliance or prudential limits.

Enter the Sandbox

An increasingly popular initiative today is the creation of "regulatory sandboxes" to allow small-scale, live testing of new technologies, services or business models within a secure and efficient environment, where specific regulatory requirements are relaxed or upheld.[120] The primary aim is to align compliance with the rapid growth of fintech companies without drowning them in rules, allowing these companies some breathing space to innovate. It seeks to enable a more open and active dialogue between regulators and innovators, in order to co-design and revise supervisory frameworks with agility. In addition, a sandbox grants companies with unique

---

[118]The Business Research Company, "Global Fintech market value is expected to reach $309.98 Billion at a CAGR of 24.8% through 2022", 26 September 2019, https://www.prnewswire.com/news-releases/global-fintech-market-value-is-expected-to-reach-309-98-billion-at-a-cagr-of-24-8-through-2022--300926069.html.

[119]Monetary Authority of Singapore (MAS), "Fintech Regulatory Sandbox Guidelines", 1.5.

[120]Deloitte and Confederation of Indian Industry, "Regulatory sandbox: Making India a global fintech hub", July 2017, p. 16.

business ideas access to market while preventing established firms from exploiting the testing regime.

Although the first sandbox-like framework was inaugurated in 2012 by the U.S. Consumer Financial Protection Bureau (CFPB), the UK Financial Conduct Authority (FCA) was the first to implement a regulatory sandbox, announcing the approach in 2015. Since then, more than 20 countries from United Arab Emirates (Abu Dhabi) to Sierra Leone have adopted the concept as a tool to support financial inclusion.[121] Shortly after the UK model was established, the Monetary Authority of Singapore (MAS) sought public consultation on the concept and launched The FinTech Regulatory Sandbox Guidelines in November 2016.

Concept in Practice: The MAS Regulatory Sandbox

To enter the sandbox, FIs and start-ups must first obtain approval. MAS will assess whether the applications demonstrate, among other requirements, that the new financial service "includes new or emerging technology or uses existing technology in an innovative way".[122] The proposed financial service should also "address a problem or bring benefits to consumers or the industry".[123] Applicants are also expected to have performed preliminary due diligence to evaluate feasibility, identify potential risks and their risk mitigation strategies. Furthermore, the applicant must show intention and ability to deploy the technology in Singapore on a broader scale upon exiting the sandbox.

Upon approval, MAS will decide, on a case-by-case basis, which form of regulatory support will be the most effective for facilitating the experimentation. Some examples of requirements which can be relaxed include credit rating, minimum liquid assets, management experience, track record and those prescribed in certain various guidelines published by the MAS, such as technology risk management guidelines and outsourcing guidelines.[124] The guidelines also stipulate requirements that MAS intends to uphold. These relate to customer information confidentiality, Anti-Money Laundering measures and the handling of customers'

---

[121] Jenik, I. and Lauer, K. "Regulatory sandboxes and financial inclusion", CGAP, October 2017, https://www.cgap.org/sites/default/files/Working-Paper-Regulatory-Sandboxes-Oct-2017.pdf.

[122] *Ibid.*, 6.1.

[123] *Ibid.*, 6.2.

[124] *Ibid.*, Annex A, p. 10.

moneys and assets by intermediaries.[125] Similarly, the approved entity must disclose that it is operating in a sandbox, properly inform all associated key risks and obtain acknowledgement from users before on-boarding them as customers.[126]

Upon successful experimentation and graduation from the sandbox, the entity can proceed to deploy the technology on a broader scale provided that "both MAS and the sandbox entity are satisfied that the latter has achieved its intended test outcomes" and the sandbox entity can fully comply with the relevant legal and regulatory requirements.[127] Nonetheless, the MAS is rather cautious in awarding sandboxes. Out of the 150 FinTech players engaged since its launch,[128] only 9 were awarded sandboxes as at end of 2019.[129]

In addition to a one-size-fits-all standard application process, a regulator may provide a fast-track process for certain applicants. MAS introduced the "Sandbox Express" in late 2018 to facilitate sandbox applications for technologies deemed to be relatively low risk or as having known risks that can be easily contained within pre-set restrictions.[130] Under the current regulations, approval involves a two-stage process and it will take about six

---

[125] *Ibid.*

[126] *Ibid.*, 8.2.e.

[127] *Ibid.*, 7.3.

[128] Lai, L. "MAS seeking feedback on proposed fintech sandbox scheme with faster approvals", *The Business Times*, 14 November 2018, https://www.businesstimes.com.sg/banking-finance/mas-seeking-feedback-on-proposed-fintech-sandbox-scheme-with-faster-approvals.

[129] Monetary Authority of Singapore (MAS), "List of sandbox experiments", listed Propine Technologies, ICHX Tech & Inzsure, https://www.mas.gov.sg/development/fintech/sandbox, accessed on 27 February 2020; "Blockchain capital markets platform iSTOX graduates from MAS fintech sandbox", *The Business Times*, 3 February 2020, https://www.businesstimes.com.sg/garage/blockchain-capital-markets-platform-istox-graduates-from-mas-fintech-sandbox. Graduates from the sandbox include iSTOX, insurtech firm PolicyPal, digital wealth management platform Kristal.ai and digital money changing startup Thin Margin; International Capital Market Association Brief: "Regulatory Approaches to FinTech and Innovation in Capital Markets", 7 September 2018, Included Insurtech Metlife, and remittance platform TransferFriend ("no longer licensed to advertise or carry on a remittance business in Singapore from 22 July 2018" according to the MAS).

[130] Monetary Authority of Singapore (MAS) "Response to Feedback Received: Sandbox Express", August 2019.

months to a year to customise a sandbox. This new initiative allows for faster processing of approvals whereby eligible applicants can begin testing within 21 days.[131]

Lingering Reservations

Nevertheless, sandboxes are not without their detractors who have raised concerns that it does not change the fact that the service providers are still experimenting with real consumers, who may suffer losses or be subject to misconduct. Future implications of the sandbox approach will obviously require a longer term study. However, MAS reckons that this is far better than sitting tight and doing nothing while wondering how to get the right framework in place for fast-evolving technology.

> *Notwithstanding the potential challenges and risks, the regulatory approach and attitude adopted by the MAS is representative of Singapore's willingness to support innovation and commitment to building Singapore into a smart financial centre. In the words of the Managing Director of MAS, "Be it countries, businesses, or people — those who are alert to technology trends, understand their implications, and harness their potential will gain a competitive edge. To be sure, many of these technologies are disruptive to existing jobs and existing business models. But if we do not disrupt ourselves — in a manner we choose — somebody else will — in a manner we will not like".*[132]

Artificial Intelligence — Boon or Bane?

Artificial Intelligence, affectionately known as AI, presents the perfect conundrum for governments who are already grappling with information technology developments. The urgency is palpable as AI is all the rage these days and its rapid evolution has implications on all fronts.

---

[131] The Straits Times, "MAS launches Sandbox Express for faster market testing of innovative financial services" 7 August 2019, https://www.straitstimes.com/business/banking/mas-launches-sandbox-express-for-faster-market-testing-of-innovative-financial.

[132] Speech by Mr. Ravi Menon, Managing Director, Monetary Authority of Singapore, at Singapore FinTech Festival — FinTech Conference on 16 November 2016.

For the economy, it would likely be manifested as the so-called fourth industrial revolution with public policy debate and private innovation pivoting around the extent to which machines will replace humans. More than half of all business organisations foresee the need to modify their business models due to AI over the short term. If nothing else, AI can help businesses reap benefits of reduced costs from automation, minimisation of human errors and raised revenues from superior customer experience.[133]

For the society, the state has to ensure that people can adapt to the ensuing restructuring of employment or are suitably equipped for new jobs. More importantly, it matters how people will interact with one another with the pervasiveness of AI in their lives. There is every possibility that AI capabilities will accentuate inequality, implying the politicians would have to be watchful and be ready to respond with appropriate social policies.

For the government as a regulator, it would be the perennial question of the degree of regulation which will be required to ensure that AI applications do not overwhelm or go rogue but fulfil their intended roles. In order to do this, the state needs to have its fair share of the requisite human resources to define scope, anticipate potential dangers and prescribe the necessary regulations or ethical standards to curtail such risks. This implies that the government would have no choice but to compete with the private sector for such talent. This is no small feat as such talent is already in short supply.

To begin with, the definition of what falls under the purview of AI keeps expanding — from the raw definition of data science to initial efforts at developing the internet of things (IOT) to robotics, to machine learning, to natural language processing, to energy-efficient AI solutions to quantum neural networks, and the list goes on.

The inherent challenge of AI is its fast-changing nature, making static regulation a non-starter. Towards that end, many governments attempt to have a dynamic response. The Singapore government released a framework on how AI can be ethically and responsibly used, modelled as a 'living document' and intended to evolve along with the frenetic pace of

---

[133] https://www.capgemini.com/2018/12/the-impact-of-artificial-intelligence-ai-on-business-and-insights/, 4 December 2018.

changes of a digital economy.[134] Positioned as detailed and implementable guidance for the private sector, the document will take in feedback from the industry and tweaked accordingly. The signalling is important as it demonstrates the government's willingness to embrace the need to change and keep pace, so as to stay relevant.

Reflections

Apart from the inherent difficulty of regulating, the diverging definition of domains, the uneven distribution of talent and social considerations, contagion risks are very real within the financial services space. This is especially so when such activity continues unfettered and grows in scale to unexpected proportions. Consequences around social ills or worse still contagion effects on the underlying economy can wreak lasting damage to the wider population.

Should a regulator of financial services be too zealous, precious innovations could be snuffed out. On the contrary, lagging too much or having too light a touch can lead to an unwieldy chain of problems to straighten out. Finding the right balance would be critical. Obviously, it's easier said than done.

Unexpected surprises present their own issues too — owing to the Covid lockdowns, online digital payments have surged and are fast becoming the norm. The huge positive is the rapid adoption of digital payments, faster than any public officer can ever dream of. The downside relates to system capacity and integrity. These are nonetheless relatively easier problems to resolve.

In Chapter 3, we review the circumstances where the government can be similarly overwhelmed, not by technology, but by the sheer enormity of its various responsibilities. These could range from the financial burden of building social and economic infrastructure, to alleviating inequality in rural areas, to crafting an ever-evolving energy policy, taking into account climate change implications, to other environmental or healthcare challenges. It also discusses some of these overwhelming challenges for which partnership provides the viable way out.

---

[134] https://www.straitstimes.com/singapore/singapore-releases-framework-on-ethical-use-of-ai/, 24 January 2019.

CHAPTER 3
PARTNERSHIP TOWARDS SUSTAINABILITY

Chapter 3

Partnership Towards Sustainability

Governments in many emerging economies frequently encounter a great deficit in financing and domain expertise when attempting to determine and execute their national priorities, both economic and social. In areas requiring heavy capital expenditure, such as infrastructural development which is crucial to growth, it is increasingly common for the state to enter into some kind of public–private partnership.

Such collaborations, while well intended, can occasionally be a quagmire; usage projections or assumptions on anticipated demand for public amenities could be wildly optimistic. This would in turn trigger an array of problems with charges to be levied on the public at large not being acceptable or collaborators could go into default or the government may be forced to review its commitments for projects not executed yet. All in all, this will typically carry a huge political burden.

Regardless of the risk of failure from the inherent difficulty of projecting demand, private sector participation remains a plus for the financing possibility and contribution of knowledge.

The participation of private sector enterprises can underpin some of the responsibilities that local governments might otherwise be overwhelmed with. There are enough examples of successful outcomes, be it from the participation of a huge multilateral financial institution or on a smaller scale, with partners in power generation or local economic development or tackling climate change.

The unprecedented fallout arising from the Covid-19 pandemic will put paid to efforts on all fronts — public coffers would be substantially weakened from having to shore up employment and sustain businesses and many private sector players are equally damaged. The unfortunate consequences point to a slowing down of private sector investment in infrastructure or any sizeable projects and a reduction in the scale of capital injection itself. In turn, this will decelerate or even stagnate economic growth aspirations for the emerging economies.

The clarion call these days is for the state to ensure *sustainable* economic viability and for the capital providers to build *sustainable* businesses. The operative word is *"sustainable"* but the efforts, given the reality of short-termism and populist politics in many countries, are anything but sustainable.

Multi-faceted Roles of Government

To begin with, there is no shortage of developments that the government is usually charged responsibility for. From the conceptualisation of infrastructure to the eventual establishment of urban townships, the burden falls squarely on the state. Ditto the many other essential services which fall under the purview of public goods. Chapter 5 deals in greater detail with the very necessary role that the state would and must play.

Economic infrastructure for compelling needs such as transportation — mass rapid systems, highways, seaports and airports — are obvious recommendations for both the emerging and developed economies. The price tags for such aspirational projects are regrettably well beyond the affordability of most governments. Yet infrastructure is essential to economic growth, so every economy cannot do without it. At last count, a big and fast-growing economy like India would require US$1.4 trillion for building the much needed infrastructure over 2020–2025.[1] The longer the lag to both building new infrastructure and maintaining existing facilities, the more impossible the ability to keep up with properly functioning public goods.

Private Sector Participation

Enter private sector participation, which sounds entirely sensible and feasible. One modality, the Public–Private Partnership, or PPP initiative, appears to be the panacea to such financial woes. Yet the experience of many governments who have gone down this route has been somewhat disappointing, for a variety of reasons.

---

[1] https://www.indiabudget.gov.in/economicsurvey/doc/vol2chapter/echap08_vol2.pdf, Para 8.19, Economic Survey 2019–20, Vol. 2, 31 March 2019.

Example 3.1: Derailment of Travel Projections

It is not uncommon these days for governments to adopt a PPP model to develop major infrastructure in the country. A collaboration with the private sector provides a variety of benefits such as reduced budgetary constraints and access to domain expertise. Availability of infrastructure will enable the government to promote business growth for the local economy, including the private sector. However, any government contemplating large-scale PPPs should always be wary of possible failures or obstacles that the financing and developing of infrastructure could bring about, and ideally, be ready with a contingency plan in place. A case illustrating the inherent difficulties of mounting a successful, large-scale PPP would be the Taiwan High Speed Rail (THSR).

The idea of the THSR was mooted during Taiwan's period of rapid economic growth as early as the 1970s. It was initially envisaged that the THSR project would be handled fully by the government. However, due to increasing public fiscal burdens, the Taiwan government decided to adopt a PPP model and have the project built by a private sector venture on a "Build-Operate-Transfer" model.[2]

Two consortiums bid for the project in 1997 — Chunghwa High Speed Rail Consortium (CHSRC) and Taiwan High Speed Rail Consortium (THSRC). There was a substantial difference of NT$250 million in bids, with CHSRC calling for the government to invest another NT$150 million into the project. On the other hand, THSRC promised zero government investment and additionally, would pay the treasury NT$100 million over the course of the concession. Not surprisingly, THSRC won the bid.[3] However, this marked the start of a tumultuous journey with the THSRC.

According to then Minister of Transportation and Communication, Yeh Kuang-shih, the THSRC's "financial structure was seriously defective" from the start.[4] To add salt to the wound, there were initially only 50,000 daily riders a day for the stretch between Taipei and Kaoshiung built at a hefty cost of more than NT$500 billion and after nearly a decade of

---

[2] https://en.thsrc.com.tw/ArticleContent/50fa391b-09a7-4728-98e7-8b7901a795d8.

[3] https://topics.amcham.com.tw/2015/04/taiwan-high-speed-rail-in-financial-crisis/, 15 April 2015.

[4] *Ibid.*

construction. This paled in comparison to the predicted 100,000 or only half of that anticipated and a far cry from the 240,000 by 2008 in the original feasibility study. This was despite the effort put in by the consortiums in coming up with five different ridership estimates during the tender bidding process.[5]

Although annual ridership has since increased to 58% of the capacity, it is nowhere close to initial predictions. A mere 130,000 riders use the THSR daily on average. This affects profits substantially, with THSRC losing an estimated NT$5–10 billion every year, after accounting for depreciation.[6]

Furthermore, at the start of the project, THSRC injected a mere NT$26 billion of its own capital into an estimated NT$400–500 billion project. This forced it to borrow significant amounts at high interest rates.[7] THSRC soon buckled under the enormous debt burden and high interest rates in the initial years of operation. By 2009, THSRC's cumulative losses were equivalent to two-thirds of its equity capital. Very soon, there was an avalanche of claims, a major one of which was by the premium shareholders. It was abundantly clear that investors would face mounting losses at the end of the 18-year concession period.

The Taiwan government really had no choice but to step in to save the project from certain ruin and started to explore ways of helping to refinance THSRC's massive loans through *inter alia* a combination of capital reduction and injection of new capital. The compromise rescue package unfortunately cost Minister Yeh his job, not least due to the ensuing politicisation of the matter.

Eventually, the government extended the rail concession from 35 to 70 years and injected NT$30 billion, boosting the government's stake to 64% from about 37% and giving THSRC more breathing space.[8]

The government gained majority control of THSRC in 2009 and injected a significant amount of funds into the THSR though they themselves were already facing fiscal concerns. This occurred despite the government partnering a private company to alleviate its burden and certainly

---

[5] https://medium.com/greater-china-review/the-beautiful-troubled-taiwan-high-speed-rail-67bcef3f2e29, 28 April 2019.

[6] https://topics.amcham.com.tw/2015/04/taiwan-high-speed-rail-in-financial-crisis/, 15 April 2015.

[7] *Ibid.*

[8] https://asia.nikkei.com/Business/Shinkansen-operation-a-flop-in-Taiwan, 5 November 2015.

not conceiving a need to pump in any more funds other than the initial sum already invested in this project.

> *No doubt, as the former Minister Yeh had accurately surmised then, the financial structure contained in the bids should not have passed muster. Likewise, the terms of the concession were not commensurate with the huge capital outlay required.*
>
> *What broke the back of the PPP was the inherent difficulty with making projections on literally, a mountain of assumptions. It was almost impossible for them to be accurate. This is particularly so for journeys and travel patterns that are new and for which there are no precedents. The underlying poor economics of the PPP/ BOT projects were aggravated by the poor financial model and capital structure. Given the impossibility of making accurate projections for such mammoth undertakings, it is imperative that the government work towards a contingency plan to factor in unforeseen circumstances and budgetary deficits to minimise the risk of failure. This could include, at the very worst, a bailout but only as a last resort.*

One should not be too quick to put the blame of any PPP failure on a sloppy government nor on a greedy private sector investor. Massive infrastructure aspirations which require private sector involvement, are by their very nature inherently difficult to conceptualise and project, in terms of utility value. The scope for "getting it wrong" is immense, something which even the best of brains cannot mitigate against. How does one predict the likely usage of a highway that never existed? A highway that could literally open up access to hitherto rural areas, freeing up potential value of the adjoining land parcels?

Here, the experience with the Central Expressway (CTE) in Singapore is instructive — when it was first conceptualised in the mid-1980s, there were reservations over a potential white elephant running north to south, with possibly enough empty lanes to remind citizens of gross fiscal wastage. Years on after its completion in 1989, new towns started popping up on both sides of the CTE and its very existence became a given. Soon arguments started over the lack of capacity planning as the heavily utilised expressway was bursting at its seams!

Even when the ability to predict ridership is better than the average, design minutiae can bring forth unexpected nightmares. The Sydney light rail system, costing almost A\$3 billion, has been criticised by detractors, with the benefit of hindsight, for poor planning for speed and duration at stops.[9] That completion was delayed by a year and the cost overrun, as much as to double the budget, only served to aggravate matters. As a consequence, the New South Wales government faced a A\$400 million class action suit from businesses disrupted by the prolonged construction.

Politics can be the Spoiler

Not all PPPs or public transport infrastructure suffer the same fate of inadequate planning. Some are in essence more straightforward undertakings, like highways to provide the much-needed connectivity between two cities. However, toll road projects are notoriously vulnerable to politics of the day. While the new amenity would often be welcomed, many users typically would cringe at or even violently object to the whole notion of paying exorbitant tolls. The reality is that governments surviving on an austerity budget frequently have no choice but to reduce subsidies, to their political misery. Often, it takes very little, like tolls, to trigger a major reaction on account of the bottled-up unhappiness over the larger issues of the rising cost of living and stagnant wages.

Example 3.2: Voting with Trucks

Protests are roiling cities across the world as fed-up citizens take to the streets to vent their grievances over rising economic and social injustices, government corruption and seemingly minor actions that came to be regarded as the final straw. Typically, what started out as a protest against a price hike for some economic staple, such as toll roads, can easily morph into a nation-wide demonstration in the streets, in an overwhelming and highly destructive manner.

The precarious poor and middle-class Chileans have been especially discontent with the rising cost of utilities, stagnant wages and meagre

---

[9]"Sydney's new \$2.8b tram line rolls into problems", *Straits Times*, 30 December 2019.

pensions in a nation that has identified with being well run and wealthy.[10] Their concerns are not unfounded — the Organisation for Economic and Cooperation and Development (OECD) has ranked Chile the most unequal of all 36 member states, despite its reputation as "Latin America's golden boy" for its historically stable and investor-friendly environment.[11]

On 6 October 2019, Chile's government hiked metro fares by 4% — raising them from the equivalent of US$1.12 to US$1.16[12] — sparking off massive street violence and turmoil that took the government by surprise. Shortly after, 1.2 million Chileans gathered at a city square in Santiago to peacefully march against the long-simmering inequalities persistent in the Chilean society, felt most acutely in how people move and work within the cities.[13]

The government, completely overwhelmed, was forced to send 20,000 soldiers into the street to take control. The government also declared a state of emergency, imposed curfews in 12 out of Chile's 16 regions and deployed tanks to the streets for the first time since the country's transition to democracy in 1990.[14]

Struggling to contain the strife, President Pinera's administration succumbed to the pressure from protestors and scrapped the subway fare increase, announced a 16% jump in the guaranteed minimum wage to 350,000 pesos (US$482) and a 20% rise in state pensions, while revoking

---

[10] Londono, E. "What you need to know about the Chile protests", *The New York Times*, 21 October 2019, https://www.nytimes.com/2019/10/21/world/americas/why-chile-protests.html.

[11] Laing, A., Sherwood, D., and Cambero, F. "Explainer: Chile's inequality challenge: What went wrong and can it be fixed?" *Reuters*, 24 October 2019, https://www.reuters.com/article/us-chile-protests-explainer/explainer-chiles-inequality-challenge-what-went-wrong-and-can-it-be-fixed-idUSKBN1X22RK.

[12] Leskin, P. "3 are dead after Chilean protesters staged violent demonstrations over a subway fare hike, burning buildings and bringing the country's capital to a standstill", *Business Insider US*, 20 October 2019, https://www.businessinsider.sg/chile-protests-subway-fare-hikes-president-fire-military-emergency-2019-10?r=US&IR=T.

[13] "Protests in Chile fueled by the historic march of 1.2 million people", *EFE-EPA*, 26 October 2019, https://www.efe.com/efe/english/world/protests-in-chile-fueled-by-the-historic-march-of-1-2-million-people/50000262-4096182.

[14] "Chile protests: Cost of living protests take deadly toll", *BBC News*, 21 October 2019, https://www.bbc.com/news/world-latin-america-50119649.

the 9.2% hike in electricity prices.[15] Pinera also announced plans to introduce health insurance for medications, which is among the most expensive in the region.[16]

Just as the Chilean government thought things could not get any worse, road chaos ensued when hundreds of trucks, cars and motorcycles looked to express their discontent over the high road tolls by putting its capital city in a gridlock.[17] The solutions offered did not appease all Chileans. Scores of unhappy Chilean truck drivers marched slowly on the access and ring roads of Santiago de Chile, which connected the capital with outlying cities and ports, setting up barricades and prompting huge back-ups in traffic. As the traffic ground to a standstill, protestors honked horns, waved Chilean flags and plastered signs that read "No more tolls! Enough with the abuse!" to the front of their vehicles.[18]

The collective "No + TAG" convened the demonstration on wheels and resorted to prompting massive back-ups on vital regional arteries after two days of unsuccessful negotiations with the government on the exorbitant level of tolls.[19] The protesters demanded an 80% reduction in electronic tolls collected under the TAG system, through a device which all vehicles must carry that will automatically make payment for the use of roads. For 120,000 pesos or US$165, a motorist can obtain a monthly pass good for unlimited use on all of the toll roads in greater Santiago.[20] Most car drivers pay between US$35 and US$130 a month to use highways around Santiago, depending on how much time they spend on the roads; and truckers have to pay much more because of the longer distances travelled as part

---

[15]"Child latest victim of Chile violence as strike begins", *The Straits Times*, 23 October 2019, https://www.straitstimes.com/world/americas/child-latest-victim-of-chile-violence-as-strike-begins.

[16]*Ibid.*

[17]Sherwood, D. and Miranda, N. "Truck drivers add to Pinera's headaches in protest-stricken Chile", Business Insider, 26 October 2019, https://www.businessinsider.com/truck-drivers-add-to-pineras-headaches-in-protest-stricken-chile-2019-10.

[18]*Ibid.*

[19]"Truckers protesting road tolls snarl traffic in Chile's capital", *EFE*, 6 November 2019, https://www.efe.com/efe/english/world/truckers-protesting-road-tolls-snarl-traffic-in-chile-s-capital/50000262-4104876.

[20]*Ibid.*

of their jobs.[21] With 7 out of 10 Chilean workers earning an average income of less than US$745 per month and half making less than US$540 a month, they are already struggling to pay for the basic needs with little room for change or contingencies, let alone access to highways.[22]

More critically, besides sharply lowering the tolls, the drivers sought to delink TAG debts from the renewal of their driving licences, which would otherwise have a direct adverse impact on their livelihood.[23] To appease or quell the protests, Transport Minister Rafael Moreno merely announced that there would be no further increases on highway toll fees.[24] This effectively only served to kick the can down the road, doing little to address all of the root problems. Not surprisingly, there remained the demand for the government to do more.

What happened in Chile is far from an act of rebellion or civil disobedience. In essence, it is closer to an emotional outburst, an explosion of a pressure cooker that has been bottling up for years. Hard work lies ahead, even as the government has acknowledged the need for structural reforms to address national inequality and acceded to calls to draft a new constitution.

> *In isolation, the charges might well have been set appropriately, relative to the cost of constructing the toll roads. However, once taken together with lingering unhappiness over other components of the cost of living, this became the proverbial straw that broke the camel's back. Standing firm on the tolls would have been politically untenable. Relenting, however, is probably fiscally unsustainable. Governments caught in such a dilemma would have to either scale back infrastructure development to what is fiscally sustainable or prepare the people mentally for the need to recover a meaningful level of costs via tolls.*

---

[21] "Chile's congress evacuated as inequality protests paralyse Santiago", *The Guardian*, 26 October 2019, https://www.theguardian.com/world/2019/oct/25/chile-protests-congress-valparaiso-police.

[22] "Truckers protesting road tolls snarl traffic in Chile's capital", *EFE*, 6 November 2019, https://www.efe.com/efe/english/world/truckers-protesting-road-tolls-snarl-traffic-in-chile-s-capital/50000262-4104876.

[23] *Ibid.*

[24] "Chile's congress evacuated as inequality protests paralyse Santiago", *The Guardian*, 26 October 2019, https://www.theguardian.com/world/2019/oct/25/chile-protests-congress-valparaiso-police.

All said and politics aside, increasingly, it can be concluded that project simplicity can be a virtue. PPP projects hitherto are mostly single purpose in nature, like a water desalination plant, toll roads or waste to energy facility. As it is, projections of utility or patronage over the longer term are frequently challenging enough to implement. Any attempt to explore a possible integration of several purposes within a single facility, even with the requisite private sector expertise, can only be for the bravehearted.

Example 3.3: Juggling Many Balls at the Sports Hub

If a public sector project goes wrong, the government is answerable to the people for its failure. However, when the government adopts a PPP with private sector investor(s), there will now most likely be a dispute over who is responsible and should shoulder the blame when things go awry. This was brought to the fore when teething problems emerged which in turn raised questions over the conceptualisation of the Singapore Sports Hub PPP.

The Singapore government took a decision to demolish the old National Stadium, which closed in 2007, to make way for an integrated hub comprising a stadium for community sports, a leisure water park, a retail mall and office space. Plans were made for the construction of the new National Stadium to begin the following year.[25] The Singapore government decided to adopt the PPP approach for such an unusual undertaking — a departure from the traditional single-purpose model being used thus far.

The partnership was between Sport Singapore, the government's statutory board, and Sports Hub Pte. Ltd. (SHPL), a consortium consisting of InfraRed Capital Partners, the majority equity partner, Global Spectrum Pico, Dragages Singapore and DTZ Facilities and Engineering. The Singapore Sports Hub was eventually completed in 2014, totalling to a cost of S$1.33 billion.[26] Despite all efforts and hopes that the PPP would succeed, the outcome was unfortunately not quite up to expectations. Therein lies the question — with so many partners in the mix, who was to blame for expectations not being met?

---

[25] https://cmp.smu.edu.sg/article/public-private-partnerships-case-study-singapores-national-stadium, 31 July 2018.

[26] *Ibid.*

The agreement made was that SHPL would receive payments from the government totalling S$193.7 million annually over a 25-year term period. In exchange, SHPL would hold the contract to build and operate the hub.[27]

However, two major problems soon became prominent — high rental fees and teething problems with facilities which put many event organisers off. The uncompetitive rental fees had led several event organisers and global sports promoters to seek alternative venues. The most unexpected example occurred when the Ministry of Defence was charged what was considered to be exorbitant fees for usage of the stadium for the 2016 National Day Parade (NDP). The Sports Hub initially wanted to charge the government S$26 million for an additional 35 days of rehearsal. This caused a major public outcry, and the figure was eventually reportedly lowered to S$10 million. The total cost of hosting the NDP at the Sports Hub was estimated to be just under S$40 million, almost double the cost of hosting it at its conventional venue at Marina Bay. To date, this remains the only time NDP was staged at the Sports Hub.[28] To many, this is ironic considering the Sports Hub is a major joint venture between the government and the private sector, yet the government is abstaining from using the venue for one of its most prominent events of the year. One of the main reasons offered was the non-feasibility of hosting the parachute team, the Red Lions, a crowd favourite at the NDPs.

The high rental fees were obviously becoming an issue that needed to be resolved as it was driving away potential customers. Besides the pricey fees, teething problems with the facilities after its grand opening were also a major issue.

In 2014, complaints about the state of the sandy pitch were made after a football match between Brazil and Japan. To fix the pitch, SHPL spent S$1.5 million on lamps to replicate the effects of sunlight to encourage the growth of the grass.[29] Meanwhile, events had to be cancelled, leading to further public discontentment. Another series of lapses involved sound system problems which plagued Taiwanese pop star Jay Chou's concerts in both 2014 and 2016. This led to concert goers petitioning for a refund.

---

[27] https://cmp.smu.edu.sg/case/3581, 7 June 2018.

[28] https://www.straitstimes.com/sport/singapore-sports-hub-the-highs-and-lows-over-the-years, 2 February 2019.

[29] https://cmp.smu.edu.sg/article/public-private-partnerships-case-study-singapores-national-stadium, 31 July 2018.

An audit conducted by KPMG[30] opined that the interests of the various stakeholders were misaligned. Sport Singapore placed more emphasis on hosting community events that would boost public welfare whereas the private sector preferred events that would maximise profits and serve their commercial interests.[31] Even among the consortium partners, there were competing interests as reflected in SHPL's intention then to terminate the venue operation contract.[32] This however did not come to pass.[33]

Meanwhile, balancing the different, and often competing, interests continued to take a toll on top leadership of the integrated development, which saw the third CEO departure.

> *With a PPP, complications are likely to occur with different stakeholders not always necessarily having the same interests and standards. In addition, projections and expectations of patronage or utilisation may be far off from the original plan, so a contingency plan is needed in case plans go askew. Often, a question of consortium leadership and responsibility arises; with so many partners in the mix, such as in the Singapore Sports Hub partnership, who is to be blamed when things go wrong? PPPs with single purpose typically encounter problems in the normal course of events, let alone those with multiple objectives. Simplicity is probably still the best way to go, especially for infrastructure projects fronted by the government since the state will always be held accountable by the public.*

Fiscal Challenges

When government coffers run dry, there is only one default option — revisit mega commitments with a view to cancellation, deferral or downsizing, especially when such promises were made by the previous

---

[30] https://www.straitstimes.com/sport/sportshub-consortium-set-for-big-internal-shake-up, 19 February 2016.

[31] https://cmp.smu.edu.sg/article/public-private-partnerships-case-study-singapores-national-stadium, 31 July 2018.

[32] https://www.straitstimes.com/sport/sportshub-consortium-set-for-big-internal-shake-up, 19 February 2016.

[33] https://www.todayonline.com/sports/alls-well-sports-hub-consortium-now?cid=h3_referral_inarticlelinks_03092019_todayonline, 20 February 2016.

government on what would appear to be increasingly questionable assumptions. This appears to be fair game, be it a U-turn on the Andhra Pradesh[34] capital city project at Amaravati by the newly elected YSR Congress Party in India or the cancellation of several big-ticket infrastructure projects by the then new Malaysian government after its electoral victory in May 2018. This proved to be short-lived with the abrupt change in political leadership in March 2020, with a new coalition alliance which included the party that was allegedly responsible for ironically massive commitments and mismanagement.

Example 3.4: Weighed Down by Massive Commitments and Mismanagement

A change in government is often accompanied by a corresponding change in policy direction and a keen sense of delivering on campaign promises. What greeted the new Malaysian government in May 2018 was more than a plateful — massive infrastructure project commitments and alleged mismanagement of key institutions. The surprise victory was however short-lived with another change in March 2020, with the assumption of leadership by a new political alliance.

In May 2018, the Opposition alliance Pakatan Harapan (PH), led by former Prime Minister Mahathir Mohamad, shocked the nation with a victory over former stronghold Barisan Nasional, led by UMNO chief Najib Razak.

Heavy Infrastructure Commitments

Prior to May 2018, the infrastructure projects agenda was a rather busy one for Malaysia — an RM50 billion Kuala Lumpur–Singapore High-Speed Rail ("HSR"),[35] an RM65 billion East Coast Rail Line

---

[34]"TDP caught on back foot over capital decentralisation row in Andhra Pradesh", *Livemint*, 5 January 2020.

[35]https://www.channelnewsasia.com/news/singapore/kuala-lumpur-singapore-hsr-rail-link-what-to-know-10284406?cid=h3_referral_inarticlelinks_24082018_cna, 6 September 2018.

("ECRL")[36] and an at least RM10 billion Trans-Sabah gas pipeline ("TSGP") project.[37] PM Mahathir Mohamad surprised the public with the announcement in October 2018 that the government was cancelling these and other major projects in a bid to save more than RM300 billion.[38] This was to uphold the principle of spending within their means, be it the assumption of debt or as a financial investment.

After a series of bilateral discussions between the Malaysian and Singapore governments, there was agreement to postpone the 350km-long HSR construction to July 2020, and completion to 2031 instead of the original 2026. Meanwhile, the ECRL project with Chinese partners was restarted in July 2019, after a year-long suspension, but on a more modest budget of RM45 billion.

Balancing the Fiscal Books

The plight of the then new government was an unenviable one — some RM18 billion of the Goods and Service Tax ("GST") collection as input taxes since 2015 were reportedly unaccounted for, most likely misappropriated by the previous regime, according to the then Minister for Finance Lim Guan Eng.[39] This was disclosed when the new government was moving a bill in Parliament to repeal the GST in August 2018, as part of its campaign promises.

Besides the deficit on both the development and recurrent budget front, the then new PH government was also presented with two other major challenges — ploughing in some RM6 billion[40] to rescue the Federal Land Development Authority ("FELDA") and another RM20 billion to restore the financial health of Lembaga Tabung Haji ("LTH").

There were no two ways about it. FELDA was a national icon, having been established in 1956 to perform a strategically important role, that of

---

[36] https://www.todayonline.com/world/china-and-malaysia-restart-massive-belt-and-road-project-after-hiccups, 25 July 2019.

[37] https://www.theedgemarkets.com/article/govt-still-talks-over-transsabah-gas-pipeline-says-guan-eng, 17 July 2019.

[38] https://www.channelnewsasia.com/news/asia/hsr-project-cancellation-save-300-billion-10853072, 22 October 2018.

[39] https://www.theedgemarkets.com/article/about-rm18b-or-93-gst-input-tax-credit-missing-lim, 8 August 2018.

[40] https://www.reuters.com/article/us-malaysia-felda/malaysia-backs-1-5-billion-in-aid-for-state-palm-oil-firm-felda-idUSKCN1RL161, 9 April 2019.

overseeing the palm oil plantation sector. The agency's mandate was to resettle and employ the rural poor in the palm oil industry. FELDA had instead chalked up losses from years of mismanagement, the making of bad, if not questionable, investments and assumption of soaring debt. FELDA's liabilities had risen 12-fold over 10 years to RM14 billion by 2017, in stark contrast to a cash balance of a mere RM35 million.

The scenario at LTH was equally perplexing. The Tabung Haji fund was set up in 1963 to assist Malaysian Muslim pilgrims to save their money to perform the haj. Owing to alleged mismanagement, again including bad investments, the Ministry for Finance transferred to another vehicle for rehabilitation, some RM9.6 billion worth of non-performing assets, comprising a mixture of listed equity holdings, properties and plantation assets. The property assets included a controversial purchase of land at the Tun Razak Exchange, at a significantly higher rate than that paid for by the vendor, 1Malaysia Development Berhad ("1MDB").[41]

In response to the need for austerity all round, the Malaysian government contemplated trimming defence spending by some RM20 billion to help bolster the FELDA and LTH rescue efforts.[42] At its Annual Budget release nonetheless, the Defence Ministry received an increase from RM13.9 billion to RM15.6 billion for 2020.[43]

Meanwhile, the 1MDB saga has continued. At stake were the missing billions which the then new Malaysian government was pursuing in earnest. Given the complexity of the various allegedly fraudulent transactions and the cross-border nature of the suits, the verdict is unlikely to be soon. Beyond the legal suits lies the all-important question of how state enterprises can become the vehicles for the ruling party to achieve political ends.

The about-turn for infrastructure projects was not simply an exercise to wilfully undo what the previous government had done, but to 'put the house in financial and governance order'. These challenges are far from trivial and will require patience on the part of the public to see resolution or an unravelling of previously ill-conceived commitments. A lot then hinged on how badly the Malaysian public wanted to see real change and their trust in the then PM Mahathir's government to deliver the ideal results.

---

[41] https://www.malaysiakini.com/news/499766, 14 November 2019.

[42] https://www.straitstimes.com/asia/se-asia/malaysias-defence-minister-says-defence-spending-diverted-to-bail-out-tabung-haji-felda, 20 April 2019.

[43] https://www.nst.com.my/news/nation/2019/10/529102/mat-sabu-muhyiddin-pleased-budget-allocation, 11 October 2019.

Patience is not a luxury as we now know. A purported internal battle for political leadership between the then PM Mahathir and the PM-in-waiting Anwar Ibrahim led to an implosion of the ruling PH coalition. An intriguing combination of defection of MPs and the formation of a new coalition alliance Perikatan Nasional (PN), including the former ruling UMNO party, culminated in an abrupt change in PM to Tan Sri Muhyiddin on 1 March 2020.[44]

The newly-minted PN government has got its work cut out for it — in addition to deciding what to do about the major infrastructure projects, plugging the gaps at FELDA and LTH, addressing the missing US$4.5 billion from 1MDB for which the former PM Najib Razak is still undergoing trial, there is the unfortunate emergence of the Covid-19 pandemic.

Many new governments expect to roll up their sleeves to undo certain public policies when they are in charge. Some, like first the newly-elected Pakatan Harapan and then the Perikatan Nasional governments, have also uncovered surprises or even nightmares along the way. The job is no doubt an unpopular and challenging one, where there is risk of politicization of the various issues all the time.

Apart from having to balance the budget each year, governments typically have to plan for the longer-term objective of raising the income level of the population at large. Inequality rears its ugly head whenever an economy expands, ironically, at a healthy pace and for a stretch. The contrast between the per capita statistics of the better located coastal cities and the rural areas will become increasingly marked over time. Yet ensuring that the disparity does not lead to potential political challenges or social strife would require vast amounts of resources, and often, time for efforts to bear fruit.

Developing the Local Economy

There is absolutely no economic interest on the part of the private sector to build social infrastructure like schools, hospitals or public housing.

---

[44] https://www.economist.com/asia/2020/03/05/malaysias-new-government-may-be-even-more-unstable-than-old-one, 5 March 2020.

Some participation may find its way as Corporate Social Responsibility (CSR) initiatives but are usually carried out on a much smaller scale than that required for the public or country at large.

Exceptions however do exist. When a business is of a scale that it becomes the sole generator of economic activity within a district or village, the local government will do well to collaborate closely with the private-sector operator for synergistic benefits. This is fairly common within the agricultural and resources sectors in land-rich areas like China, India, Australia and Indonesia. Under such circumstances, the town identity and well-being would bear a strong correlation to the sense of responsibility of the local business owners.

Example 3.5: Introducing Kerinci

Many countries with large expanse of land face the challenge of ensuring even economic progress, which can be elusive, if not impossible for the pockets that are not readily accessible. There however exists the potential for collaboration with the private sector in some cases to bring about synergistic benefits.

Not many have heard of the small town of Pangkalan Kerinci in Indonesia — known affectionately by the locals as *Kerinci*. Considered as the nerve centre of the Royal Golden Eagle (RGE) Group, Kerinci is home to APRIL and Asian Agri in the pulp and paper mill and palm oil plantation industries, respectively. Although relatively small in size, Kerinci has transformed in a remarkable way, a growth story that speaks volumes on how the government, businesses and the communities they operate in can collaborate meaningfully to boost the infrastructure, economy and ultimately, the well-being of an entire city.

Before RGE arrived on the scene in Kerinci some 30 years ago, the town was a sleepy village of 200 odd dwellings whose inhabitants were either fishermen or illegal loggers.[45] With no proper paved roads, the only way to get to Kerinci then was by boat or foot, rendering the remote town a bleak prospect for locals to make their fortunes.

The contrast cannot be starker today. The town has since prospered to serve a community of about 100,000 inhabitants, boasting more than 11,000 km of new roads laid out in the area, a local power generating plant

---

[45] https://www.aprilasia.com/en/our-media/articles/before-and-after-the-growth-of-kerinci-in-pictures, 12 March 2018.

working on sustainable resources, a small airport and two shipping ports to distribute the pulp and paper produced in Kerinci to global destinations.[46]

An important factor in the transformation of Kerinci is the 5Cs philosophy that guides RGE chairman and philanthropist Sukanto Tanoto's businesses: that its operations should be good for Community, Country, Climate and Customer, and only then will they be good for the Company.

For the last two decades, APRIL's community development programmes, a hallmark of the pulp and paper giant, have been well received. Implemented by APRIL's operating unit, PT Riau Andalan Pulp and Paper (PT RAPP), the Small and Medium Enterprise (SME) programme supports aspiring entrepreneurs in the community, within and outside the forestry industry, through vocational training, and mentorship in obtaining financing from local banks and opportunities to market their product and services.

Sulaiman is one of the many local entrepreneurs that has benefited from this programme. From his workshop in Pangkalan Kerinci, Sulaiman manages the production of coco peat, to be used as seedlings for acacia and eucalyptus trees in APRIL's plantations. "I joined PT RAPP's community development programme in 2013. My first order was 30 tons of coco-peat within the first month of my company's operation. Now I can supply as many as 600 tons to PT RAPP", said the 38-year old whose company now turns in a rather healthy profit.[47]

Asian Agri, an RGE constituent firm focusing on the production of palm oil in Sumatra, has also been working closely with the communities to raise their standard of living significantly. The firm is one of the pioneers in support of the government's 1987 Plasma Transmigration Scheme. Under the scheme, villagers from the rural parts of Indonesia were relocated to oil palm growing areas and given two hectares of land to farm. To date, Asian Agri is in partnership with 30,000 such plasma smallholders.[48] The partnership grants these smallholders training on agricultural best practices to optimise production, assistance in acquiring bank loans used to start their plantations or to repay debts and entrepreneurship skills to gain additional income. In turn, previously undreamed-of opportunities are now

---

[46] *Ibid.*

[47] "Emerging trend of successful local entrepreneurs in Riau", *The Jakarta Post*, 8 May 2017, https://www.thejakartapost.com/adv/2017/05/08/emerging-trend-of-successful-local-entrepreneurs-in-riau.html.

[48] Asian Agri, "Asian Agri and Apical unveil 'sustainable palm oil everywhere everyday' at trade expo Indonesia 2019". Press release, 16 October 2019, https://www.rgei.com/attachments/article/1401/20191016-press-release-tel-2019-en.pdf.

the reality for many of smallholder farmers and their families. Not only was Asian Agri able to further the government's efforts to improve the overall quality of life in these communities, it also supports the third point of the country's National Priority Agenda (Nawa Cita) about building Indonesia up from the village level.

As both examples have shown, the government need not always be the sole facilitator of economic growth. The private sector can be well positioned to alleviate poverty and provide opportunities for the community it operates in, creating an economic multiplier effect. Asian Agri also exemplified the importance of carefully calibrating the symbiosis between both parties; the community trusts them enough to allow them to use their resources, while Asian Agri repays that faith by continuously improving the community.

> *Kerinci is proof that such a concept of a public, private and community partnership, tapping on their respective strengths and leveraging on one another's work, can be successful, truly synergistic and even catalytic in the pursuit of common goals. On its own steam, the government would have to artificially create sources of growth or entice investors to build economic and social infrastructure in faith. Likewise, a private enterprise like RGE would achieve nought if the local government were not enlightened. This is a perfect example of a win–win–win proposition.*

Tapping Private Sector Expertise

Very often, multinational corporations with experience across several geographies are the repositories of technical knowhow. They are well placed to add value to evolving public policies in an emerging market situation. In particular, multilateral development banks (MDB) such as the World Bank (WB),[49] Asian Development Bank and the relatively new Asian Infrastructure Investment Bank (AIIB) have accumulated a wealth of experience in developing both economic and social infrastructure.

Wise is the country that capitalises on such deep knowledge to leapfrog development cycles. Apart from the traditional roles of providing financial support, many MDBs also focus on specific policies such as

---

[49]"The effectiveness of multilateral development banks", *International Banker*, 10 October 2019.

agricultural reforms. The overall agenda is ultimately one of sustainable growth, taking reference from the 17 Sustainable Development Goals (SDGs). Enlisting the assistance of MDBs is all the more important as it also promises continual and meaningful engagement with the private sector.

Example 3.6: Harnessing True Energy from Collaboration with AIIB

The Bangladesh government formulated a Power System Master Plan 2016,[50] sponsored by Japan International Cooperation Agency, which encapsulated an extensive energy and power development plan up to 2041. Such a plan will underpin Bangladesh's aspiration to become a high-income country by then. Apart from building domestic capacity, importation was also considered. What is obvious is the promotion of international cooperation in all respects.

Ability to function after dark ✓.
Ability to do well in school ✓.
Ability to live a better life ✓.

Let there be light — figuratively, thanks to a milestone decision by the Board of Directors at AIIB in June 2016,[51] and US$165 million later in 2018, some 12.5 million people in the rural regions of Bangladesh received reliable access to electricity.

Dubbed as the Distribution System Upgrade and Expansion Project, the project has enhanced power distribution capacity and increased the number of rural and urban electricity consumers in Bangladesh, mainly in the form of a provision of about 2.5 million service connections to rural consumers and upgrading two grid substations and conversion of 85 km overhead distribution lines into underground cables in north Dhaka.

Finances and good intentions can only go so far. What is instrumental in this AIIB aspirational project is the close working relationship between

---

[50] https://powerdivision.portal.gov.bd/sites/default/files/files/powerdivision.portal.gov.bd/page/4f81bf4d_1180_4c53_b27c_8fa0eb11e2c1/(E)_FR_PSMP2016_Summary_revised.pdf, 2016.

[51] https://www.aiib.org/en/projects/approved/2016/bangladesh-distribution-system.html, 24 June 2016.

AIIB and the two implementation agencies, namely the Bangladesh Rural Electrification Board (BREB) and Dhaka Electric Supply Company Limited (DESCO). It is obvious that without the right positive attitudes, timelines may have slipped indefinitely. The successful completion of the project, along with the outpouring of delight of the beneficiaries in the form of the ability of children to read at night, to do well at school,[52] is an excellent testimony to a critical success factor of MDB-led projects — pro-active and constructive support of local government agencies.

In the larger context of a current population of around 164 million in Bangladesh, this project's reach will go a long way towards achieving complete electrification. As of July 2018, around 90% have access to electricity.[53] The access is understandably uneven, reaching 92% of the urban population but only 67% of the rural population as of 2015.

This access has been achieved on the back of an almost doubling of capacity over the past nine years to 16,000 MW, supported by the installation of 195,000 km of electricity line. The government's target is to generate an aggregate of 24,000 MW by 2021, and 40,000 MW by 2030, so as to sustain its buoyant growth rate of between 6% and 7%.

AIIB continues to play a supportive role in the Power System Master Plan on various initiatives — in the form of US$60 million credit for the construction of a greenfield 220 MW dual-fuel combined cycle plant in Bhola, costing US$271 million and to be completed in early 2020[54]; a US$120 million upgrade of 46 km transmission lines to the power grid to counter frequent collapses of equipment and network from overload in Chittagong, costing US$177 million and to be ready by end 2022.[55]

Much work remains ahead in terms of raising the reliability of the entire energy supply chain from new planting, to plant efficiency, to curbing erratic power supply, theft and blackouts. This is indeed a multi-faceted challenge for the Bangladesh Government.

---

[52] https://www.chinadaily.com.cn/a/201911/29/WS5de0af1ba310cf3e3557aed2.html, 29 November 2019.

[53] http://bdnewsnet.com/2018/07/12/bangladesh/economy/booming-energy-sector-of-bangladesh-90-percent-have-access-to-the-elctrecity/, 12 July 2018.

[54] https://www.aiib.org/en/projects/approved/2018/_download/Bangladesh/PSI-Bangladesh-Bhola-IPP-120118.pdf, 9 February 2018.

[55] https://www.aiib.org/en/projects/approved/2019/_download/bangladesh/summary/bangladesh-power-system.pdf, 26 March 2019.

> *Thankfully, it is a government who's cognisant of the financial and expertise constraints to the pace of building such basic economic infrastructure if it were to go it alone. The positive approach to partnership with the MDBs and private sector operators is therefore realistic and fruitful, if not exemplary one.*

While multilateral financial institutions have a solid track record at helping emerging economies level up, through both the extension of finance and knowledge transfer, several private sector operators espouse the same values of sustainable development as governments. In their own distinctive ways, they map out longer-term strategies and plod on assiduously, regardless of the mounting challenges.

Even as the multilateral banks concern themselves with the developmental aspirations of the Bangladesh government and people, design details around developing the regulatory framework, structuring the power/energy sector and determining the degree of competition are where a private sector or even state-owned operator can add substantial value.

Example 3.7: Government's Push towards a Powerful Finish

> *More often than not, the government of an emerging economy will have to struggle to build appropriate infrastructure so as to catalyse economic expansion. Yet most states would have neither the financial resources for the scale envisaged nor the expertise to build and operate an efficient public good. The huge difference, from embracing an active collaboration with the private sector, can be seen in the stance taken by the Government of Bangladesh towards the goal of wide access for the public to affordable electricity. A constructive partnership of this nature and scale no doubt would require plenty of effort and consistency.*

The circumstances confronting Bangladesh over the past few decades were not very different from those of many emerging countries — economic expansion was contingent on the availability of basic infrastructure, especially of power.

Genesis of Power Privatisation

In the late 1980s and early 1990s, there was a wave of privatisation in electricity sectors around the world, starting in Latin America and then spreading to Asia. The private power mantra was spread by the WB and to a significant extent by the US government, with a rather effective carrot and stick approach. The carrot was the financial assistance provided in the form of low cost, long-term sector development loans from the World Bank Group, including the International Development Association, to fund development of essential infrastructure. In addition, the US government provided grant money to pay for technical and legal consultants to help host governments develop private power structures and negotiate effectively across the table from foreign companies. The stick was the conditions to aid. Conditions to qualifying for the financial assistance included the requirement that essentially the WB's preferred power sector privatisation model had to be adopted and procurement of new projects had to be undertaken in a transparent manner.

By way of context, the model that was being propagated actually originated in the power sector reform that took place in the US in the 1970s to break up the large utilities' dominance over the sector. The reform was enacted as the Public Utility Regulatory Policy Act, 1978.

Model for Emerging Economies

In Asia, the Philippines was the first country to adopt private power with a model that is now well known in Bangladesh — long-term Power Purchase Agreement (PPA), coterminous Fuel Supply Agreement (FSA) and Land Lease Agreement (LLA), backed by a sovereign guarantee. Other countries, such as Thailand, Pakistan, India and Sri Lanka, adopted variations of this model. The contractual structures that were applied across the region looked remarkably similar, not least because the institutions, advisors and investors were often common across the countries.

In Bangladesh, the government received assistance from the US Trade & Development Agency as well as the WB in its efforts to encourage private investment. Not surprisingly, the law firms and technical consultants who did a lot of the work were US sourced. Several of the early investors were also US companies — AES, El Paso and Coastal Corporation.

Multilateral and bilateral lenders were vitally important in those early days. Many of these lenders and investors plugged the market failure that would otherwise have prevented projects from ever materialising. One such example was the Summit Group's Khulna project for which Coastal Corporation eventually funded 84% of the total project cost in the form of cash and loan guarantees, clearly underscoring WB's clout in attracting sceptical investors.

Recognition of the Private Sector's Role

Just as important was the fact that the Government of Bangladesh (GOB) was committed to opening up the then state-owned power sector to private investment. The adoption of the Implementation Agreement (IA), which provides for an explicit sovereign guarantee of the payment obligations of state enterprises involved, was a huge step. Such a guarantee was instrumental in reassuring highly sceptical investors who had no shortage of investment alternatives elsewhere. The rapid growth in the Bangladesh power sector over the past 10 years has largely been due to the fact that the GOB left the original financial model largely intact, while giving investors assurance that sanctity of contract was a principle that they took very seriously.

This stance amply demonstrates how the GOB has been enlightened enough to reach out to both the multilateral lenders and private sector in order to develop the power/energy sector, on a scale and at a speed otherwise not possible on its own.

There were overlapping objectives. WB had been advocating privatisation of the power sector, an essential criterion for development, and where government resources may not be readily available. To this end, the International Finance Corporation (IFC) has been instrumental in helping the GOB to build the aforementioned model, wrap these agreements and provide for government's incentives and evacuation of generated electricity under the IA.

While the LLA was typically signed with Bangladesh Power Development Board (BPDB) to lease the required land, the FSA was contracted with either PetroBangla[56] for natural gas supply or with Bangladesh Petroleum Corporation (BPC) for petroleum products supply. The PPA, which is perhaps the most important document of all, would have all the sale and purchase arrangements as well as operational contracts for the power project. On the other hand, the IA provided a guarantee from the state of Bangladesh, signed with the authorisation of the President of the Republic, guaranteeing or ensuring performances of the

---

[56] PetroBangla is the government-owned national oil company which explores, produces, transports, manages and sells oil, natural gas and other mineral resources.

government-controlled contracting parties and stepping in where necessary, to mitigate or perform the obligations. The IA also provided certainty of evacuating the generated electricity. These agreements as a whole were defined as "Project Agreements".

Private Sector a Major Generator

Collectively, as of 2020, private sector investors have provided the foundation for the implementation of generating projects of more than 10,000 MW of capacity to the national grid of Bangladesh. These agreements have enabled Bangladesh to eradicate electricity shortages, with a total current grid capacity of more than 20,000 MW. These agreements are enshrined in the "Private Sector Power Generation Policy" which came into effect in late 1996, testifying to the foresight of the GOB.

Summit's participation was borne out of necessity and sensible economics. As a commodity, mostly chemicals, importer into Bangladesh, the Summit ships conveying these imports would often require much more time than the contracted discharge time as per the charter party. A shortage of electricity would make the cranes unworkable, hence the delay. The demurrages levied by the shipping companies and the ensuing acrimony would often severely cut into profit and goodwill then.

Back then in 1995, Summit proposed to the authorities a plan to build their own 100 MW coal-based power plant so as to enable the port to function round the clock. This was however not proceeded with.

Separately, at about the same time, initiatives were under way for private power generation. In 1996, the first tender for four barge-mounted power plants to be implemented urgently, within nine months of contracting, was floated by the BPDB. Summit decided to partner Wärtsilä of Finland and its then agent in Bangladesh, United Enterprises, to bid for a 100 MW project at the port city of Khulna. This culminated in a 110 MW project which was implemented on schedule in September 1998, within the requisite nine months of contracting.[57] The Khulna Power Co. Ltd. project, comprising two barges each mounted with 55 MW of generating capacity, a fuel oil storage terminal of 15,000 metric tonnes, a jetty and a 132 KV evacuation facility, made history as the first private power generator in Bangladesh.

---

[57] https://summitpowerinternational.com/khulna-power-company-ltd, 27 January 2020.

Keeping Collaboration Constructive

Since then, the Summit's generating capacity has climbed to 2,000 MW as of 2020, with another 600 MW under construction and 3,600 MW under consideration. The portfolio of the Summit's power assets are booked at around US$1.6 billion. This would not have been possible without the close collaboration between Summit and its principal counter-party, the BPDB, working hand in glove for the development of the sector. The cooperation has not only been to support the implementation of a national initiative but also to enhance the goodwill and perception of the sector in particular, and Bangladesh in general.

That is not to say that negotiations have been easy; in fact, very often, it was a game of nerves. Coming out of socialism then, BPDB was for the first time allowing and contracting out to the private sector, generating capacity that the public sector hitherto monopolised. Summit had the honour of being the first private sector player to negotiate these four pioneering contracts. It was undoubtedly a hard-earned honour — the Summit representatives struggled and endured more than a year of long days of hard negotiations, which were only finalised at the eleventh hour. They literally argued over every point, para and perhaps every word.

To be fair, it was a steep learning curve for both the BPDB and Summit, neither of whom had experience in PPAs. The lack of knowledge stacked up against both parties. As an example, Summit's supplier partner-financier Wärtsilä had required "capacity payment" and "fuel cost pass-through" as conditions precedent to signing anything, which Summit insisted on behalf of the consortium. The BPDB was initially adamant that there be no "take or pay" sort of arrangement as market and grid conditions were beyond their control. BPDB finally relented. Fuel cost as a pass-through remained a contentious issue. Likewise, the calorific content, cost of transportation and maintenance of inventory seemed insurmountable challenges. Summit ended up importing its own oil as a compromise. Today, these have become "model contracts" which are widely deployed in the entire market, sometimes even beyond the boundaries of Bangladesh, a far cry from those acrimonious days and nights of tense negotiations.

In hindsight, it would not have been possible for the two parties to settle were it not for the urgency arising from the acute shortage of electricity that prompted the then and present Prime Minister Sheikh Hasina to instruct both parties to sign an agreement that she would personally witness.

Resolve of the Government Creditable

Practically the whole Bangladesh government has been involved from the beginning — from the Ministry of Power, Energy & Mineral Resources (MPEMR), to the Ministry of Finance for providing incentives to foreign currencies, to the Ministry of Commerce for allowing imports and exports, to the Ministry of Environment for operating conditions and to the numerous local governments. All in all, about 100 different permissions/approvals, consents, licences would be required just to establish a power plant. The scale of coordination is therefore far from trivial.

The energy and power sectors of Bangladesh have greatly benefited from the 1996 "Private Sector Power Generation Policy", overseen by the Independent Commission "Bangladesh Energy Regulatory Commission" and guided by MPEMR's "Power Cell" and a private sector industry-specific association "Bangladesh Independent Power Producers Association". The market is currently stable and well organised.

Striking a Balance

The next phase of collaboration would manifest itself more significantly as projects approach the end of the respective contractual periods. At expiry, these contracts have to be re-negotiated, usually at a lower tariff. Given the robustness of arguments borne out of experience gained over the years, on both sides, many contracts may wind up in the courts. The Summit currently has an outstanding case with the Bangladesh Rural Electrification Board.

All said, as one of the pioneer private sector participants, the Summit was able to establish a commendable track record, having been associated with these huge developments and working alongside multilateral/bilateral lenders and industry experts. The GOB has struck a good balance between working with competent and financially sound private sector partners and building an essential grid to provide quality electricity at a reasonable price to all its citizens.

The Government of Bangladesh's resolve to seek out private sector participants, who provide both financial resources and domain expertise, is not without its challenges. It recognises however that the alternative of going it alone would take much longer, require a whole lot more resources and yet may not yield a better outcome. Recognising that such grid infrastructure is crucial to economic

> *growth, it has opted to address the risks of allowing private sector participation instead. Consistency is everything — it is a position that the enlightened Government of Bangladesh understands very well, one that brings long-term credibility benefit.*

Overcoming Hiccups

Collaboration with the state are not without their challenges. Sometimes, it is far from being straightforward and not always economically sensible. Such is the particularly daunting experience for the agricultural owners in Indonesia and Malaysia in their joint efforts with the respective governments to combat widespread deforestation through indiscriminate burning. Haze is a curse that some plantation owners bear more than their fair share of blame whereas others get away somewhat scot-free. But the right public–private collaboration can be a beautiful, and healthy, thing.

Example 3.8: When Regulations Are not Enough

There exists a legally binding agreement[58] among the ASEAN members on Transboundary Haze, signed in 2002, requiring the member countries to strengthen international cooperation by developing national policies for preventing and monitoring such haze pollution, and undertake individual and joint mitigating measures against land and forest fires. In reality, rules and good intentions can only go so far. Where a government is supported in its efforts by private sector players, it can make a real difference and the impact can hopefully be more sustainable.

In 2015, forest fires blanketed the Southeast Asia region in a choking haze.[59] In Central Kalimantan of Indonesia, the Pollutant Standards Index (PSI) hit a record 1,936, way more serious than 350 or what is already

---

[58] http://haze.asean.org/?wpfb_dl=32, 10 June 2002.
[59] "Haze crisis set to be one of the worst on record", *Straits Times*, 3 October 2015, https://www.straitstimes.com/asia/haze-crisis-set-to-be-one-of-the-worst-on-record.

considered hazardous.[60] The Transboundary Haze crisis gripped the region, flaring diplomatic tensions among neighbours even as flights were grounded, schools closed and pollution levels continuing to break new hazardous highs. The fires, which contributed to the worst haze air-pollution crisis ever seen in Southeast Asia, devoured some 2,000 hectares of carbon-rich peatland.[61]

Back since 2011, in response to the annual haze, Indonesia had already issued a moratorium that limits new concessions in millions of hectares of forests and peatlands. The government had also initiated a "One Map" process to resolve overlapping land claims and was committed to recognising traditional land rights. Yet the root causes of the annual haze are complex and there was no single, quick solution to the problem.

In order to address haze on a timescale that is sustainable as a long-term solution, the Indonesian government decided to tap on the strengths of companies in the forestry sector by identifying the underlying causes and implementing a multi-stakeholder effort in fire prevention, forest conservation and restoration programs.

As part of the $20 billion RGE Group of corporations under the direction of Founder-Chairman Sukanto Tanoto, Asia Pacific Resources International Limited (APRIL) is among the world's leading producers of pulp and paper products. Very early on, APRIL recognises the benefits of working closely with the Indonesian government, local communities and other key stakeholders towards fire management.

Initiated by APRIL in 2013, the *Restorasi Ekosistem Riau* (RER) is one of the largest landscape-level restoration efforts in Southeast Asia. In order to protect the 150,000 hectares of natural peatland forests, APRIL established plantations of acacia trees around RER, acting as a protective buffer for these unprotected forested areas prone to deforestation, burning and illegal logging. In addition, RER works with local non-governmental organisations (NGOs) such as BIDARA to teach communities alternative forms of livelihoods such as chilli farming, as a means to prevent forest encroachment and degradation.

To mitigate fire risk on dry peatlands, APRIL uses a water management system to maintain sufficient water levels in its plantations, particularly during the dry seasons. This approach has been informed by science-based consultations and industry best practice — to ensure that

---

[60] *Ibid.*

[61] Hicks, R. "How a palm oil company is fighting slash and burn culture", *Eco Business*, 11 April 2017, https://www.eco-business.com/news/how-a-palm-oil-company-is-fighting-slash-and-burn-culture/.

peatlands remain wet for both long-term plantation productivity and a reduction in fire risk.

At the core of APRIL's strategy to fight fires is to tackle the underlying cause of the haze-spewing blazes: the tradition of fire-based agriculture and land as a primary source of income. According to the World Resources Institute,[62] it is estimated that around 50–60 million Indonesians depend directly on the forests to support their livelihood, and that some 25 million[63] in the country still live below the poverty line. Burning is by far the quickest and cheapest way to clear land, and has been a traditional method in Kalimantan and Sumatra for generations.

Officially launched by APRIL in July 2015, the Fire Free Village Program (FFVP) is a fire prevention initiative in Riau, Indonesia, founded in close collaboration with local communities. Through a process of socialisation, education, training and economic incentives, the programme not only increases awareness of the negative impact of burning but also provides alternative sources of income. The rationale is that if the villagers can live off the land productively, they will be less likely to encroach onto new land or burn it.

Local communities receive assistance from APRIL to adopt sustainable agricultural alternatives — such as mechanical land clearing tools — *in lieu of* fire for land clearing. Plenty of thought has also gone into the education of young minds. At the heart of their programme in elementary schools is a comic book that would capture the interest of students and help them appreciate the importance of the issue and the benefits of a fire-free landscape. Educating younger generations will help to shape the right behaviours for the longer term, key to countering the age-old practice of burning to clear land. More significantly, participating villages are incentivised to abandon traditional agricultural methods, through funding for community infrastructure projects. The projects funded are identified in close consultation with the community and, therefore, in alignment with their needs.

APRIL's holistic approach has shown promising results for them in the fight against fire — for the fourth consecutive year since its launch, the RER conservation area has been free from encroachment and fires and evidence has shown that the burnt area in neighbouring communities had

---

[62] World Resources Institute, Research on "Forests and landscapes in Indonesia", https://www.wri.org/our-work/project/forests-and-landscapes-indonesia, 7 February 2020.

[63] Jati, Wasisto, "It's okay to be poor: Why fighting poverty remains challenging in Indonesia", *The Jakarta Post*, 20 August 2019, https://www.thejakartapost.com/academia/2019/08/20/its-okay-to-be-poor-why-fighting-poverty-remains-challenging-in-indonesia.html.

been reduced by a commendable 90%. An extensive fire prevention effort like this, though not cheap, costs a lot less than putting fires out. It is estimated that for every dollar APRIL spends on prevention, five can be saved on suppression. Nonetheless, to date, APRIL has also invested more than US$9 million in fire suppression resources including helicopters, airboats, lookout towers, water pumps and training efforts for full-time fire fighters.

Essentially, the initiative by APRIL illustrates how root cause analysis can enable governments to identify and implement effective solutions to complex issues. Post-2015, Indonesia's Coordinating Ministry of Economic Affairs released a Standard (Standard Pencegahan Kebakaran, Hutan, Kebun dan Lahan — December 2016) for plantation companies, including palm. The Standard was developed by consulting the industry, including APRIL, whereby the outline of APRIL's FFVP was essentially adopted.

> *The increasingly successful adoption of the FFVP highlights the opportunity for a government to focus on developing enabling regulatory frameworks that encourage more public–private sector collaboration. Most importantly, efforts that were well supported by a government's open attitude, towards fostering a long-term partnership as a solution, can have a dramatic effect. It is thus quite fitting that APRIL was duly honoured for its commitment to the UN SDG in the form of a Best Program Award.[64] Meanwhile, the battle against slash-and-burn continues, as was evident in another round of haze in 2019, with more than 400 hotspots detected in several provinces and 1.6 million ha of forests and peatland burned.[65]*

Circular Economy and Climate Change

The same collaboration between the public and private sectors can potentially reap success in the area of achieving a circular economy (CE),

---

[64] https://www.rgei.com/attachments/article/1162/20190107%20-%20APRIL%20 Group%20honoured%20for%20commitment%20to%20UN%20SDGs.pdf, 7 January 2019.

[65] https://www.straitstimes.com/asia/se-asia/find-lasting-solution-to-forest-fires-jokowi, 7 February 2020.

which is in itself a huge topic. Current debate revolves around a reduction in waste, which has to be properly managed especially where there are pollutive or other hazardous consequences, and recycling as much as possible. Many businesses are aiming towards approximating a CE as it can potentially bring about better economics too.

Example 3.9: Paving the Path to a CE

The principles of the CE have gained increasing prominence in recent years. The large environmental effects associated with agri-industrial development in Indonesia are both striking and material, especially with the rising demand for biofuels and the rapid extension of oil palm plantations. Inevitably, there is a common quest towards the circular approach.

In recent years, Indonesia has undergone a series of planned transformations in the regulatory regime for the palm oil industry with the decentralisation of authority for land and forest management to the district level and a shift towards new mandatory certification schemes, such as the Indonesia Sustainable Palm Oil (ISPO) certification system.[66] These certification standards were subsequently harmonised with the Roundtable on Sustainable Palm Oil under the UNDP auspices.[67] While these rules can be prescribed by the government to encourage circularity, their specific implementation and pace of change will have to be driven by the private sector.

Asian Agri, as an affiliate of the Royal Golden Eagle (RGE) group of companies and one of Indonesia's largest palm oil producers, is one such company that has built core competencies in the circular design of their business to facilitate product reuse, recycling and cascading. Under their Zero Waste Policy, Asian Agri is committed to recycling both solid and liquid wastes from the crude palm oil (CPO) production processes.

Leftover solid waste such as palm fibres and shells are used as boiler fuel to run turbines in the mills, thereby providing a renewable source of

---

[66] UNDP Indonesia, "Sustainable palm oil initiative — Indonesia", Green Commodities Programme Factsheet, https://www.undp.org/content/dam/undp/library/Environment%20 and%20Energy/Green%20Commodities%20Programme/Indonesia%20Factsheet%20pdf. pdf.

[67] https://www.undp.org/content/dam/gp-commodities/docs/ISPO-RSPO%20Joint%20 Study_English_N%208%20for%20screen.pdf, 2015.

energy. Around half of their palm shells are on-sold to third parties rather than being disposed of as passive waste. Other by-products are applied to the soil as organic fertilisers in their plantations to boost nutrient levels, prevent soil erosion and help manage moisture levels.

More significantly, liquid waste or Palm Oil Mill Effluent (POME), generated from the processing of fresh fruit bunches, is treated at their biogas plants to produce clean, renewable energy, both powering their operations and local communities, and helping to reduce emissions. Each biogas power plant is capable of generating 2.2 MW of power, of which 700 W are used internally to power the company's mills.[68] The remaining 1.5 MW of electricity is supplied to the local electricity grid, thereby powering many households in the surrounding communities.[69]

Prior to the construction of these biogas plants, POME would only be used for land applications as a fertiliser. To date, the company has 10 biogas power plant units in operation and plans to increase the number subject to energy demand.[70] Not only do the biogas plants support the Indonesian government's commitment to achieve a 23% renewable energy rate in the country by 2025 but are also integral to creating a CE by closing the loop between waste and resources.

As Asian Agri has shown, the roles of stakeholders and non-governmental actors are crucial in the transition to a CE. In adapting regulation to assist the transition towards more circularity and hence higher resource productivity, governments need to strike a balance between guiding waste towards the highest value use and protecting citizens and the environment. Driven by market demand and business economics, the private sector can lead the way to accelerating the transformative process. Above all, innovation is the key — the government can leverage on the expertise of the private sector's researchers, business efficiency and resources to invest in circular innovation and in upscaling successful projects.

---

[68] Inside RGE, "Asian Agri opens 7th biogas power plant to generate clean energy", 9 February 2019, https://www.inside-rge.com/updates/asian-agri-opens-7th-biogas-power-plant-reduce-ghg-emissions-generates-clean-energy.

[69] *Ibid.*

[70] Asian Agri, "Asian Agri's commitment to clean energy with biogas plants", https://www.asianagri.com/en/media-en/articles/asian-agri-s-commitment-to-clean-energy-with-biogas-plants, 7 February 2018.

To the credit of several governments, many have fully embraced the urgency of the climate change agenda and are in the midst of implementing their own game plans, towards their own stated goals. According to the United Nations,[71] new data have shown the climate emergency as getting worse every day, and is impacting people's lives everywhere, whether from extreme heat, air pollution, wildfires, intensified flooding or drought. Chapter 6 has a fuller discussion on some of the national initiatives that can only be contemplated by the government.

There is generally tension between competing goals — between well-being for existential reasons and say, social goals of redundancy from the cessation or reduction in certain activity.[72] The push to remove or reduce carbon dioxide emissions meanwhile continues.

Some of the more straightforward measures can be found in attempts to reduce the carbon footprint/pollution such as policies towards a reduction in vehicular traffic in the cities. This has the twin advantage of reducing traffic congestion which is the scourge of every modern city.

Example 3.10: A River Runs Through

The thought of depriving a city of its major arterial road may sound far-fetched or even politically suicidal. The Seoul Metropolitan Government (SMG) did just that and persevered through the whole host of objections. The result? A beautiful green waterfront park that is now not only a tourist destination but also a great testimony to the patience the local government had towards realising a far-sighted vision of a global metropolis with a mind for sustainability.

Now a must-see tourist attraction of 90,000 visitors daily, the Cheonggyecheon, a 5.8 km linear, green river park at the heart of Seoul is a model for urban renewal projects worldwide. Prior to its restoration in 2003, the stream was paved over to create a highway which promptly became a nightmare of congestion and stress for inhabitants in the vicinity.

---

[71] "Madrid Climate Change Conference, 2–13 December", United Nations, https://www.un.org/sustainabledevelopment/climate-change/.

[72] "The drive to a conclusion", *United Nations Blogs.* https://blogs.un.org/blog/2019/12/13/the-drive-to-a-conclusion/, 13 December 2019.

Led by the SMG, championed by Lee Myung-Bak, Seoul's Mayor at the time who later became the country's President, the Cheonggyecheon was restored to create both ecological and recreational opportunities. Although the idea of destroying a major traffic artery of the city in favour of an eco-cultural playground faced strong criticism, the SMG remained focused on the goal and got the public on board with patience, education and extensive cooperation among stakeholders. The project eventually proved catalytic, spurring economic growth and development in an area of Seoul that had languished over several decades.

What It Was Before

Connected to the Han River, the Cheonggyecheon was originally an 11 km-long stream which was developed into 14 waterways in 1412, at the beginning of the Chosun Dynasty. By the early 20th century, as Seoul was burgeoning into the megacity of around 10 million that it is today, the river was bordered by shanties and used as a convenient dumping ground, resulting in an eyesore of polluted water.

By 1971, it seemed a perfectly logical decision to accommodate the urban population growth and the boom in traffic by covering up the stream and building an elevated highway over it. Gathering momentum from the new roadway, numerous facilities were erected on both sides of the road to form a large commercial district, including high-rise shopping malls, traditional markets and numerous industrial tool shops. There was a saying that "nothing is impossible to obtain or make in Cheonggye".[73] The area represented Korea's modern industrial development.

Falling Into Disrepair

Three decades after its construction, the once-proud elevated highway carrying approximately 168,000 vehicles a day was found to be posing safety and health hazards for the surrounding communities.[74] Traffic congestion at downtown Seoul was severely polluting the air with unsafe levels

---

[73] Chang Yi and Yoon-Joo Jung, "Role of governance in urban transformation of Seoul (2017)", The Seoul Institute, https://www.seoulsolution.kr/sites/default/files/gettoknowus/Role%20of%20Governance%20in%20Urban%20Transformation%20of%20Seoul_Chang%20Yi_2017-BR-04.pdf.

[74] Walsh, B. "Saving Seoul", *TIME Magazine*, 15 May 2008, http://content.time.com/time/world/article/0,8599,2047965,00.html.

of particle matter, nitrogen oxide and benzene.[75] In addition, engineers from the Korean Society of Civil Engineering found the expressway to lack structural integrity — due to the sewer and drain flowing below the elevated road, there was an accumulation of gases such as carbon monoxide, methane and other underground gases that led to an accelerated corrosion of the highway's foundation.[76]

There was also concern about socio-economic inequality; while development had taken place on the south side of the Cheonggyecheon, the north side had become uncompetitive and dilapidated.[77] Rather than repair the highway at a projected staggering cost of US$95 million, the SMG was motivated to remove the highway and restore the river, using it as an opportunity to address several of these problems at the same time.

Opposition to Radical Idea

However, the government met with a great deal of resistance from several quarters; essentially removing the highway was seen as a radical move. Situated at the industrial network across the country, the highway served more than one million merchants in the business circles of the area, which was home to 6,000 buildings, 210,000 workers and 1,000 street vendors.[78] Almost all of the 3,265 area merchants surveyed opposed the Cheonggyecheon Restoration Project (CRP).[79] To businesses, removing the highway meant the removal of access, diminished consumer foot traffic and a likely increase in rental. To the street vendors, it meant abrupt joblessness or relocation of stores away from where their families had been long attached to. As the SMG persisted with launching the project in earnest, the merchants started to organise protest groups and held demonstrations. A group of citizens, environmentalists, archaeologists and historians also disagreed with the city government over what and how to restore, criticising the project for its capitalist-driven urban redevelopment and inhumane eviction.

---

[75] Asian Development Bank. "Revitalizing a city by reviving a stream", *Development Asia*, https://development.asia/case-study/revitalizing-city-reviving-stream.

[76] Shin, J. and Lee, I. (2006) Cheong Gye Cheon restoration in Seoul Korea, Civil Engineering 159, pp. 162–170, Institute of Civil Engineers, November.

[77] *Ibid.*

[78] Kwon, K. K. (n.d.) Cheong Gye Cheon Restoration Project: A revolution in Seoul. Seoul Metropolitan Government.

[79] Lah, T. J. (2011) "The Huge Success of the Cheonggyecheon Restoration Project: What's Left?" Citizen Participation: Innovative and Alternative Modes for Engaging Citizens.

Overcoming Opposition

To manage the overwhelming resistance, the SMG established a triangular governance structure comprising the Cheonggyecheon Restoration Headquarters, a Citizens Committee and a Research Group. The Restoration Headquarters, made up of civil servants, was the main project implementation arm and sought multi-stakeholder input.

The Citizens Committee was instrumental in suggesting policy direction based on inputs from the general public, and in promoting the project. Essentially, it was an official channel to engage citizenry to canvass opinions and concerns from the public with regard to the restoration project. Some 4,200 meetings in various forms were held for negotiations between the city officials and the merchants affected. In addition, the Committee engaged the private sector and NGOs by inviting them to form a partnership and alliance. Efforts were directed at explaining the value behind restoring the Cheonggyecheon stream over investing in a replacement expressway, citing how it will address safety problems and mobility demand; reinstate history and culture through the preservation of relics and street beautification; and re-energise businesses.[80] The Research Group, comprising 58 researchers, provided expertise on issues such as land use plans, restoration strategies, culture and traffic management schemes.

Post consultation with the public, the SMG implemented a multitude of measures who had been collectively devised and implemented. Besides providing financial support to businesses affected, such as loans and grants, the SMG also drew up detailed relocation plans including the provision of free shuttles during work to minimise travel inconveniences. Merchants operating in the area were accorded favourable rights to move into a new commercial complex. They also implemented parking reforms to stimulate commercial activity. Since traffic congestion was another primary concern, the city accelerated its efforts on public transportation reform, created circular-route buses, increased parking fee to discourage traffic and cracked down on illegal parking as solutions. Conceptualisation was thus as holistic as possible.

Cost-Benefit Analysis

Against the project's hefty US$360 million price tag and an estimated US$1.9 billion of social costs, some US$3.5 billion worth of social benefits

---

[80] Asian Development Bank, "Revitalizing a City by Reviving a Stream", *Development Asia*, https://development.asia/case-study/revitalizing-city-reviving-stream.

were expected to be accrued.[81] Economic benefits were to be delivered in the form of an increase in the number of businesses and employment density within 1.2 km of the Cheonggyecheon corridor,[82] and as property prices increases, estimated at double the rates found elsewhere in the city.[83] The reduction in passenger cars and enhanced used of public transport also translated into an improvement in the area's air quality. Specifically, small-particle air pollution in the area had fallen from 74 to 48 micrograms per cubic metre.[84] The restoration has re-established lost habitats, and as a result the number of fish species increased from 4 to 25, bird species from 6 to 36, and insect species from 15 to 192.[85] The greening of the Cheonggyecheon not only reintroduced the ethos of the natural environment but also highlighted the importance of an eco-friendly approach to urban design. Without a doubt, the rebirth of Cheonggyecheon became a win–win situation for all the stakeholders.

The success of the Cheonggyecheon restoration holds many lessons for cities aspiring to pull off an ambitious project such as this. The thought of depriving a city of its major arterial road may sound far-fetched or even politically suicidal. Political will, innovative governance and interagency coordination as exemplified by the SMG's multistrategy were critical to the successful implementation of such a large-scale project within 29 months. Regulators should not shy away from facilitating, if not driving the whole development process by encouraging open, two-way communication with feedback loops to consolidate public opinion. When meeting with resistance, listening carefully to major

---

[81] Lee, Y. (2005) "Cheonggyecheon restoration and urban development", http://management.kochi-tech.ac.jp/PDF/IWPM/IWPM_Lee.pdf.; CRP (Cheonggyecheon Restoration Project) (2009), https://inhabitat.com/how-the-cheonggyecheon-river-urban-design-restored-the-green-heart-of-seoul/, 18 November 2014.

[82] Kang, C. (2009) Land market impacts and firm geography in a green and transit-oriented city — The case of Seoul, Korea. Ph.D. Dissertation submitted to the Department of City and Regional Planning, University of California, Berkeley, AAT 3410922.

[83] Commission for Architecture and the Built Environment (2011) "Cheonggyecheon restoration project: Evaluation", https://webarchive.nationalarchives.gov.uk/20110118114019/http://www.cabe.org.uk/case-studies/cheonggyecheon-restoration-project/evaluation.

[84] Revkin, A. (2009) "Peeling back pavement to expose watery havens", New York Times, https://www.nytimes.com/2009/07/17/world/asia/17daylight.html.

[85] *Ibid.*

> *stakeholders to build a consensus and embracing an inclusive governance structure will also help all parties appreciate the larger public good.*

Reflections

That a government realises it does not have a monopoly on ideas, innovation or domain expertise, and reaches out to the private sector for collaboration, is a stance to be lauded. As can be seen in the earlier chapters, the state could often find itself falling behind as a regulator in fast changing situations. Instead of viewing the private sector as money-grabbing capitalists, a government would do well to tap such expertise and evolve public policies together. That is not to say that decision-making has to be collective; in matters of macro strategy, such as climate change, or national security, the state must continue to reserve the right to decide on what is the larger good. It must continue to drive public policy positions.

There exist many situations, especially for emerging economies, where collaboration with the private sector makes eminent sense. This is particularly true for the establishment of major infrastructure to facilitate economic activity or expansion. Many governments encounter a vicious cycle of not having enough revenues to sustain a building programme which will in turn restrain growth. On the contrary, if a successful collaboration can be struck for a private sector operator to realise an acceptable, commercial long-term return, it becomes a win–win proposition. Many toll-roads and railway projects represent good examples, though not without their teething or politicisation vulnerabilities.

The multilateral development banks have been active collaborators to many emerging economies, as have many private sector participants in infrastructural projects for transportation and utilities. Unfortunately, the Covid-19 scourge is expected to deal such development aspirations a harsh blow. Many governments would be preoccupied with both the consequential healthcare and unemployment challenges. Infrastructure projects would inevitably take a back seat. Meanwhile, contributions to the multilateral banks would likely be dampened and the finances of private sector operators would also be severely handicapped.

In reality, Covid or otherwise, the state often finds itself as the sole, if not lonely decision-maker, either as a default option or the consequence of real politics. When national icons fail, sometimes repeatedly, all attention will be trained on the government, with the expectation that a bailout must happen, in some shape or size. We shall examine in detail in the next chapter the kind of rescue efforts that many governments are expected to mount, regardless of the merits of a rescue nor their fiscal well-being.

CHAPTER 4
BAILOR OF LAST RESORT

Chapter 4

Bailor of Last Resort

Whenever national icons fail, a case will be made for the government to consider a bailout. The more symbolic of national pride or identity the enterprise is, the more vehement the argument would be. The performance of that failing enterprise is often barely relevant. Neither is the question of whether the state needs remain a shareholder.

Airlines and banks tend to populate this cluster of too-big-to-fail icons. If anything, the ongoing Covid-19 pandemic-triggered economic crisis once again brings to the fore the inevitable predicament that governments find themselves in. Owing to the lockdowns virtually globally, tourism has literally fallen off the cliff and travel bans really mean that airlines no longer have any business to speak of. The bailing out of national airlines, almost regardless of the fiscal well-being of the government, is the default course of action.

Continual bailing out can be a hard habit to break. Coupled with a lack of political will to enforce commercial discipline over a sustained period, the bleeding of state enterprises can balloon to unmanageable proportions. Be it inefficiency from a bloated bureaucracy or endemic corruption, once these have persisted for a long enough period, these problematic state enterprises would present an everlasting series of political headaches.

The pressure on government for rescue efforts is not limited to state-owned enterprises. Where there are adverse repercussions for a big part of the population should a private business go under, there will similarly be calls for the government to act.

Bailouts frequently have a long tail. Thus far, governments like the US and UK who have made the conscious decision to rescue non-state enterprises for pure contagion prevention reasons have largely been patient, disciplined and responsible. The hard slog should however not be underestimated. The bailouts, particularly of the airline companies in the wake of the Covid-19 pandemic, would pose substantial pressure on governments, as the ticket sizes are humongous. Regardless of how such bailouts are funded, an overly high debt-to-GDP burden or dented public coffers would become the reality for many countries.

Plight of State Enterprises

Over the past decade or so, the spotlight on state-owned enterprises, or SOEs as they are commonly referred to, has intensified. There is no shortage of literature on what SOEs should not be; on the contrary, there are very few examples of good, purposeful state enterprises that invoke national pride.

Unfortunately, the narrative has not changed all these years. During boom times, SOEs would explode disproportionately with the economy. It is after all, easy to justify allocating more national budget to support yet more economic activity. During downturns, SOEs would struggle with a trimmed budget but otherwise have very little room to restructure, let alone lay workers off. Restructuring almost never happens, let alone properly.

More Indebtedness, Drain on Public Resources

Many have taken on more debt or remain heavily indebted — SOEs remain a consumer of vast amounts of public and private capital, and regrettably, there continues to be ineffective use of both financial and human capital. SOE debt is estimated to account for more than 60% of all non-financial corporate debt in many emerging markets, from a manageable 20% in Turkey to a high 85% in South Africa.[1] As at end third quarter of 2019, SOEs had in aggregate raised some US$12 trillion additional debt over the past decade alone.

Reflecting the impact of the ongoing SOE reforms, debt accrued by the Chinese SOEs grew at a slower pace of just under 14% by end 2018 to reach aggregate of RMB 135 trillion (US$19 trillion). The reforms are part of the efforts by the State-owned Assets Supervision and Administration Commission (SASAC) to trim gearing by 2 percentage points from end 2017 to end 2020.[2]

---

[1] https://www.iif.com/Portals/0/Files/content/Global%20Debt%20Monitor_January2020_vf.pdf, 13 January 2020.

[2] http://www.chinadaily.com.cn/a/201910/24/WS5db10417a310cf3e355723dd.html, 24 October 2019.

More Corruption, Poor Accountability

What is more worrying and exploding into a challenge of unmanageable proportions is the persistence of corruption, a leakage that many countries can ill afford. The scale of corruption continues to astound, running into billions, denting public finances so badly that many governments so afflicted are unable to function properly.

Take the well-publicised series of misdeeds purportedly committed under the auspices of 1MDB of Malaysia over the period 2009–2014. Since May 2018,[3] the then newly elected government has been diligently and extensively probing into 1MDB for missing funds of at least US$10 billion, a scale which has hampered the Malaysian government from carrying out many essential infrastructure projects. Or that the Defence budget had to be cut by around US$6 billion so as to rescue two state-related entities — Tabung Haji, the haj-related fund and Federal Land Development Authority (FELDA), which have many public stakeholders.[4]

Or take Operation Carwash in Brazil where widespread corruption caused at least US$5 billion to be leaked from the system through a web of Petrobras executives and politicians.[5] Though this was uncovered only in late 2015, the impact continued to be felt for several years thereafter.

Over in South Africa,[6] TransNet was investigated as part of the State Capture Commission's work for corruption, money laundering and fraud. This included dodgy locomotive transactions. So far, the tally has exceeded R1.3 billion or US$90 million, not as staggering as the wrongs committed elsewhere, but nonetheless symptomatic of the underlying scourge.

---

[3] https://www.scmp.com/week-asia/explained/article/2186477/explained-malaysias-1mdb-scandal, 16 February 2019.

[4] https://www.straitstimes.com/asia/se-asia/malaysias-defence-minister-says-defence-spending-diverted-to-bail-out-tabung-haji-felda, 20 April 2019.

[5] https://www.theguardian.com/world/2017/jun/01/brazil-operation-car-wash-is-this-the-biggest-corruption-scandal-in-history, 1 June 2017.

[6] https://www.iol.co.za/news/politics/transnet-could-be-linked-to-first-state-capture-prosecution-38053790, 27 November 2019.

More Inefficiency, Unjustified Market Dominance

The litany of woes goes on — SOEs often exhibit a glaring governance deficit in the form of a lethal mix of inefficiency, cronyism and populism. Bloated bureaucracies have long been the norm, often leading to organisational distress and even insolvency. Even UK Parliamentarians had admitted as much for the famous British Broadcasting Corporation (BBC)[7] which many would consider to be one of the better-known state enterprises.

Owing to history, many SOEs continue to dominate the sectors they are operating in, somewhat unfairly but unwittingly, rendering a segment unable to benefit from true competition.

Add to the role design flaws, cronyism and populism, and the situation will be ripe for SOEs to fail repeatedly. When this happens, the public at large and the private sector will look to the government as both shareholder and regulator for remedies or redress.

This pretty much sums up the huge tasks ahead for the new Indonesian Minister of State-Owned Enterprises Erick Thohir[8] (appointed in October 2019), who has been seeking to clean up the act — close some 70 out of the 750 SOEs, recruit talent to boost governance and focus on the new emerging sectors of Big Data and Artificial Intelligence, and stamp out corruption or financial misdeeds. Transformation would be key as the publicly listed SOEs alone already account for a significant 26% of GDP.

As much as the public will typically be seeking a more efficient and effective SOE portfolio of their government, their sentiments can shift whenever big SOEs, of the national-icon type, threaten to collapse. Expectations will then illogically shift towards rescue efforts.

Bailouts — A National Response

Bailouts do not occur only during downturns. If anything, the Covid-19 pandemic-triggered fallout illustrates this reality unfortunately. They are a proposition whenever loss of national pride or systemic failure or both are

---

[7] https://www.independent.co.uk/voices/editorials/leading-article-bloated-entitlement-at-the-bbc-1688470.html, 21 May 2009.

[8] https://www.straitstimes.com/asia/se-asia/indonesias-state-owned-firms-face-big-overhaul, 11 March 2020.

real possibilities. It goes without saying that whenever a bailout is undertaken to save a big, national icon, there would be the inevitable financial drag on the economy, coming obviously at the expense of public coffers and ultimately, taxpayers.

Here, some airline bashing is in order — but there is unfortunately good justification. The airline industry is inherently difficult a business to run, being so capital intensive while heavily regulated, resulting in unfavourable economics. Politicisation of airline companies as national flag carriers further aggravates the financial distress. National pride will always exact a cost in this instance.

Example 4.1: Failure to Take Off, Again

A national airline is a special thing in many countries. Akin to a national flag, anthem or currency, a national airline is a prominent way for a country to define itself. Flag carriers are known for showcasing a nation's cuisine, flaunting the pennant colours, and presenting a unique cultural brand. Unfortunately, many of the world's airlines are in a perilous state and governments are being pressured to intervene with financial aid. Given the abysmal performance of some state-owned airlines to which their governments have been extending multiple lifelines, the justification of repeated state bailouts continues to be under the spotlight. Does it make any more strategic economic sense — especially if the aid provided has merely propped up weak and inefficient firms at the expense of taxpayer monies, arguably delaying their inevitable failure?

Privatisation of Air India

Founded in 1932 by J.R.D. Tata as Tata Airlines, the airline became a public limited company under the name of "Air India" after World War II.[9]

---

[9]"64 years after Air India's nationalisation, Tata Group looking at bid to fly its bird back home", *The Economic Times*, 10 October 2017, https://economictimes.indiatimes.com/industry/transportation/airlines-/-aviation/64-years-after-air-indias-nationalisation-tata-group-wants-to-fly-its-bird-back-home/articleshow/61020088.cms.

Post India's independence in 1947, the Government of India acquired a 49% stake in the airline and, in 1953, purchased the majority stake from the founder, J.R.D Tata. Beginning mid-2000s, the national air carrier of India started bearing the brunt of jokes, be it for delayed flights, stale food or their hardly state-of-the-art facilities. This was a far cry from what it used to stand for — it was awarded several national and international awards from consumer services to corporate social responsibility; in fact, Air India was previously synonymous with luxury and sophistication.

Today, it is no secret that Air India is in deep trouble — plagued by non-profitability for over a decade and a crippling debt of around ₹58,000 crores (US$7.8 billion).[10] Air India has been on life-support via two rounds of state bailouts within five years and a failed attempt to divest. While myriad factors have contributed to Air India's undesirable leverage — post-merger integration failure, rising fuel costs, political opposition to privatisation and network consolidation, bureaucracy, and the global slowdown — the Indian government has been taken hostage by the fear of losing its now-bankrupt national icon. The key question that begs answering is whether there remains a case for the government to continue to keep Air India afloat.

In 2012, the government approved a debt-restructuring plan worth nearly US$6 billion[11] and planned to inject equity ₹30,000 crores (US$4.3 billion) over eight years. In 2013, the idea of privatisation was first mooted by then Civil Aviation Minister Ajit Singh but summarily slammed by the opposition. Despite the capital injection, the airline turnaround was unsuccessful, with the airline barely breaking even at the operating level in subsequent financial years (2015–2017).[12]

---

[10]"Total debt of Air India is Rs 58,351 crore: Civil Aviation Minister", *The Economic Times*, 26 June 2019, https://m.economictimes.com/industry/transportation/airlines-/-aviation/total-debt-of-air-india-is-rs-58351-crore-civil-aviation-minister/articleshow/69963774.cms.

[11]Kannan, S. "Air India: Problems run deep in India's national airline", *BBC News*, 16 May 2012, https://www.bbc.com/news/business-18082903.

[12]Kaushik, M. "A loss-making airline for almost a decade, Air India has no reason to exist", *Business Today*, 30 August 2018. https://www.businesstoday.in/current/economy-politics/a-loss-making-airline-for-almost-a-decade-air-india-has-no-reason-to-exist/story/281813.html.

Privatisation was once again suggested by the Aviation Minister Ashok Gajapathi Raju.[13]

In 2018, the government attempted to sell a 76% stake in Air India but the 31 May deadline for private players to express interest came and went without a single bid.[14] Potential buyers were mainly put off by the sale's rigid conditions and hefty US$5 billion debt obligations. Those conditions included the government retaining a 24% stake and a rule that the new owner could neither lay off any employees nor merge Air India with another airline.[15] The unattractive deal structure deterred interest and the failed attempt at disinvestment presented the government with a difficult question — should it continue to pump billions of taxpayer money to save the airline or allow the national carrier to be privatised in its entirety, thereby changing the deal structure?[16]

The Indian government chose the latter. On 27 January 2020, the government made yet another announcement on its intention to privatise the ailing national carrier Air India. As the saying goes — once bitten, twice shy. The Modi administration prepared a fresh proposal to address the key sticky issues, the biggest one being the airline's huge debt load. To tackle that, half of Air India's debt or ₹29,000 crores (US$3.9 billion), as well as non-core assets and non-operational assets will be transferred out into a special purpose vehicle (SPV), known as Air India Asset Holding Ltd (AIAHL).[17] The government is also prepared to sell its entire stake in Air India since the previous partial stake sale failed to garner interest and as it is no longer tenable to continue to pump in fresh capital.

---

[13] Iyengar, R. "India is willing to privatize its loss-making national airline", CNN, 14 February 2017. https://money.cnn.com/2017/02/14/news/india/air-india-privatization-aviation-minister/?iid=EL.

[14] Shah, A. and Ahmed, A. "India renews push to sell Air India, puts entire stake on the block", *Reuters*, 27 January 2020, https://www.reuters.com/article/us-india-air-india-sale/india-renews-push-to-sell-air-india-puts-entire-stake-on-the-block-idUSKBN1ZQ0DJ.

[15] Iyengar, R. "Can Air India survive its botched privatization?", *CNN*, 15 June 2018, https://money.cnn.com/2018/06/15/news/companies/air-india-privatization-what-next/; Thompson, M. "India tried to sell its national airline. It got zero bids", *CNN*, 1 June 2018, https://money.cnn.com/2018/05/31/investing/air-india-privatization-fails/?iid=EL.

[16] *Ibid.*

[17] "Cabinet approves transfer of Air India's Rs 29,464 crore loans, subsidiaries to SPV", *Business Today*, 1 March 2019, https://www.businesstoday.in/sectors/aviation/cabinet-approves-transfer-of-air-india-rs-29464-crore-loans-subsidiaries-to-spv/story/323485.html.

Jet Airways a Relic of a Bygone Era

With losses in 8 out of the last 10 years and an inability to compete with ruthlessly efficient low-cost carriers such as IndiGo and SpiceJet,[18] Jet Airways created a huge amount of turbulence and crash landed in slow motion as it missed repayments, piled up as much as ₹8,500 crores (US$1 billion) in debt, declared bankruptcy, and left tens of thousands of employees without a livelihood.[19] Those were the days, when Jet Airways was the "shining face of Indian aviation" during the late 1990s and 2000s.[20]

Jet Airways was born in 1993, two years after India liberalised its economy and opened its doors to private investments. With a fleet of 123 aircraft offering 650 flights across the country and continents, Jet Airways was, until their grounding earlier in 2019, the second-largest airline in India after its national carrier.[21] Its downward spiral began way back in 2012 when IndiGo managed to dislodge Jet Airways from its top market position, flying 27% of the total Indian passengers as opposed to 26.6% flown by Jet Airways.[22] In order to regain market share, Jet Airways dropped airfares — often well below cost — despite continuing to be a full-service airline. Coupled with rising fuel costs and India's currency plunging to record lows in 2018, the hurdles soon proved too onerous and

---

[18] Shah, A. and Daga, A. "The downfall of Jet Airways: How India's premium airline crumbled", *Reuters*, 9 April 2019, https://www.reuters.com/article/us-jet-airways-debt-lessors-insight-idUSKCN1RL1UC.

[19] Naidu, K. "The ₹10 trillion Tata Group may want some of Jet Airways' parts after the airline's employees decided to bid", *Business Insider*, 1 July 2019, https://www.businessinsider.in/tata-group-may-bid-for-jet-airways-assets/articleshow/70022109.cms?utm_source=contentofinterest&utm_medium=text&utm_campaign=cppst.

[20] "Jet Airways: The riches to rags story of India's oldest private airline", *BBC News*, 23 March 2019, https://www.bbc.com/news/world-asia-india-47664059.

[21] "With 15 more grounded, jet Airways has just 20 planes in operations now", *The Economic Times*, 3 April 2019, https://economictimes.indiatimes.com/industry/transportation/airlines-/-aviation/jet-airways-grounds-15-more-planes-over-non-payment-of-dues/articleshow/68692494.cms?from=mdr.

[22] Upadhyay, A. "How Indigo managed to topple Jet Airways to gain top position in market share", *The Economic Times*, 21 August 2012, https://economictimes.indiatimes.com/industry/transportation/airlines-/-aviation/how-indigo-managed-to-topple-jet-airways-to-gain-top-position-in-market-share/articleshow/15577979.cms?from=mdr.

Jet Airways began defaulting on its debt payments to banks in December 2018.[23]

Even though Jet Airways is a private airline, the government wanted to keep it afloat to avoid the potential loss of thousands of jobs at a politically sensitive time. It pleaded with state-run banks to step in with a bailout plan. State Bank of India (SBI) and other lenders were preparing to extend a fresh loan of US$218 million. On its part, the government would lift the foreign ownership limit of 49%.[24] Meanwhile, Jet Airways was forced by the cash crunch to ground more than three-quarters of its fleet as it was unable to pay aircraft lessors.

Not everyone was convinced that Jet Airways was worth saving. In a setback to its revival plans, existing shareholder Etihad Airways, with a 24% stake, declined to inject more capital in the airline and instead offered to exit its investment, to make way for foreign stakes in Indian airlines.[25] With no buyer in sight due to concerns about the airline's long-term viability, the planned bailout by the banks was left in limbo, and Jet Airways' creditors announced plans to start insolvency proceedings in a last-ditch effort to recover any dues.[26]

If Jet were to go under, and Air India were eventually shuttered should privatisation efforts fail, the only full-service airline for India's growing aviation market is Vistara — a joint venture between the Tata Group and Singapore Airlines Ltd.[27] If Jet survives, it should do so without aid from the government; Indian taxpayers have already been burdened with one debt-ridden national icon.

---

[23] "India's Jet Airways defaults on debt payment to banks", *Reuters*, 2 January 2019, https://www.reuters.com/article/jet-airways-debt/indias-jet-airways-defaults-on-debt-payment-to-banks-idUSL3N1Z20H6.

[24] Shah, A. and Daga, A. "Jet Airways lenders lay out bid terms for 75 percent stake in airline", *Reuters*, 8 April 2019, https://www.reuters.com/article/us-jet-airways-debt-sale/jet-airways-lenders-lay-out-bid-terms-for-75-percent-stake-in-airline-idUSKCN1RK0AE.

[25] "Jet Airways: The riches to rags story of India's oldest private airline", *BBC News*, 23 March 2019, https://www.bbc.com/news/world-asia-india-47664059.

[26] Bahree, M. "With no buyer in sight, Jet Airways lands in Bankruptcy Court", *Forbes*, 18 June 2019, https://www.forbes.com/sites/meghabahree/2019/06/18/with-no-buyer-in-sight-jet-airways-lands-in-bankruptcy-court/#45054d785954.

[27] Sharma, M. "What Jet's collapse says about India", *The Business Times*, 18 April 2019, https://www.businesstimes.com.sg/transport/what-jets-collapse-says-about-india.

Malaysian Airlines: No Further Bailouts

Another beleaguered national carrier that is slated for privatisation is the 72-year-old Malaysia Airlines (MAS), having been unable to turn a profit since it was taken private, or essentially nationalised by the sovereign wealth fund Khazanah Nasional, in 2014. As MAS struggled to compete with nimble, upstart low-cost carriers such as AirAsia and VietJet, the airline was reportedly burning through its cash reserves of more than US$2 million a day.[28] MAS's unprofitability was capped off by two disasters in 2014 — first when flight MH370 mysteriously disappeared in what remained an unresolved case and another when MH17 was shot down over Ukraine.[29] The state fund then offered RM1.4 billion (US$426 million) in the same year to buyout the remaining minority stake and requested that it be delisted from the Malaysian stock exchange.[30] This would help facilitate the radical restructuring that was required in order to return the carrier to profitability.

However, it proved to be an uphill task. MAS announced a loss of RM3.7 billion (US$1.8 billion) in 2018 as it continued to haemorrhage,[31] and went through three chief executive officers between September 2015 and October 2017.[32] In August of 2019, Khazanah Nasional pumped in another RM300 million (US$72 million) cash to keep the airline afloat, even as it was considering offers from buyers to take MAS off the government's hands.[33] Given that the Malaysian state had already pumped in RM800 million (US$187 million) in 2019 itself into MAS over four failed

---

[28] Mosbergen, D. "Malaysia Airlines burning more than $2 million in cash reserves every single day: Report", *The Huffington Post*, 26 August 2014, https://www.huffpost.com/entry/malaysia-airlines-losing-money_n_5715783.

[29] *Ibid.*

[30] "Minority shareholders back $526 million privatisation buyout of Malaysia Airlines", *The Straits Times*, 6 November 2014, https://www.straitstimes.com/asia/se-asia/minority-shareholders-back-526-million-privatisation-buyout-of-malaysia-airlines.

[31] "After years of bleeding money, aviation industry analysts are saying it's time to shut down or sell off Malaysia Airlines", *Yahoo! News*, 7 March 2019, https://sg.news.yahoo.com/years-bleeding-money-aviation-industry-062209539.html.

[32] Raghuvanshi, A. and Ngui, Y. "Malaysia Airlines loses third CEO since 2014", *The Wall Street Journal*, 17 October 2017, https://www.wsj.com/articles/malaysia-airlines-loses-third-ceo-since-2014-1508247012.

[33] "Khazanah injects $72 million in Malaysia Airlines as it considers offers", *Reuters*, 19 August 2019, https://www.reuters.com/article/us-malaysia-airlines-khazanah/khazanah-injects-72-million-in-malaysia-airlines-as-it-considers-offers-idUSKCN1V90N6.

attempts at restructuring without meaningful results, the calls have been growing louder for the government to sell off or shut down MAS.[34] Nationalisation regrettably did not work in the case of Malaysia Airlines. Moreover, there is a limit to how much public resources the government can tap and allocate since MAS needed a recurrent amount of RM1 billion (US$240 million) per year to stay afloat under its current structure.[35]

Bumpy Journey Ahead

Liquidity-flushed investors hoping to turn around Air India or Malaysia Airlines may still emerge out of the blue. If however no buyer shows up, the respective governments could be forced to continue stanching the red-ink of their national carriers or reluctantly allow the national carrier to be shut down and the underlying assets sold off.

> *Although the appeal of owning a national airline or the idea that governments should protect large icons from failure make for compelling arguments, state bailouts should only be relied on as a last resort. The Covid-19 pandemic would be justified as an exception, but rescues must be limited to only players who were otherwise performing creditably.*
>
> *Even then, good intentions are not enough as success cannot be guaranteed simply by the infusion of new capital. When there is neither economic or financial rationale for maintaining these icons nor political will to effect painful reforms, the business should not be allowed to continue indefinitely. Governments owe it to taxpayers to ensure that the value of pride that these national icons elicit does not go beyond economic logic.*

What is the cost of national pride? Many rounds of bailouts until a government is financially crippled and unable to continue pumping in capital any longer? It is instructive to see how some other governments have swallowed the bitter pill and undertake painful restructuring exercises in a bid

---

[34]Chong, J. and Idris Naqib, A. "Malaysia Airlines needs RM1b cash injection a year to survive", *The Edge Financial Daily*, 24 October 2019, https://www.theedgemarkets.com/article/malaysia-airlines-needs-rm1b-cash-injection-year-survive.

[35]*Ibid.*

to save their beloved airlines and themselves. By the same token, some will accept the inevitable, remain pragmatic on the real cost of national pride and put their airlines up for sale, albeit most reluctantly.

Example 4.2: Economics Over Sentiments

The fate of many struggling national carriers makes for painful reading. However, the dilemma faced by their government–shareholders contains even more excruciating details of repeated bailouts, usually to no avail. Some national icons carry the burden of inefficiencies imposed by unreasonable politicians, especially of extensive domestic network coverage, or from a lack of proper accountability and governance. When governments have exhausted their public coffers or can no longer justify another bailout, they are really left with two unpopular options: undertake painful restructuring, which may reduce the standing of their national icon and involve mass retrenchment or divest their stake in part or in full.

Tough Love on Qantas Airlines

While other governments endeavour to keep their rickety national carriers in the air for as long as possible, the Australian government treated Qantas' request for assistance rationally and practically, not ideologically or purely sentimentally.

In 2013, Qantas Airlines, or the "flying kangaroo" as it is affectionately known in Australia, flew into financial turbulence when its coveted investment-grade credit rating was downgraded to "junk" after warnings that it would lose up to A\$300 million for the half-year ending 31 December.[36] The main culprits behind potentially the worst financial performance in its 94-year history were its profit-draining battle with rival Virgin Airlines and continued poor performance from its ailing international division. Within the same year, the airline was forced to cut costs by slashing 1,000 full-time jobs in early December, scale back unprofitable routes and defer or sell their aircraft.[37] This triggered a strong warning to

---

[36]"Qantas downgraded to junk status by credit ratings agency Moody's", *The Guardian*, 9 January 2014. https://www.theguardian.com/business/2014/jan/09/qantas-downgraded-to-junk-status-by-credit-ratings-agency-moodys.

[37]*Ibid.*

investors and the downgrade ultimately increased the airline's borrowing costs.

Out of fear that it would slip into bankruptcy, just as Ansett Airlines did back in March 2002, Qantas requested for a A$3 billion (US$2.7 billion) unsecured loan from the Australian government, as one of the options to help them work towards profitability.[38] After the airline posted a first-half loss of A$252 million (US$225 million) in 2014, the Australian government decided against helping Qantas out with the loan.[39] The rejection was based on expert advice from accounting firm PricewaterhouseCoopers that Qantas did not need a line of unsecured credit from the government.[40]

Instead, the government proposed repealing the Qantas Sales Act, which till then prohibited majority foreign ownership of the airline. The 1992 Qantas Sales Act — a nod to union pressures designed to ensure the privatised Qantas remained in Australian hands — restricted any single foreign investor from holding more than a 25% stake in Qantas, aggregate foreign airlines to 35%.[41] The legislation also mandated 51% Australian ownership.[42] Qantas' Chief Executive Officer Alan Joyce believed that the old rules were putting the airline at a disadvantage when raising capital against competitors such as Virgin Airlines, which were not subject to the same onerous foreign ownership limits. Foreign shareholders Air New Zealand, Etihad Airways and Singapore Airlines have a combined 63% stake in Virgin.[43]

Given the government's decision to reject the proposal for an unsecured loan, Qantas announced that it would accelerate its "Qantas transformation programme" to achieve A$2 billion in cost reductions over the following three years by cutting 5,000 redundant positions across-the-board, equivalent to 15% of the Qantas headcount, freezing wages until the Group is profitable again, withdrawing Qantas from the low-yielding routes, re-timing of services to minimise ground time at London Heathrow

---

[38] "Australian government rejects Qantas $2.7bn loan request", *BBC News*, 5 March 2014. https://www.bbc.com/news/business-26445272.

[39] *Ibid.*

[40] *Ibid.*

[41] "Australia seeks to relax Qantas Sale Act to allow foreign ownership", *The Straits Times*, 3 March 2014, https://www.straitstimes.com/business/australia-seeks-to-relax-qantas-sale-act-to-allow-foreign-ownership.

[42] *Ibid.*

[43] "Qantas chief Alan Joyce demands stop to virtual takeover of Virgin Australia", *The Straits Times*, 18 November 2013. https://www.straitstimes.com/business/qantas-chief-alan-joyce-demands-stop-to-virtual-takeover-of-virgin-australia.

and deferring the delivery of or selling more than 50 aircraft it had on order.[44] Understandably the programme meant hardship all round and was not embraced by all. Although unions were furious that Qantas' employees had to bear the brunt of poor management, everyone understood that the airline had to make the tough decisions necessary so as to overcome the challenges and hopefully build a stronger core business.

From turbulent times to clear blue skies, Qantas's plan worked well and the sacrifices paid off. Qantas completed its turnaround in 2017 and posted its second-highest underlying profit of the national airline of A$1.4 billion (US$1.11 billion).[45] Qantas proved its mettle, that it was able to work its way through its problems, without resorting to government loans or guarantees. Although Qantas is the quintessential Australian icon, the government understood the risk of bailing out the national icon. It remained focused on supporting businesses in a sustainable manner and explored tweaking regulations instead of providing a bailout. All said, the then Prime Minister Tony Abbott's tough love helped stiffen Qantas's resolve to get back on its feet. As with any failing business, the best way to guarantee its survival is to radically improve its efficiency and force reforms.

Rebirth of Swissair

Before its somewhat humiliating demise, Swissair had long been one of the most venerable airlines in the world. Formed in 1931, the Swiss national carrier was a "symbol of the country's prosperity and financial acumen".[46] By the 1960s, Swissair's high liquidity and returns earned it the nickname "the flying bank".[47] Thus, when on 2 October 2001, the inevitable demise of the Swissair Group was made clear, it sent shockwaves through the nation.[48]

---

[44]"Qantas has today announced details of its $2 billion in cost cutting", *The Daily Telegraph*, 27 February 2014. https://www.dailytelegraph.com.au/business/qantas-has-today-announced-details-of-its-2billion-in-cost-cutting/news-story/d35cde215f63c1294da24307cf7ae924.

[45]"Qantas rises as it reports second-highest profit on record", *Financial Times*, 24 August 2017. https://www.ft.com/content/06b1dd5d-88dc-31c7-bea6-9c0d434f5361.

[46]Karras, C. "March 26, 1931: Swissair, the 'flying bank' airline, is founded", *Yahoo! News*, 27 March 2014. https://www.yahoo.com/lifestyle/bp/march-26--1931--swissair--the-%E2%80%9Cflying-bank%E2%80%9D-airline--is-founded-202907183.html.

[47]*Ibid.*

[48]Olson, E. "Lacking cash, Swissair grounds all its flights", *The New York Times*, 3 October 2001. https://www.nytimes.com/2001/10/03/business/lacking-cash-swissair-grounds-all-its-flights.html.

Burdened by over-expansion, increased competition and the economic downturn, Swissair filed for bankruptcy as it could no longer scrape enough cash to keep operations going. Chaos then ensued when some 262 flights were cancelled and 39,000 passengers found themselves stranded.[49]

In fact, the crisis possibly had its genesis in 1992, when the Swiss population voted against joining the European Union (EU). This meant that Swissair had to remain globally competitive or run the risk of becoming an insignificant regional airline. Under pressure, Swissair embarked on an ambitious but ultimately disastrous expansion programme. The group aggressively acquired stakes in several regional airlines including Poland's LOT, Belgium's Sabena Airways, South African Airways and other smaller airlines — mostly unprofitable airlines, despite their good reputation.

In 2000, the company recorded its first ever loss, amounting to Fr 2.9 billion (US$1.8 billion) which consumed almost its entire capital reserves.[50] Deep in debt and desperate for cash, Swissair was hit even harder in 2000 by high fuel costs and slow trading conditions which affected business travel.[51] The 9/11 terrorist attacks then pulled the rug out from under when virtually all passengers steered clear of air travel. Consequently, the Fr 2.9 billion (US$1.7 billion) worth of assets the airline group had been hoping to sell to reduce its gearing slumped miserably in value.[52] Teetering on the edge of insolvency, the company's debts ballooned to reach Fr 15 billion (US$9.2 billion) by September 2001, doubling that barely a year earlier.[53]

Expectations were there for the Swiss government, as well as the two largest banks UBS and Credit Suisse, to help bail out Swissair. The Swiss government offered to play a supporting role in a rescue, but the big banks, UBS and Credit Suisse, were reluctant to bail out the entire airline and

---

[49] *Ibid.*

[50] Olson, E. "Its strategy off course, Swissair looks for a new bearing", The New York Times, 16 March 2001, https://www.nytimes.com/2001/03/16/business/worldbusiness/IHT-its-strategy-off-course-swissair-looks-for-a-new.html.

[51] "How Swissair landed in trouble", Wharton School of Business, University of Pennsylvania, 24 October 2001. https://knowledge.wharton.upenn.edu/article/how-swissair-landed-in-trouble/.

[52] Milner, M., Harper, K., and Clark A. "Financial crisis grounds Swissair fleet", *The Guardian*, 3 October 2001. https://www.theguardian.com/business/2001/oct/03/theairline-industry.internationalnews.

[53] Rahesch, "Swissair — Meltdown of a national icon", Harvard Business School, 9 December 2015. https://digital.hbs.edu/platform-rctom/sumission/swissair-meltdown-of-a-national-icon/.

wanted to pitch in only enough to sustain a much slimmer affair. The two banks mounted a Fr 1.36 billion (US$840 million) salvage operation for the group's 70% stake in Crossair, the company's more financially healthy subsidiary, which later became the new national carrier known as Swiss International Air Lines. In between, the government injected Fr 450 million (US$280 million) to tide Swissair over the transition till the deal on Crossair was sealed. The European Commission objected to the dishing out of aid without prior consultation. Eventually, the original Swissair faded into history and the new flag carrier assumed the national iconic role, right down to taking over the codes, routes and operations.

In 2008, Lufthansa took over the airline for Fr 339 million (US$339 million), thus ending its Swiss ownership and consequently, the Swiss national identity. This was however not the only instance of ceding national identity as represented by a flag carrier; in 2007, KLM, the Dutch national carrier, was acquired by Air France.[54]

Demise of Air Berlin

Not too far away from Switzerland, Germany's Air Berlin went on a similar shopping spree that sent the airline into a tailspin. Unlike Swissair, part of which survived and started a new chapter, Air Berlin did not share the same fate. After having successfully operated since 1979, in August 2017, the airline was forced to file for insolvency following years of losses and eventually ceased operations after its biggest shareholder, Gulf owner Etihad Airways, withdrew its financial backing.[55]

Prior to its downfall, the Germans' second-largest carrier was loss-making almost every year since 2008[56] as it embarked on a largely growth-by-acquisition strategy. This included significant stakes or mergers with German leisure airline LTU, German carriers dba and TUIfly, Austrian airline Niki and Swiss airline Belair. With this expansion came the indigestion challenges of financial struggles and debt — Air Berlin reported a net loss of €782 million (US$854 million) in 2016, up a hefty 75% from

---

[54]"Lufthansa pays €217m for Swiss takeover", *Financial Times*, 26 March 2008 https://www.ft.com/content/e1d4e966-fa89-11dc-aa46-000077b07658.

[55]Bryan, V. and Sheahan, M. "Air Berlin files for insolvency after Etihad withdraws support", *Reuters*, 15 August 2017, https://www.reuters.com/article/us-air-berlin-lufthansa/air-berlin-files-for-insolvency-after-etihad-withdraws-support-idUSKCN1AV14E.

[56]*Ibid.*

the year before. It also racked up €1.2 billion (US$1.3 billion) worth of debt.[57]

In the wake of the impending doom, Etihad pulled its funding plug after having already poured an estimated €1.76 billion (US$2 billion) into Air Berlin since 2011.[58] To make matters worse, EU state aid rules only allowed rescue and restructuring aid to companies that are in financial difficulty. However, such aid was subject to strict conditions known as the "one time, last time" principle.[59] The German government came under pressure to safeguard some 8,500 jobs and granted Air Berlin a temporary loan of €150 million (US$176 million) in order to keep operations going in the short run, as per the European Commission guidelines.[60] This bridging loan was expected to tide Air Berlin over the three months while it attempted to conclude ongoing negotiations with Lufthansa to buy out their assets.[61]

Following Air Berlin's end of operations and desperate to recoup some of the cash owed, the German authorities tried to auction Air Berlin's assets for as much as possible, including the now-defunct airline's business class seats and the signature chocolates.[62]

---

[57]Newton, J. "Aeroplane seats for £1,333 and branded chocolates for £195: Air Berlin is selling off its entire stock after going bankrupt with £700million of debt", *The Daily Mail UK*, 17 January 2018. https://www.dailymail.co.uk/travel/travel_news/article-5279125/Bankrupt-airline-Air-Berlin-selling-entire-stock.html; "Air Berlin administrator sues Etihad for up to €2bn", *Financial Times*, 14 December 2018. https://www.ft.com/content/05c68878-ff9e-11e8-aebf-99e208d3e521.

[58]Petzinger, J. "The German government buys time for bankrupt Air Berlin after investor Etihad bails", *Quartz*, 16 August 2017. https://qz.com/1055001/german-government-gives-air-berlin-a-loan-after-its-biggest-investor-etihad-airways-pulls-the-plug/.

[59]European Commission, "Guidelines on State aid for rescuing and restructuring non-financial undertakings in difficulty" p. 70, 3.6.1, https://ec.europa.eu/competition/state_aid/legislation/rescue_resctructuring_communication_en.pdf.

[60]"State aid: Commission approves German rescue aid to Air Berlin", European Commission [Press Release] 4 September 2017, https://ec.europa.eu/commission/press-corner/detail/en/IP_17_3083.

[61]"Air Berlin may drop more long-haul routes next week — Sources", *Reuters*, 8 September 2017. https://www.reuters.com/article/air-berlin-lufthansa-longhaul/air-berlin-may-drop-more-long-haul-routes-next-week-sources-idUSL8N1LP3HV.

[62]Newton, J. "Aeroplane seats for £1,333 and branded chocolates for £195: Air Berlin is selling off its entire stock after going bankrupt with £700million of debt", *The Daily Mail UK*, 17 January 2018. https://www.dailymail.co.uk/travel/travel_news/article-5279125/Bankrupt-airline-Air-Berlin-selling-entire-stock.html.

Although critics have faulted the respective governments for their seemingly nonchalant attitude, it should be pointed out that they were not responsible for the poor management or misspending at Swissair or Air Berlin. A bailout would not have necessarily helped them operate better; worse still, senior management might have misinterpreted this as a safety net and continue with their reckless behaviour.

> *Regardless of the extent of state ownership, governments are often expected to consider bailing out national flag carriers, for national pride reasons or to prevent massive job losses. Governments must consciously reduce the moral hazard associated with acting under pressure and avoid excessive risk-taking from the extension of taxpayers' monies and any ensuing market competition distortion. Such rescue and restructuring government aid should only be granted to airline companies when their very existence is justified and they have exhausted all other market options.*

The challenges are already in existence during peacetime. The onset of travel restrictions on virtually a global scale, arising from the Covid-19 pandemic, is an unprecedented hard stop unlike any recession before. The entire aviation sector has been haemorrhaging. Many airlines, especially the ones that run on a low-cost budget model, have gone belly-up from a combination of virtually nil revenues, sticky overheads and expensive aircraft loans to service.

No airline company has been immune to the plunge in air travel; travel bans have affected the good, the bad and the ugly.[63] Even hitherto well-managed airlines like Singapore Airlines[64] and Cathay Pacific are confronted with massive operating challenges and required radical restructuring and heavy capital injection. The aggregate bailout bill size has grown to an once-thought impossible magnitude of at least US$200 billion, and counting.[65] IATA has projected that airlines were

---

[63] https://www.straitstimes.com/business/companies-markets/the-airlines-most-in-danger-of-going-under-during-the-coronavirus-crisis, 27 March 2020.

[64] https://www.reuters.com/article/us-health-coronavirus-airlines/singapore-airlines-latest-to-get-massive-rescue-amid-coronavirus-crisis-idUSKBN21D3UW, 27 March 2020.

[65] "Coronavirus; airlines face unprecedented crisis", *Financial Times*, 3 May 2020.

heading for a massive loss of US$84 billion in 2020.[66] Post Covid-19, the shake-up will be unmistakable — the demise of many a non-national carrier, especially budget players, and much trimmer but highly indebted survivors.

Prior to the Covid-19 scourge, the narrative was that national airlines simply "cannot be sold" for reasons of national pride. With many governments seriously disabled financially from carrying out such bailouts, this narrative has quietened somewhat.

Covid-19 aside, the cost of being in denial extends far and wide, in tandem with the continued justification of a national icon and the spirit of not allowing any to fail. In South Africa, the pattern of rescuing SOEs is unfortunately the painful norm, which when carried out repeatedly, creates a costly, vicious circle.

Example 4.3: State Capture in South Africa

Owing to political legacies, the South Africa government remains saddled with a gaping hole in its fiscal books from sustaining a whole stable of inefficient and bloated SOEs. Endemic corruption which has been festering over the years has made the task of reform quite impossible. Unfortunately, there remains no way out but the painful process of restructuring and transforming the entire public enterprise sector.

The government of South Africa has more than a plateful of SOEs that require a radical restructuring of core and non-core businesses, huge capital injection to stave off insolvency and anti-corruption measures to staunch the financial bleeding, all at the same time. At the heart of these challenges is a lack of governance and an unsavoury mix of politics and business. Cronyism is rampant as is bloated bureaucracy from prolonged inefficiency and adding to the ranks, often for political reasons.

As is common in many economies, state enterprises have been around for the longest of time, frequently playing a crucial role in security or nationally strategic domains. The difference has less to do with the extent of privatising SOEs than with whether they are fulfilling their original mandates, commercially run and held accountable for the vast amounts of

---

[66] https://www.straitstimes.com/business/companies-markets/airlines-heading-for-116b-loss-this-year-iata, 11 June 2020.

public capital that have been poured into sustaining them. There are also concerns about the wastage of talent.

Plight of SOEs over Last Few Years

As at 2017, South Africa government guarantees to SOEs on account of their liabilities reached a massive R450 billion (or US$36 billion). The grave situation not surprisingly led the Reserve Bank[67] to sound the warning of financial instability from just a mere couple of defaults by the massively indebted SOEs. It is regrettably a long list of patients for resuscitation and plenty of red ink all over the fiscal books.

South African Airways's (SAA) challenges are well known. It has been loss-making since 2012 with no clear route out of the turbulence. As of 2019, it is estimated to be burning through R450 million or US$31 million a month. Between 1999 and 2017, a staggering R29 billion or around US$3 billion has been ploughed into the airline.[68] Post 2017, the government continued to dish out loans or inject capital directly, all in a bid to save a national icon. There is no light at the end of the public capital tunnel which is encountering simultaneous and pressing needs for funding for other equally desperate SOEs.

Eskom: The aggregate bailout for SAA would pale in comparison to that being and to be chalked up by Eskom, the national power utility company which supplies 90% of the country's ballooning demand — a ginormous R150 billion or US$10 billion over the current decade to stay afloat. Eskom runs an unsustainable debt-to-equity ratio of more than 200%, with debt currently toting up to a massive R420 billion or US$30 billion, requiring an annual cashflow of R23 billion (or US$1.6 billion) to survive over the next three years.[69] No doubt, a condition was attached to the bailout — an explicit mandate to implement the recommendations of the presidential task team at Eskom. In essence, these proposals revolved around a restructuring or unbundling of Eskom into three companies to deal with generation, transmission and distribution, as a prelude to relinquishing

---

[67] https://www.biznews.com/asset-management/2018/04/26/soe-debt-threatens-financial-stability, 26 April 2018.

[68] https://www.thesouthafrican.com/news/saa-bailout-how-much-last-20-years/, 19 January 2019.

[69] https://www.businesslive.co.za/bd/national/2019-02-21-eskom-bailout-to-reach-r150bn-in-10-years/, 21 February 2019.

Eskom's near monopoly. Questions remained over the pace of unbundling,[70] apportioning of debt and revaluation of assets, including two poorly designed new power stations. In all fairness, the unbundling was indeed a non-trivial exercise which could be a long and challenging series of processes, even if the government were prepared to exempt the related taxes arising from the asset transfer. The legal implications over titles and liabilities can be extremely complicated. There was of course also the issue of continuity of essential services to the public, in the midst of all the transformation.

South Africa Broadcasting Corporation (SABC), the national public broadcaster which would need around R3.2 billion (US$230 million) to survive,[71] received partial bailout funding of R2.1 billion in October 2019.[72] Eight pre-conditions were stipulated for the funding which would help SABC to settle outstanding debts, invest in technology and local content, as well as maintain buildings satisfactorily. Through the last two decades, the broadcaster has had its fair share of restructuring involving television and radio services. In the meantime, it continues to endure accusations of being pro-government (ANC) and engaging in heavy censorship.

Transnet,[73] the national rail, port and pipeline company, had a litany of corruption, money laundering and fraud charges filed against it by the Organisation Undoing Tax Abuse (Outa). These included suspicious Transnet contracts covering dodgy locomotive transactions of not insignificant amounts, amounting to R56 billion (US$3.5 billion).[74] It is debatable how long these prosecutorial efforts would lead to a certain outcome.

Unfortunately, the narrative of bloated and inefficient state enterprises has not changed all these years. More often than not, the SOEs are guilty as charged and given the dominant role they play collectively in the economy, the state has to tread very carefully. It is indisputable that mounting multiple bailouts on such a

---

[70] https://www.reuters.com/article/safrica-eskom/south-africas-eskom-new-ceo-warns-against-hasty-unbundling-of-firm-idUSL8N29V03R, 26 January 2020.

[71] http://www.sabc.co.za/sabc/sabc-board-and-management-provide-an-update-on-key-issues-to-the-deputy-minister-ms-pinky-kekana/, 17 December 2019.

[72] https://www.iol.co.za/business-report/companies/sabc-board-management-meet-deputy-minister-pinky-kekana-39405070, 18 December 2019.

[73] https://www.iol.co.za/news/politics/outa-hands-evidence-of-graft-at-transnet-to-zondo-commission-22545529, 4 May 2019.

[74] https://www.fin24.com/Companies/Industrial/new-transnet-ceo-faces-tough-task-to-get-transnet-on-the-right-track-20200204-2, 4 February 2020.

scale will cripple any country, not just South Africa. The ability to restructure, re-position SOEs into commercially viable and sensitive business entities is nonetheless a prerequisite to achieving a stable and sustainable economy for the long term.

Realistically speaking, there is very little choice apart from bailing out the most essential of services but without the resolve and discipline to rid SOEs of corruption and their unproductive malaise, any funding effort will be futile. Where corruption has weakened enforcement institutions, attention should be paid by the state to finding the right leaders, creating sufficient incentives and providing protection for their unpopular tasks. A focus on establishing transparent procurement processes and the execution of huge public projects would be imperative to the fostering of accountability.

Non State-owned Icons Need Bailouts Too

The rationale for a rescue of state-owned national icons is easily understood, even if unjustified. It can be argued that the nexus between state ownership and bailout is clearly defined by virtue of ownership. Hence, expectations of a financial response by the state, regardless of the enormity of the need, are the norm across many jurisdictions.

However, the long arm of the government is often expected to stretch towards ailing national icons, too-big-to-fail non-state owned institutions as well. As recent cases have shown, the state is compelled to act where many members of the public would be badly hurt if a major catastrophe were not averted.

Example 4.4: Expectation of Universal Protection by Government

Anbang Insurance Group is a familiar firm to many, not just in China but also within the international sphere. It comes as no surprise that when news of the potential failure and bankruptcy of this industry giant emerged, many turned expectantly to the

> *Chinese government, waiting for public officials to do something to save this national icon, and by extension the economy from ruin.*

In 2018, Anbang Insurance Group received a US$9.7 billion bailout[75] from the government-run Insurance Security Fund (CISF) after ex-Chairman Wu Xiaohui admitted to fundraising fraud and embezzlement. This was part of the Chinese authorities' crack down on the financial industry to guard against excessive borrowing and risk.[76]

At that point in time, Anbang reportedly controlled about US$310 billion in assets and catered to some 35 million customers. Standard & Poor's ranked Anbang third in size in 2017 among Chinese insurers.[77] The company is known for its aggressive global expansion, including the near US$2 billion acquisition of New York's Waldorf Astoria hotel in 2014.

The takeover of the company by China's insurance regulator was to ensure Anbang's solvency as well as protect public and policyholders' interests, which included millions of retail investors, according to the China Insurance Regulatory Commission (CIRC).[78] The money from the CISF, an industry-funded body that bails out troubled insurers, was to facilitate the takeover of Anbang only temporarily and after equity restructuring, would let Anbang remain a privately owned company. This takeover of Anbang, which was intended to last one year, was predicated on the management of the company by a group of officials from the CIRC, the central bank and other key financial regulators and government bodies.[79]

The key reason for the Chinese government's intervention in Anbang was because the company was regarded as "too big to fail". Anbang was a key financial institution and so interconnected with the rest of the system that a systemic failure would be catastrophic for the greater economic system.[80] Not surprisingly, public expectations are that these major non-state

---

[75] https://www.scmp.com/business/companies/article/2140250/china-rescues-anbang-insurance-us10-billion-bailout-after-ex, 4 April 2018.

[76] https://www.bbc.com/news/business-43207506, 27 February 2018.

[77] https://www.wsj.com/articles/anbangs-rescue-is-chinas-too-big-to-fail-moment-1519641004, 26 February 2018.

[78] https://www.straitstimes.com/business/companies-markets/china-rescues-anbang-with-127b-bailout-after-fraud-claims, 5 April 2018.

[79] https://www.reuters.com/article/us-china-anbang-regulation/china-seizes-control-of-anbang-insurance-as-chairman-prosecuted-idUSKCN1G7076, 23 February 2018.

[80] https://www.wsj.com/articles/anbangs-rescue-is-chinas-too-big-to-fail-moment-1519641004, 26 February 2018.

companies, such as Anbang, must be supported by the government if they face potential failure and drag along millions of retail investors.

With most of Anbang's investors being individuals who have put their hard-earned savings into instruments such as insurance policies,[81] the public would be hit the hardest by Anbang's insolvency. It was thus no surprise that the Chinese public, perceiving the government as a safety net, also turned expectantly to them for a bailout to ensure public welfare.

If the government had regarded Anbang's potential problems as simply another big corporate failure and Anbang had gone bankrupt with no means of paying back their investors, the consequences could be devastating. Anbang's failure would have triggered and caused serious, systemic problems for the rest of the financial services sector and eventually have economy-wide repercussions. By bailing Anbang out, the government has justifiably prevented an economic catastrophe, even though Anbang is not state-owned.

> *The social implications of the possible failure of Anbang as an industry giant were much too far-reaching to be ignored. The government had no choice but to save this national icon from ruin, as letting it crumble and struggle to save itself would have much more disastrous consequences for the welfare of the people. Ignoring the problem was simply not an option as it would have major repercussions for the financial services sector as a whole. The public obviously agreed — expecting the state to bail Anbang out even though Anbang was a private company and not a government-owned company. Although the government had to use the insurance security fund to bail Anbang out, it can be argued that they made the right call as they saved a lot more than just the individual company — they also saved the financial industry and the economy from ruin.*

The political burden of not allowing many members of the public to suffer cannot be overstated. Even an otherwise run-of-the-mill business failure, like Thomas Cook or FlyBe both of the UK, can heighten the need for a government to act, to make good on behalf of the failed business operator(s). The public outcry would otherwise cause enough discomfort,

---

[81] https://www.bbc.com/news/business-43207506, 27 February 2018.

if not political pressure, for the government to feel an obligation to respond.

Example 4.5: Navigating Turbulence in Travel

When a national icon is on the verge of failing, the public naturally looks to the government to save it, regardless of ownership. The reality is that the government cannot simply bail out large corporations just because the public expects it to do so. The government would have to factor in the implications and repercussions the failure of the supposed icon would have on the rest of the industry and wider economy. It would also have to assess the effect on public welfare or social norms. Most critically, it needs to consider how public funds could be best used in such a scenario and if such funds are readily available before making a decision. This was the exact predicament the UK government found itself in when home-grown Thomas Cook descended into ruin. Given its wide reach of customers, many were looking to the government expectantly to bail the travel agency out.

Travel giant Thomas Cook needs no introduction in the UK and indeed, to many travellers around the world. Established for almost 180 years, the household name and the world's oldest travel agency offered a one-stop service for its customers — from flights to tours and meals, travellers simply need not worry about their getaway plans. The company even owned its own hotels and operated its own airline, flying to at least 82 destinations around the world.[82] Over the years, it built up a reputation as one of the world's best-known holiday brands.

However, it all started unravelling in September 2019. Thomas Cook collapsed under the weight of its £1.7 billion debt into liquidation after rescue talks failed to secure the necessary £200–250 million in emergency funding, leaving some 600,000 of customers stranded, including as many as 150,000 in the midst of their packages with Thomas Cook. More than 20,000 employees lost their jobs consequently.[83] The collapse of a national icon such as Thomas Cook was unthinkable — so how exactly did it happen?

---

[82] https://www.nytimes.com/2019/09/23/travel/why-thomas-cook-travel-collapsed.html, 23 September 2019.

[83] https://time.com/5683934/thomas-cook-travel-collapse/, 23 September 2019.

What Went Wrong

Industry analysts were quick to diagnose the problems at Thomas Cook — from the disastrous merger in 2007 of Thomas Cook with MyTravel, a UK-based package travel company, which led to the assumption of massive debt that culminated in a record loss of £1.5 billion in May 2019; to stiff competition from the emergence of lower cost rival Jet2Holidays; to a steep drop in summer sales from the prolonged Brexit-related uncertainty; to the rise of online travel players posing competition to brick and mortar firms like Thomas Cook and significantly, the shift in travel patterns away from package tours.[84]

Thomas Cook's problems were not entirely new. In 2011, the company's debt had already ballooned to £1.1 billion and it only managed to survive after an emergency additional cash injection. However, this had only served to pile on more debt. Since 2011, more than a quarter of the revenues went towards annual debt servicing.[85]

For a couple of years in between, a reprieve came in the form of an investment by the Chinese group Fosun International. Fosun bought its (first) stake in Thomas Cook in 2015.[86] In August 2019, there were talks of a £900 million deal to avert bankruptcy.[87] This deal, however, fell through. Soon after, the lenders requested for £200 million to keep the company afloat. Fearing bankruptcy, the travel agency turned to the UK government for help.

Features of Proposed Bailout

Three specific requests were made of the government: guarantee a new money facility, exert pressure on other stakeholders into funding the money or if all else fails, the government itself would support Thomas Cook so as to delay the initiation of the insolvency process. Understandably, the open-ended commitment to provide unlimited support to an imminently insolvent company was untenable, hence, the government refused to accept the

---

[84] *Ibid.*

[85] *Ibid.*

[86] https://www.theguardian.com/business/2019/sep/23/thomas-cook-as-the-world-turned-the-sun-ceased-to-shine-on-venerable-tour-operator, 23 September 2019.

[87] https://www.theguardian.com/business/2019/aug/28/thomas-cook-agrees-terms-of-900m-rescue-deal-with-fosun, 28 August 2019.

agency's request.[88] When Thomas Cook eventually went out of business in September 2019, it was drowning in about £1.7 billion in debt to its banks with a further £1.3 billion owing to suppliers.[89]

Pro-nationalisation critics lamented that the cost of rescue flights and compensation due to the shutting down of Thomas Cook may far exceed the £200 million of short-term funding that Thomas Cook needed to survive.[90] How could the government let the nation's iconic travel agency go to ruin after all the years it had faithfully served the British public?

The public was neither being facetious nor unreasonable. In fact, there was a precedent — Thomas Cook was nationalised in 1948 after facing bankruptcy during the Second World War. The government then could not countenance the failure of an institution that was very much a part of the fabric of British life.[91]

This time round, however, the government stood firm, arguing that this was purely a commercial matter and that customers of Thomas Cook would be protected by the Atol protection scheme and insurance.[92] Transport secretary Grant Shapps said that the operation to repatriate customers would cost £100 million, less than the sum requested by Thomas Cook to bail it out.[93] Spending taxpayer's money on bailing out an insolvent company was not something the government was prepared to do. By the time Thomas Cook failed, it had chalked up over £3.1 billion in liabilities against cash reserves of less than £1 billion. The CEO of Thomas Cook estimated that it would run out of cash by early October, or even sooner.[94] In reality, a government bailout would not have sustained the company for a long period anyway.[95] It would merely have delayed, for just a little while, the inevitable failure of regrettably, a national icon.

---

[88] https://www.forbes.com/sites/francescoppola/2019/09/29/why-the-u-k-government-was-right-not-to-bail-out-thomas-cook/#692cfb6217b9, 29 September 2019.

[89] https://www.independent.co.uk/travel/news-and-advice/thomas-cook-collapse-travel-abta-corporate-finance-failure-mark-tanzer-a9146851.html, 8 October 2019.

[90] https://www.theguardian.com/business/2019/sep/23/thomas-cook-as-the-world-turned-the-sun-ceased-to-shine-on-venerable-tour-operator, 23 September 2019.

[91] *Ibid.*

[92] *Ibid.*

[93] https://www.theguardian.com/business/2019/sep/23/row-breaks-out-government-refusal-rescue-thomas-cook, 23 September 2019.

[94] https://www.forbes.com/sites/francescoppola/2019/09/29/why-the-u-k-government-was-right-not-to-bail-out-thomas-cook/#692cfb6217b9, 29 September 2019.

[95] https://www.huffingtonpost.co.uk/entry/thomas-cook-government-bail-out_uk_5d886b7ce4b0849d472bc138?guccounter=1&guce_referrer=aHR0cHM6Ly93d3cuZ29vZ2xlLmN vbS8&guce_referrer_sig=AQAAADnayFScMk9aWnHlDFG2YKtAR75z0APIYXQ0kF-

Flybe Grounding to a Halt

Even before the dust had settled for the Thomas Cook fiasco, another loss-making regional carrier Flybe, which supplied the majority of the UK domestic flights, was about to be grounded. The response of the British government was ostensibly one of a rescue plan where support would be given on "strictly commercial terms".[96] This support came in the form of an agreement to review air passenger duty (APD), giving breathing room to Flybe's shareholders to inject extra capital to sustain the business. Some 2,400 jobs were at stake. Flybe's consortium of shareholders included Virgin Atlantic.

This review was part of a plan to add more feeder flights, one which attracted a range of criticism, including a formal complaint by British Airways to the EU of "state aid" by the British government. Alas, all the efforts came to nought as Flybe had no answer to the Covid-19 disastrous impact on air travel.[97]

The public often turns to the government as a safety net when investments they have made go awry or a service that they have gotten used to runs the danger of cessation — such was the case for Thomas Cook when it failed and left thousands stranded. The government sometimes has the unpleasant or unpopular task of going against public expectations to make the correct political call. This was clearly a case of inevitable insolvency and many would agree that the government made the right judgement call by not bowing to public pressure but instead, by letting this national icon, Thomas Cook, disappear altogether. The intended rescue support for Flybe, on the other hand, was taken with the larger public good of enhanced regional connectivity across the UK.

Oz6nNzbb4lXpxFkO3NZhlJF1pagOaFVP1RMJKwhdXmytFv4mPVi1Y9d4tfmDfcdn5B
t8rxJA7E7-NZ-v_Njf-fhs00EIfKD48mXS8P-DLiRR_9EJCxdaxmdxtH1rdGLWNA948h,
23 September 2019.

[96] https://www.clactonandfrintongazette.co.uk/news/national/18162619.british-airways-owner-lodges-complaint-eu-flybe-rescue-deal/, 15 January 2020.

[97] https://www.independent.co.uk/travel/news-and-advice/flybe-news-flights-administration-collapse-coronavirus-outbreak-bust-latest-news-a9376421.html, 5 March 2020.

Bailouts to Stave Off Systemic Risks

The Global Financial Crisis (GFC) is a truly apt description in that it encapsulated the wide and deep extent of systemic damage that the integrated global marketplace underwent, most noticeably in 2008. When the phenomenon started unfolding, it compelled many governments to pump in their wherewithal towards bailing out their critical economic pillars, from banks to insurance companies to mortgage corporations to auto companies, regardless of whether they were state-owned or otherwise. Even countries whose governments have long divested whatever national business interests they had, essentially re-nationalised some of these ailing pillars to save the economies at large.

Example 4.6: Massive Support for the Long Haul

When an economy not just is about to be brought to its knees but also would imminently have its pillars of activity collapsing into smithereens, the government would have no choice but to intervene, regardless of its ideology about state capitalism or the amount of financial resources it has or does not have at its disposal.

Such was the inconvenient plight that governments of many large economies found themselves confronted with back then around 2008. The previously stoic defenders of a less-government-more-private-sector model for the economy like the UK, US and Switzerland concluded that not bailing out failing national icons was simply not an option. Their respective economies would suffer widespread systemic damage that could be far worse than political pain in the short term.

Pain in the US

The US government had the unenviable responsibility of rescuing a whole slew of companies across various industries from financial institutions — already a very large category including hundreds of banks, insurance companies, mortgage servicers — to auto companies. The total cheque size? A staggering US$700 billion was initially aimed at buying the otherwise defaulting mortgage-backed securities, to relieve almost a thousand beneficiaries of this colossal burden. This was roughly equivalent to a quarter of the Federal Budget in 2008.

Eventually, a combination of channels was designed to extend help given the exigencies and lack of political appetite to assume the mortgage-backed securities in whole — preferred stock purchase, direct bailouts to AIG, which itself consumed a big chunk (US$68 billion) as did the auto companies (US$81 billion), loan facility through the Federal Reserve to member banks and a stability plan for homeowners. Many provisions were added to ensure that taxpayers were not simply bearing the brunt of bad banking decisions but that help was extended meaningfully to avert a total collapse of the financial system, and the larger economy as a consequence.[98]

All in all, the initial principal amount has since been recovered in aggregate terms. To date, more than US$100 billion is estimated to be still outstanding after a decade.[99]

Pain in the UK

Regardless of the debate around how much the UK government actually spent rescuing the banks, the government did issue a statement in November 2016 that taxpayers would face a £27 billion loss from the bank bailout during the 2007–2009 financial crisis.[100] Against the estimated total outlay of £137 billion spent rescuing household names like Royal Bank of Scotland (RBS), Lloyds and Northern Rock, this was material.

The intervention included the giving of financial guarantees by the Treasury which totalled more than £1 trillion, a massive undertaking in the event of any loss in confidence in the banks.[101] In 2016, the government had only managed to recoup just over half of the bailout quantum (not including the guarantees). The recovery was made more complicated by Brexit, the UK's decision to leave the EU, which adversely impacted the share prices of these financial institutions. By 2017, the National Audit Office indicated that only some £58 billion remained un-recovered[102]; a House of Commons Briefing Paper updated this to an almost full recovery, save for the

---

[98] https://www.thebalance.com/what-was-the-bank-bailout-bill-3305675, 22 August 2019.

[99] https://projects.propublica.org/bailout/list, 31 January 2020.

[100] https://uk.reuters.com/article/uk-britain-eu-budget-banks/british-taxpayers-face-27-billion-pound-loss-from-bank-bailout-idUKKBN13I1FJ, 23 November 2016.

[101] "Bank rescues of 2007–2009: Outcomes and cost", *House of Commons Briefing Paper*, 8 October 2018.

[102] https://www.express.co.uk/finance/city/840265/Government-bank-bailout-credit-crunch-cost-recovery, 13 August 2017.

crystallised loss of £27 billion on the RBS bailout as at March 2018. Outstanding guarantees had also been whittled down to £14 billion.[103]

Pain Elsewhere

The narrative is the same in Switzerland and many other economies. This is not surprising as the financial markets are now so inter-linked and borderless that systemic risk has no nationality. This was played out in full for the Swiss government with its top two banks UBS and Credit Suisse mired in the subprime bubble. Together, both banks held some 60% of the market for loans to the small and medium-sized enterprises.[104] Given the dominant role that the financial services sector plays in Switzerland, contributing more than 10% of GDP, the government ploughed in "trillions of dollars and euros" on a bank rescue and economic recovery plan. Thanks to the high level of private investment, a lean and trim bureaucracy, and a solidarity towards resolving the crisis, the country was able to emerge without the baggage of more public debt. However, its financial sector had been reduced in size internationally.[105] UBS managed to stage an impressive recovery outside of the US, returning the US$60 billion injected, together with a good profit.

In the wake of the GFC, many new regulations were layered on. One major development was the implementation of the Volcker Rule which generally prohibits banks from conducting certain investment activities with their own proprietary accounts and restricts their relationships with hedge funds and private equity. The Basel capital and liquidity standards were adopted by countries around the world. Consequently, investment banking gradually lost its shine.

To the credit of these governments, there was the discipline to divest their newly acquired stakes systematically over time. This, with the benefit of hindsight, demanded loads of patience as it was a long-haul exercise for most governments. These bailouts have a long unwinding period Take the US automakers GM, Chrysler and Ford for example. Out of

---

[103] "Bank rescues of 2007–2009: Outcomes and cost", *House of Commons Briefing Paper*, 8 October 2018.

[104] https://www.swissinfo.ch/eng/2008-crisis_the-day-ubs--the-biggest-swiss-bank--was-saved/44474630, 16 October 2018.

[105] https://www.swissinfo.ch/eng/10-years-after-the-collapse-of-lehman-brothers_the-financial-crisis-of-2008-and-the-swiss--miracle-/44397608, 14 September 2018.

the US$80.7 billion that the US government disbursed in 2008, tax-payers lost some US$10.2 billion when the bailout programme ended in 2014.[106]

> *The responses of the governments of the larger economies will be extremely crucial in any major global crisis. Given the interconnectivity of today's global marketplace especially in financial services, their rescue efforts, or the lack of, would have huge implications for the rest of the world. Suffice it to say, domestic political pressure would have ordinarily extracted an immediate and hopefully effective response from the government to a brewing crisis at home anyway, but the potential contagion effects mean that increasingly, a collective response around the world would have to be the norm. In short, bigger players like the US, UK and Switzerland can no longer act alone.*

Bailouts are getting much bigger by the day, in contrast to the shrinking public coffers. Occasionally, there are no two ways about it, especially when it relates to an ongoing major undertaking. The UK government had to plough in another £$1.4 billion[107] into what is possibly Europe's biggest infrastructure railway project, the Crossrail, in a bid to get the line operational and revenue generating, past its due completion date of December 2018. The new target completion date is March 2021, implying the inevitable chalking up of more budget overruns.[108]

Not all triggers are traced to a lack of market regulation or economic cycles, some countries buckle under a prolonged state of weak fiscal health which may manifest itself as weak economic underpinnings such as banks or real-estate developers. Greece found itself in such a situation.

---

[106] https://www.thebalance.com/auto-industry-bailout-gm-ford-chrysler-3305670, 27 January 2020.

[107] https://www.bbc.com/news/uk-england-london-46507417, 10 December 2018.

[108] https://www.bbc.com/news/uk-england-london-49646570, 16 September 2019.

Example 4.7: A Greek Tragedy?

When a country is at risk of collapsing under great financial stress, it is incumbent upon the government of the day to step in and do everything in its power to prevent such a disastrous consequence from happening. The importance of the government's role in such a scenario cannot be overstated. In fact, the precarious state is exacerbated when the country's failure could create devastating contagion effects for related international businesses. The Greek government's effort in helping to bail out its banks is an example that perfectly illustrates this point.

The Greek financial crisis has been going on for over a decade and was finally starting to show hopeful signs of making a recovery, starting with its exit from its third successive bailout programme in 2018. To put in perspective, since late 2009, in the aftermath of the 2008 GFC, the Greek economy had shrunk by a quarter. It also had an undesirably high debt-to-GDP ratio of 188% in 2017.[109]

Greece has struggled to make a recovery, with the country needing bailout loans in 2010, 2012 and 2015 from the International Monetary Fund (IMF), Eurogroup and European Central Bank. In fact, Greece is the first developed country to fail to make an IMF loan repayment on time.[110]

Banking System Continued to Flounder

Despite the bailout exercises, the Greek banking system continued to pose concerns. The inordinately large number of non-performing loans (NPLs) remained a challenge. According to data from Bank of Greece, NPLs averaged a staggering 50% of all loans. This stood in stark comparison to the average NPL ratio of 4% across the EU.[111] It is noteworthy that some of the NPL predicament was aggravated by the distress at the governmental level, leaving banks with no choice but to write off government bonds.

---

[109] https://www.worldfinance.com/banking/greeces-banking-woes-continue-despite-exiting-bailout-programme, 11 April 2019.

[110] https://www.straitstimes.com/business/economy/greece-becomes-first-developed-country-to-default-on-imf, 1 July 2015.

[111] https://www.worldfinance.com/banking/greeces-banking-woes-continue-despite-exiting-bailout-programme, 11 April 2019.

Furthermore, post the banking debacle, it was revealed that the quality of the banks' capital was fundamentally questionable, despite their having passed "stress tests" by the European Central Bank on adequacy of capitalisation. More than half of the combined capital of Greece's four largest banks was made up of deferred tax assets, and the return on the banks' equity was negative,[112] as the economy continued to be depressed by stubborn costs.

Since then, Greek banks have been trapped in a vicious cycle and have been unable to resuscitate themselves. They need to be able to lend to get the economy running again, but they also need a functioning economy to resolve some of their NPL challenges. Consequently, the banks were unable to access sufficient funding for loans, but on the other hand, demand itself had also not been forthcoming.[113]

Reasons for EU Bailouts

Greece accepted loans from the EU in 2010 in order to avoid default on its debt. This would enable Greece to continue making payments so that the viability of the eurozone would not be threatened. However, the condition for the loans was that Greece would have to carry out austerity measures to, *inter alia*, improve its management of public finances. It would have to modernise its financial statistics and reporting, lower trade barriers, increase exports and reform its pension system — its pension payments soaked up 17.5% of GDP, higher than for any other EU country. These austerity measures, comprising lower spending and an increase in taxes however precipitated a recession till 2017.[114] The ensuing 25% contraction in the economy stoked social unrest as unemployment climbed to 25%, with youth unemployment at a glaring 50%.

The Greek government laboured hard to improve the country's financial situation and in 2011, the European Financial Stability Facility added another €190 billion to Greece's bailout. By 2014, Greece's economy appeared finally to be on the mend, growing by 0.7% and with the

---

[112] https://www.businesstimes.com.sg/banking-finance/the-greek-banking-tragedy-and-how-to-end-it, 14 December 2018.

[113] https://www.worldfinance.com/banking/greeces-banking-woes-continue-despite-exiting-bailout-programme, 11 April 2019.

[114] https://www.thebalance.com/what-is-the-greece-debt-crisis-3305525, 14 December 2019.

government successfully selling bonds and balancing the budget once again.[115]

However, a crisis started brewing again in 2015. The Greek public voted against the onerous austerity measures in a referendum which had brought about widespread hardship. The instability caused banks to close and Greece to sustain extensive economic damage, threatening the progress they had only recently made. Fortunately, the European Central Bank agreed to re-capitalise Greek banks with €10 to €25 billion, allowing them to re-open. Banks imposed a €420 weekly limit on withdrawals, preventing depositors from emptying their accounts and exacerbating the problem. This helped reduce tax evasion and federal revenue increased by €1 billion a year, with people turning to debit and credit cards for purchases. The same year, Greek parliament passed the (much-needed) austerity measures despite the referendum outcome. This was necessary for it to receive a further EU loan of €86 billion. The European Central Bank and IMF subsequently agreed to an easier repayment of Greek's debt over a longer time period.[116]

In January 2018, the Greek parliament agreed on new austerity measures to qualify for the next round of EU bailouts. This in turn helped banks reduce bad debt, and resuscitated the economy, leading to the end of the €86 billion bailout program in August 2018.[117]

A key step forward is the layout of a blueprint by the government in 2019 to reduce the country's €75 billion debt. The plan was aimed at speeding up the sale of NPLs by Greek lenders, repackaging them into securities with the state guaranteeing the safest portions. The program, coined Hercules, is expected to contribute around €200 million annually to Greece's public budget from the fees it generates. This marks the initial phase of the government's plan to reduce NPLs by some €30 billion from the balance sheet of Greek banks, making up around 40% of the total backlog.[118]

Role of Government Crucial

If Greece had refused to accept the series of EU's bailouts, totalling €320 billion, it is almost certain that it would not have been able to remain

---

[115] *Ibid.*

[116] *Ibid.*

[117] https://www.ft.com/content/3e7dac80-5050-11e8-b3ee-41e0209208ec, 5 May 2018.

[118] https://www.bloomberg.com/news/articles/2019-10-15/mezzanines-waterfalls-and-fees-in-greece-s-bank-rescue-plan, 15 October 2019.

a member state of the eurozone. This would mean a return to its previous monetary system including issuing its own currency, the drachma, again.[119] This would have its own set of unfavourable consequences — the likely cheaper currency, though initially helpful for exports and tourism, would debase the value of payments in their own currency and some banks would go bankrupt. Reduced drachma values would also cause the cost of imports to increase, possibly leading to hyperinflation, further worsening the economic and social situation in the country, potentially leading to social unrest.[120]

Furthermore, foreign investors from the continent would have to write off all debts to Greece, causing heavy losses and possibly causing the eurozone's reputation to take a hard hit, leading to another possible economic crisis in the continent. Greece would have to wave foreign investments goodbye.

The Greek government's intervention was not only necessary, but also crucial. Without the government stepping in to seek EU financial support and agree to the EU's conditions for austerity measures, the systemic risk from the continued Greek financial crisis would have been disastrous. It would have brought down not only the Greek economy but also the lenders within the eurozone, as well as possibly trigger a contagion effect into the international maritime sector. Going it alone, leaving the EU, was simply not viable. For pure economic survival reasons, the government has no choice but to step in, even if it means adopting unpopular reforms.

Avoidance of Bailouts

Can bailouts be avoided altogether? Can the concomitant financial burden be minimised? Ideally, bailouts should be undertaken only when systemic effects are real and pose threat to the entire economy if nothing is done.

---

[119] https://www.express.co.uk/finance/city/581754/What-happens-if-Greece-defaults, 5 June 2015.

[120] https://www.thebalance.com/what-is-the-greece-debt-crisis-3305525, 14 December 2019.

There is an increasingly loud call in many countries for SOEs to be transformed, to stem the bleeding and more importantly, to return them to their original missions. Bailouts should then be limited to those brought on by macro triggers such as Covid-19, well beyond the ability of an SOE to respond to, and even then, selectively for the cost that it would exact. Bailouts arising from inefficiency and a lack of accountability of SOEs should not be the default for governments to address.

Stewardship and Transformation of SOEs

Before addressing the question of what sort of reforms SOEs need, we should re-visit the fundamental question of why they should even exist, and if so, how should they be stewarded for optimal effect.

Why SOEs

SOEs are typically borne out of a need for the state to effect policies of national strategic importance or for security reasons. In the provision of social services such as healthcare, education, public housing (to a varying degree, as high as more than 80% for Singapore), the state plays a key role.

Where there is market failure, owing to heavy capital outlay or a long gestation period, such as in the building of high-speed rail across vast stretches of land or climate change initiatives, SOEs represent logical policy implementation means. Occasionally, they are also instrumental in furthering the development of private enterprises or seeding new industries.

During a crisis, "new" SOEs could emerge when the state has no choice but to bail out the too-big-to-fail national icons.

Mandate for SOEs

At the risk of stating the obvious but all governments should regularly review the criticality and strategic relevance of all SOEs. In short, is state participation in business really necessary?

In 2002, the first Temasek Charter was drawn up by Temasek Holdings in Singapore as a public document — it defined what strategic, security interests would be, as well as the intention to be an active investor and shareholder. Subsequent revisions emphasise the aim to deliver sustainable value over the long term. The availability of the Charter document means the possibility of constant public scrutiny and accountability.[121]

The context is relevant — the review of any SOE's vision and mission must take into account the underlying industry structure and competition framework. Patience is a virtue here as the execution of restructuring or transformation itself might need to be phased out.

Even if the SOE is a dominant player, there is a need to compare and contrast against peers, not just in the home country but globally. Ironically, not having a big hinterland has long inspired the likes of Singapore Airlines (SIA) and Port of Singapore Authority (PSA) to be benchmarked against global standards.

In the early days of the transformation efforts, besides helping to define a financial viability framework, Temasek also scoured globally for suitable candidates for the different boards — the aim was to build boards with a diversity of professional, business and market expertise. Over time, each board acquired its own capabilities to carry out its own management and board succession.

Ultimately, there must be a focus on competitive positioning and viability. The government must never be a backstop by default. Whenever possible, it should be made abundantly clear that the state will not mount any bailout unless national economic survival was at stake.

Scope for Privatisation

Assessing the scope for privatisation is probably the toughest policy decisions of all. This is no trivial matter as even the best-laid plans can be scuttled by disruption, need for restructuring, business cycles or simply the wrong or outdated assumptions.

The Singapore government undertook a major review of privatisation candidates and in 1987, published a list of 41 GLCs to be divested over the following 10 years. The important point is not so much whether a list has been properly drawn up and kept to. It is the discipline of constantly satisfying oneself that each SOE continues to fulfil its strategic role and where state ownership remains essential.

---

[121] https://www.temasek.com.sg/en/who-we-are/our-purpose, 16 March 2020.

Privatisation is a key part of sustaining an economy's well-being as it taps both the expertise and capital beyond the public sector. When pursuing privatisation, the state needs to assess the state of the economy and the relative maturity of each sector, i.e. identify sectors where state involvement continues to be catalytic.

Next, the industry structure and competition framework are key considerations. Is the sector large enough to provide scope for both state and private actors to compete meaningfully? Are current SOEs too dominant? Should there be a refinement of the competition rules before privatisation takes place?

The availability of private capital, be it local or in the form of FDIs, is key to a successful divestment exercise. Are capital markets deep and wide enough especially for bigger offerings? Equally important is the capacity of the private sector to provide the necessary expertise to run the business. Is there a need to build a talent pool first?

How to Steward and Transform

Governments deciding on how to steward SOEs to good effect would do well to adopt the following guiding principles.

Define Clearly Authority and Accountability

There should be no doubt as to who the Shareholder is. Equally important is spelling out clearly who would appoint or influence the appointment of board members and senior management. Unless absolutely necessary, ownership should **not** be vested in the (national) regulator. It is however the established practice in many countries to park an SOE under the relevant regulator. Doing so is just availing the SOE as a convenient policy implementation tool.

The SOE's very existence will always be subordinate to the policy priorities. The inevitable conflation of roles of the state as both regulator and capital provider will mean that the regulator's priorities will always prevail. Take for example a political quest towards cheaper electricity tariffs to ensure success of a re-election. Typically, the regulator will just lean over to instruct the energy SOE to effect lower tariffs. If the enterprise is however not owned by the state-cum-regulator, the conversation will be very different. The efforts at, say, driving productivity would not simply be nullified by a mere stroke of the political pen to lower tariffs.

Is board and management drawn from a common pool of civil servants, or worse still, is the stint at the SOE part of career development? Where there is no ownership or sense of responsibility for the fate of the SOE, there will be no pulling in the same direction.

Who are the stakeholders? Where there is a monopoly, there is a tendency to take the public for granted, an oft cited example being municipal bus services where there is no concept of service standards. All stakeholders receiving public services should be identified and their needs addressed accordingly.

All governments attempting a transformation of their SOEs should begin by tackling these questions at the very minimum. They should then endeavour to make the following political moves and take the relevant policy decisions.

Set Appropriate Political Signature

Given that issues around SOEs are always highly politicised, top-level support for both the transformation and continual stewardship is an absolute must.

China recognised this back in the early 2000's and established the State-owned Assets Supervision & Administration Commission (SASAC), which reported directly to State Council. In Singapore, Temasek Holdings was established in 1974 to hold all government-linked companies (GLCs) under the Minister for Finance. The Elected President's responsibility for direct oversight as part of Preservation of Past Reserves serves as a check and balance against a rogue government.

Nominate Change Agent

The need to identify clearly the change agent, for any restructuring or transformation, is of paramount importance. The Singapore Ministry of Trade & Industry undertook the energy industry restructuring — a separation of roles from generation to distribution to retailing, which included the definition of the competition framework and regulations, while the generating companies (gencos) were transferred over to Temasek Holdings before being divested over time.

Here, Temasek Holdings is the designated change agent for the gencos. Temasek led the review as part of its ongoing role as a shareholder, taking into account any regulatory changes or industry restructuring while imposing commercial, financial discipline before the eventual divestment. In fact, this does not apply only to the gencos. Separately, many Temasek portfolio companies are listed entities which are themselves subject to the rigours of being public companies. In short, they are subject to the same commercial standards as the rest of the privately owned businesses.

Disallow Conflation of Roles

Governments should resolutely disallow conflation of roles or exercise of political influence over SOEs. There is a very real temptation as regulators typically can and will influence without needing any ownership legitimacy. The government holding company should deal with the different regulators at arms' length, as any private sector operator would. Any change in regulation that leads to unfavourable economics would be properly and professionally debated upon and challenged, if need be. For instance, when the Singapore government wanted to accelerate the liberalisation of the telecommunications market in the early 2000s, for which Singtel had already been granted a licence to build and operate the infrastructure, the government had to compensate the company more than S$600 million.

Politics Around SOEs

Transformation of state enterprises is a long and arduous task, mainly because it is always a political journey. Moreover, as political parties these days may not last many terms, there is neither continuity nor priority given to any long-term transformational effort.

Bloated and Unwieldy

The plight of many a government can be characterised by a potent mix of factors. Social considerations loom large as SOEs usually employ massive numbers of people and are usually so heavily unionised that retrenchments are virtually impossible. Moreover, political concerns are heightened as many SOEs have either ballooned into national giants that simply cannot be allowed to fail or are providing essential services for which there is a political cost to any disruption.

Poor Performance

Most SOEs flounder because they are mere policy tools of their regulator-cum-shareholder or from a lack of proper corporate governance or a lack of accountability for performance. Ultimately, SOEs succeed or fail depending on the political will that governments have, to take hard decisions to define Key Performance Indicators clearly and then to deal with under-performance resolutely.

Nest for Corruption

More critically, SOEs in many countries are unfortunately also where corruption has been festering on an increasing scale over time. Substantial vested interests, usually involving political leaders, will take a long time to dismantle, if at all.

Revenue collections are inherently difficult to raise, least of all taxes, given the tough competition for Foreign Direct Investments (FDIs). Resorting to taking on more national debt has led many countries to grief. There is therefore a strong case to tap private sector capital and to collaborate on the larger projects. Collaboration is not without its challenges as this is where corruption has become rampant in many countries, especially given the big ticket sizes involved. To circumvent this and reduce vulnerability to corruption, many countries have adopted transparent procurement and project execution processes.

Towards Fiscal Health

In many countries, subsidies are usually commonplace for certain public goods even though they can accumulate into a huge fiscal burden, if not a curse over time. Politically speaking, subsidies, once given, are almost impossible to be reduced, let alone done away with.

However, subsidies pale in comparison to bailouts, which may not always be the consequence of a cyclical downturn. An increasingly bloated SOE, purportedly of national importance, could easily present the need for a bailout, when the day of reckoning is here. Think of the national airlines that repeatedly get bailed out, come what may.

It is difficult enough balancing the budget in an era where socialism ranks high and capitalism is considered evil. It is even tougher striking the balance when subsidies would not go away and a government is under pressure to rescue iconic SOEs to save jobs and national pride.

Sustainability is everything. Efficient, effective and commercially viable SOEs would constitute a strong underpinning for the economy at large. Such SOEs do not just happen; there needs to be sufficient political will to undertake massive transformation from time to time.

Reflections

State enterprises are often critical enablers of growth of developing economies. They form a repository of expertise that serves the national good.

For many emerging economies where there are no FDIs forthcoming in the earlier stages, state enterprises clearly play an important strategic role.

In many countries, the problem with troublesome state enterprises lies in the lack of discipline and political will over time to scrutinise their strategic relevance and subject their operations to commercial or financial discipline. Many become bloated after repeated bailouts/financial support, which is the reality we have today.

What sort of SOEs should we aspire to nurture? Any transformation will be long and tedious, but it must always begin with the political will to want to restructure. Only with SOEs functioning efficiently, effectively and purposefully can governments hope to lower the risk of costly bailouts.

It is almost impossible to avoid off-cycle bailouts, but it is the government's responsibility that when such an eventuality materialises, a good example being the Covid-19 pandemic's stalling of the global economy, it will have as much resources as it can muster. Far too much precious resources are currently being frittered away by poorly mandated and badly run state enterprises, leaving very little for genuine restructuring efforts.

There is evidence that increasing amounts of financial resources are being deployed towards politically convenient, if not populist responses.

The next chapter discusses how the curse of populism or short-termism is plaguing governments the world over, leading some to deliberately conflate their different roles towards political ends. Meanwhile, changing expectations *vis-à-vis* state enterprises and social services are emerging as a genuine challenge to even the longer-sighted politicians.

CHAPTER 5
WHEN POLITICS DOMINATE

Chapter 5

When Politics Dominate

Prior to the Covid-19 pandemic triggered crisis, political parties had already been living and dying by the ballot box. Many may not last more than a term, explaining the oft seen eagerness by politicians to pander to short-term demands by the electorate. Emblematic of the pace of technological advances, gratification has to be immediate. This had led some political leaders to act in uncharacteristic ways or abandon long-established economic principles.

In attempting to meet more immediate preferences, some governments consciously conflate their multiple roles as regulator and capital provider. The Chinese government considered the eradication of widespread corruption among the state-owned enterprises (SOEs) to be top priority and acted resolutely. Others rank social priorities above all things else. Providing employment for the masses, especially within the lower income segments, is a burden that many governments carry, to the detriment of the state enterprises that are used as the policy execution means, say within the railways sector.

What's perhaps the most challenging conundrum for many governments is the shifting expectations of the public. This could take the form of expectations of the design and public amenities that state-provided housing should have. Or a shift in the extent of desired state ownership of certain businesses, toggling between essential services and an uneven playing field. Over time, as to whether the government should begin divesting as many businesses as possible can purely be an emotional debate that swings back and forth.

The Covid-19 pandemic crisis has put paid to such healthy debate or even conflated the various roles that the state should play. All at once, the government now has to address issues of polarisation by class, stem immigration flows, plug gaps in healthcare services and most of all, provide the necessary relief to staunch spiking unemployment and stimulus to get the economy going again. Should an important election be imminent, populism would rear its ugly head (again) or worse still, be justified in some places.

Long Arm of the Government

Populism is commonplace these days. Politicians live and die by the ballot box. Their tenure is typically a term of 4–5 years. This gives perfect meaning to the old adage "make hay while the sun shines". In practice, it means extending the already long arm of the government into every conceivable sphere of influence, be it in the government machinery or the business and social communities at large. It means scoring quick wins so that re-election is assured. Unfortunately, in many countries, it also means lining one's pockets when the opportunity arises. In sum, it means short-termism in every sense of the description, from policy formulation to execution to immediate gains for the stakeholders that matter, including of course the voting public.

It is a vicious cycle that the world can do without. What incentive is there for a political party to plan long term for the economy when it might not be around to take the credit when their fruits of their labour become visible? Or worse still on the flip side, which politicians would push for tough labour restructuring in a bid to enhance employability in a fast-changing economy?

When countries have to adopt austerity measures as a condition for aid from the multilateral banks, the politicians in charge frequently pay the price when they do precisely what is needed. This is the plight of Portugal's ex-Prime Minister Pedro Passos Coelho (2009–2014), who diligently formulated and executed austerity measures. He lost at the polls despite doing the responsible thing.

Examples of populism abound. That is not to understate the tremendous pressure that many political leaders now face especially when the state coffers run dry. We have witnessed many previously strong leaders being re-elected either on a laser-thin majority or with an inability to form a properly functioning coalition government. Their work ahead is unfortunately all cut out — an impossible task of getting agreement on anything.

Firstly, to govern properly under a coalition arrangement, there would be active horse-trading for cabinet positions and, ultimately, a compromise on political leanings and national priorities. This will essentially lead to a race to please as many voters as possible. Nationalism is often a popular emotional theme.

Example 5.1: Shipyard at Brittany — Preparing for Stormy Seas

It all began on a harmless enough note — the financial failure of a major shareholder of France's core asset in large-scale shipbuilding. When an Italian state enterprise became the sole bidder, alarm bells started ringing, triggering populist calls to nationalise the facility. After prolonged, tough negotiations, the transaction now has another hurdle to overcome — anti-trust concerns.

President Macron of France is well-known to be pro-EU and pro-globalisation, essentially a free-marketeer. It therefore came as a surprise in July 2017 when he acted somewhat out of character. President Macron intervened[1] in the sale of a major shipbuilding facility at Saint-Nazaire in Brittany to an Italian state-owned enterprise, Fincantieri, purportedly to *"defend France's strategic interests in shipbuilding and security issues"*. The nationalisation is meant to be temporary.

For the record, Fincantieri was then Europe's biggest boat-builder and a rival to the Saint-Nazaire shipyard, which is the only one in France with facilities large enough to build aircraft carriers and was then owned by STX, a South Korean interest that recently went bankrupt. In fact, a South Korean court had already blessed the sale to Fincantieri, the sole bidder, for 79.5 million Euros.

What was it about this incident that contradicted his stand or underscored his challenges? By threatening to nationalise the shipyard, in a bid to avoid selling to the Italians, unless the Italians agreed to a 50–50 joint venture, the President was essentially acting anti-EU, almost xenophobic.

Further, by using state ownership to control a strategic asset, when hitherto he had been known to be a free-marketeer, and at a time when French SOEs were already employing far more people than those in US and UK, the move smacked of populism.

The stated concern was ostensibly over the threat to France's sovereignty. President Macron was understandably concerned about job cuts and, ultimately, the impact on popular support. The shipyard directly employed 2,600 people and work for more than 4,000 others. There were real fears that jobs would be lost to Italy and technical know-how, to China,

---

[1] http://www.rfi.fr/en/economy/20170727-france-nationalise-shipyard-block-italian-bid-report, 27 July 2017; http://www.rfi.fr/en/economy/20170730-france-offers-italy-naval-shipbuilding-deal-shipyard-purchase-row, 30 July 2017.

on the back of a technology-transfer agreement with the China State Shipbuilding Corporation.

President Macron's position was clearly hard to defend as STX, a foreign (South Korean) company had owned 66 percent of this facility since 2008 anyway, albeit through a series of acquisitions in Aker Yards beginning with a 39 percent stake in 2007. In September 2017, after prolonged negotiations, and (indeed) a temporary nationalisation of the shipyard, Fincantieri settled for a half stake, with the French Naval Group and the French government holding the other half. And the name, for sentimental reasons, was reverted to Chantiers de l'Atlantique.

In January 2019, the EU's Competition Bureau agreed to review the proposed acquisition,[2] a transaction that the Commission considers "could harm competition at European and global level", particularly in the global cruise shipbuilding market. In October of the same year, the Commission registered preliminary competition concerns over an already concentrated and capacity-constrained market,[3] and the inability of large customers to counteract any risk of resultant price increases. A decision is pending as of 17 March 2020. Should the EU Commission object to the transaction, it remains for the French government to cough up the full 80 million Euros or more to fully nationalise the shipyard, again.

> *Strategic and security reasons may often require the sustained protestations on the part of the government when intervening in a corporate action involving foreign parties. The challenge is one of consistency of reason. It is also a question of being forthright about underlying concerns, say of massive job losses or loss of intellectual property.*

The effectiveness of using nationalism can take gigantic proportions when skilfully delivered. We are all too familiar with the ramifications of the US–China trade war on the global economy. The dispute which has led to four rounds of tariffs imposed by the US on some US$360 billion worth of Chinese goods, matched (not in full) by China's retaliatory imposition on more than US$110 billion worth of US products.[4] No one's holding the breath beyond the "phase one" deal signed in January 2020.

---

[2] https://ec.europa.eu/commission/presscorner/detail/en/IP_19_262, 8 January 2019.

[3] https://ec.europa.eu/commission/presscorner/detail/en/ip_19_6205, 30 October 2019.

[4] https://www.bbc.com/news/business-45899310, 16 January 2020.

Diversification of manufacturing capabilities has taken on heightened importance as has the re-alignment of supply chains.

Given the widespread impact of the trade war on the rest of the world, this is not something that can be summarised in a chapter; it's a huge topic that deserves an entire detailed discussion in itself.

Suffice it to say, the very objective of re-asserting the US' pre-eminence in all spheres is a simple and direct message that any American can understand. Or the exhortation to "buy American". Take for example how President Trump offered steel tariffs exclusion as a bargaining chip to Canada and Mexico on the new North American Free Trade Agreement (NAFTA) deal.[5]

The overall narrative is extremely important. It must take cognisance of the political expectations of the day — nationalism as in "buy local", importance of employment for low-skilled workers and villainisation of foreign contributors.

Little Appetite for Unpopular Policies

Secondly, these days there is very little appetite to implement tough unpopular policies. This can range from suspending an unpopular but fiscally justifiable Goods and Services Tax as in Malaysia,[6] to lethargy at a much-needed curtailing of subsidies to back-tracking on toll charges for a highway built under the Public–Private Partnership arrangement.

Example 5.2: The Road is Long, with Many a Winding Turn

Governments of emerging economies are frequently confronted with the real challenge of funding their infrastructural project ambitions. These typically run the gamut from transportation systems to schools to hospitals to public housing. The bigger ticket items tend to be concentrated in transport infrastructure,

---

[5] https://www.bloomberg.com/news/articles/2018-03-06/steel-tariffs-transform-into-nafta-chip-as-trump-plays-dealmaker, 6 March 2018.

[6] https://www.channelnewsasia.com/news/asia/malaysia-gst-no-reason-to-reintroduce-the-tax-mahathir-11980480, 8 October 2019.

particularly stretches of roads and highways over a large land expanse to connect communities to economic centres. The high capital expenditure challenge is compounded by the inherent difficulty of projecting usage trends or consumer demand. Many a public–private collaboration will end up in grief owing to poor conceptualisation or inaccurate projection or bad politics or all of the above.

Three decades ago, Vietnam was one of the poorest countries in the world. From 2000 to 2015, Vietnam emerged as a rising star, boasting an average GDP growth rate of 6.9%. It comfortably clocked in at 7% in 2019,[7] placing it among the fastest growing economies in the world. Such growth momentum has been underpinned by significant resources needed to meet the growing demand from its population of 95.5 million people for infrastructure services. To relieve the strain on limited public coffers and reduce budget deficits, the Build–Operate–Transfer (BOT) model, a form of Public–Private Partnership (PPP), has become very popular in attracting private investment to bridge the financing gap required for sustainable development in Vietnam.

Teething Problems Aplenty

As is typical of BOT projects, the Vietnamese government would contract a private company to build and operate a project — for example, a section of a highway or a new highway bridge — in exchange for a stipulated concession to collect tolls or fees from the commuting public, usually via pre-agreed toll booth locations. The developers will retain all revenues from the project before transferring ownership to the government at the end of the concession.

As of December 2017, there were 88 toll stations on Vietnamese highways and expressways installed by investors under BOT schemes to facilitate toll collection.[8] BOT investments, especially in transport infrastructure ventures, tend to achieve only middling success; in the case of Vietnam, considerable problems abound. Implementation revealed major obstacles for all stakeholders, including excessive imposition of fees and

---

[7] World Bank national accounts data, and OECD National Accounts data files.

[8] "Vietnam reviews toll road after rare protests", *The Straits Times*, 8 December 2017, https://www.straitstimes.com/asia/se-asia/vietnam-reviews-toll-road-after-rare-protests.

unreasonable positioning of toll booths, among others, which have aroused indignation among users.

Political Pressure from Protests

First opened on August 1, 2017, the Cai Lay toll station in the province of Tien Giang has become one of the most controversial BOT projects in Vietnam. Investors had spent VND1 trillion (over US$43 million) on a project to re-asphalt 26.5 km of a highway and build a new bypass stretching 12 km around a local town.[9] Barely four months later, Prime Minister Nguyen Xuan Phuc was forced to intervene, instructing the suspension of the toll station following a series of staged protests by local truck drivers for its unfair location, repeatedly paralysing the toll station's operations.

The toll station came under fire for being inappropriately located such that a fee is collected regardless of the route chosen by drivers, rather than only from drivers wanting to use the new bypass. As part of the protest, drivers came up with various ways of expressing their disapproval of the toll fees, from paying in small notes to blocking the roads, most of which have resulted in major tailbacks. Drivers took to using VND200 (US$0.01) and VND500 notes, the smallest denominations in local currency, to pay the VND25,000 (US$1.50) to VND140,000 toll fees, forcing staff to spend a lot of time counting their payments, thus creating long delays on the highway on many days.[10] Many drivers even put the small notes into bottles to create further difficulties for the toll station staff.[11]

With all the lanes effectively blocked when the money was being counted, traffic was jammed for hours. At times, the toll station had to be closed several times a day to allow all the vehicles through.

Following an urgent meeting between the Prime Minister, the Ministry of Transport (MOT) and leaders from the Tien Giang province, a decision

---

[9]Loan, D. "Vietnam to reopen controversial tollgate on southern highway", *Vietnam Express International*, 17 January 2019, https://e.vnexpress.net/news/news/vietnam-to-reopen-controversial-tollgate-on-southern-highway-3869296.html.

[10]*Ibid.*

[11]"Prime Minister requests temporary halt of controversial tollgate", *Dantri International*, 5 December 2017, http://dtinews.vn/en/news/024/54133/prime-minister-requests-temporary-halt-of-controversial-tollgate-.html.

was made to halt all operations at the station until both the local and central governments can finalise a plausible, alternative solution.[12]

Re-opened with Several Concessions

Closed for more than a year following protests, the Cai Lay toll was scheduled to re-open in March 2019 with lower toll charges. The MOT announced in January 2019 that the fee for cars under 12 seats and trucks under two tons was to be more than halved from VND35,000 to VND15,000 and toll fees for other auto types were also reduced proportionally.[13] Meanwhile, the MOT granted residents living within a radius of 10 km from the toll gate a waiver of the toll fees, up from the previous 5 km radius.[14]

In return, the concession period for toll collection was more than doubled from 7 years to 15 years and 9 months. Despite these concessions, the Tien Giang's transport department continued to receive more than 500 petitions from locals, asking that their vehicles be exempted from paying toll altogether.[15]

Bidding Process under Scrutiny

Further highlighting the need to address shortcomings in BOT projects, the government called for a review and audit of the entire investment and implementation of contracts. Inspection conclusions revealed some recurring and grave errors that BOT road projects have committed, such as the arbitrary appointment of investors without a bidding process; investment decisions inappropriately and inconsistently made vis-a-vis the country's master plan, wrong calculation of investment needed; inaccurate prediction of the traffic flows and others, affecting the viability of projects.

According to the National Assembly, Vietnam's standard distance between toll stations is 70 km, but in reality there are stations every 62 km,

---

[12]"Vietnam orders suspension of controversial tollbooth amid driver protests", *Radio Free Asia*, 4 December 2017, https://www.rfa.org/english/news/vietnam/tollbooth-12042017155839.html.

[13]Loan, D. "Reopening of controversial tollgate in Vietnam delayed", *Vietnam Express International*, 24 March 2019, https://e.vnexpress.net/news/news/reopening-of-controversial-tollgate-in-vietnam-delayed-3898873.html.

[14]*Ibid.*

[15]*Ibid.*

some even as close as 15 km apart.[16] In addition, no bidding process for the selection of contractors was carried out for more than 70 of the BOT projects implemented so far. Some appointed had limited financial capabilities and failed to meet project requirements.[17]

Disruption to Infrastructure Roll-Out

Since the controversy over the Cai Lay project, 39 other projects have had tolls reduced, and 14 other road-upgrading projects have come to a halt.[18] The problems have brought about revenue losses to many BOT operators, with some even facing risk of bankruptcy. Noting that the state budget could only finance 11% of the funding needed for transport investment projects from 2016 to 2020, Transport Minister Truong Quang Nghia affirmed that the BOT model would remain highly relevant to infrastructure development in Vietnam.[19]

Essentially, the scheme would require better oversight and a consistent legal framework for the investment model. The key to success in these projects lies in the ability of the state to impose strict selection criteria on investors for projects and appropriate management measures to ensure transparency, especially in the collection of toll fees. Furthermore, imposing strong sanctions on any violation in BOT projects or even blacklisting violators can help improve the overall efficiency of project planning and implementation. In the long run, however, governments should aim towards a more sustainable PPP structure where the need for intervention or granting of concessions can be minimised.

Infrastructural development is rife with conceptualisation, funding and post-completion execution challenges. Predictability of government behaviour and a sense of equity would be critical

---

[16]Chinh, G. "Northern Vietnam highway blocked in protest against toll", *Vietnam Express International*, 12 June 2019, https://e.vnexpress.net/news/news/northern-vietnam-highway-blocked-in-protest-against-toll-3937273.html.

[17]"Lack of transparency rife in BOT, BT projects", *Viet Nam News*, September 2017, https://vietnamnews.vn/society/393499/lack-of-transparency-rife-in-bot-bt-projects.html.

[18]"Build-operate-transfer ventures look for boost", *Vietnam Investment Review*, 26 June 2019, https://www.vir.com.vn/build-operate-transfer-ventures-look-for-boost-68816.html.

[19]"Transport sector seeks a smooth road for BOT investment", *Vietnam Law Magazine*, 30 June 2016, http://vietnamlawmagazine.vn/transport-sector-seeks-a-smooth-road-for-bot-investment-5418.html.

> *success factors for potential private sector participants. Certain public amenities tend to be easily politicised. The government needs to be able to resist the temptation of giving in to the demands of the masses. When contracts are no longer sacrosanct, sovereign risk will be introduced which ultimately will exact a higher overall investment cost.*

All said, we should recognise and accept that, to govern effectively, the government must be all-pervasive in as constructive a manner as can be. The long arm of the government, when extended in a nimble and supportive way, can yield the economy, and ultimately society, substantial lasting benefits.

Traditional Roles of Government

What exactly is the role of government in business? Does it wind up being a friend or foe? One can never have a truly satisfying nor complete discussion of the role of government in business nor be able to get away with certain pronouncements for too long. This is an evergreen debate, across economies both big and small, mature and emerging, resource-rich and resource-poor.

Infrastructure Development

At one end of the spectrum, there are clearly areas where state participation is expected or even welcomed; in infrastructure, this is without dispute. Typically, a long lead time is required so a responsible government must plan way ahead for the kind of roads, highways, ports, schools, hospitals that an economy would need.

Infrastructure development is extremely capital intensive. As of 2019, projections of the capital required to build new or repair existing infrastructure reached trillions and were climbing, with the shortfall estimated at US$15 trillions.[20] The sad truth is that the price tag is usually beyond

---

[20] https://www.weforum.org/agenda/2019/04/infrastructure-gap-heres-how-to-solve-it/, *World Economic Forum*, 11 April 2019.

what an economy can afford. As is typical, fast-growing emerging economies require a massive amount of infrastructure, all at the same time. Infrastructure is required for growth, which in turn can fuel the building of yet more infrastructure.

The longer the lag in development and maintenance of infrastructure, the more impossible the task. Even developed economies like the United States, which built an excellent highway system decades back but left it for too long, now find catching up such a breathless task. Ditto the United Kingdom.

Healthcare Coverage

Healthcare is another area where state participation is the only viable norm, appropriately classified as a public good in most countries. Governments are expected to ensure that either national healthcare insurance is in place or there is a sufficient network of healthcare facilities to meet the needs of the bulk of the population, especially the poor, or better still, they fulfil both. Ultimately, the goal is that the public has access to a minimal, acceptable level of healthcare services, at affordable rates.

Longer life expectancy changes some of the underlying planning parameters — advances in healthcare have contributed to this increase in life expectancy but which in turn also requires higher spending to sustain improvements. The reality is that the bulk of the healthcare dollars are spent at the tail end of one's life. Likewise, rising affluence raises expectations of the quality of healthcare. Hence, an ageing population like Singapore's would only serve to compound such trends.

Unlike infrastructure development, healthcare is more frequently politicised. In the US, it continues to be a major bipartisan concern. President Obama's healthcare reform which began in 2010 had been unravelled by President Trump since he took office in 2016. Understandably, it takes substantial effort, maybe even more, to undo the earlier planned reforms, essentially repealing the Affordable Care Act.[21]

All said, public policy changes, in such an important area as healthcare where the government is expected to play a key driver role, will have extensive implications for the private sector participants.

---

[21]"Obamacare: Has Trump managed to kill off Affordable Care Act?", https://www.bbc.com/news/world-us-canada-24370967, 29 March 2019.

Traditional Fiscal Management

The traditional roles of Government revolve around the planning and management of the national budget and ensuring fiscal soundness.

For strategic and security reasons, the state typically regulates a broad range of essential services like defence, public transportation and education. In fact, in circumstances where there is market failure, the state winds up providing some of these essential services itself.

As the steward of the national economy, the state also undertakes the development of targeted sectors, directing resources to promote growth, both domestic and overseas. This is particularly relevant to a small economy like Singapore.

Provider of Capital

The second cluster of roles revolves around the provision of capital which is most widely manifested as SOEs. This may be for the protection of strategic interests, for public policy reasons or where there is market failure such as building infrastructure like high-speed rail across vast stretches of land or any project that requires heavy capital outlay or involves a long gestation period.

Many governments also act as a catalyst for new industries or for the nurturing of local champions into regional/global leaders. At the other end of the spectrum is irregular participation during a crisis, in the form of bailouts of too-big-to-fail national icons.

Conflation of Roles

The wearing of many hats can obviously breed confusion and encourage a conflation of roles when politically convenient. Where a state does not consciously define and discharge its various roles clearly, the blurring of edges will confuse all stakeholders concerned when a conflict arises. Very often, this arises not from a lack of clarity but a sheer lack of discipline to differentiate conflicting roles.

Many governments conflate roles for policy execution convenience — such as the common habit of directing a state-owned electricity-generating entity to lower tariffs when the economy is not doing well.

To be fair, the public is often equally guilty of imposing on the state the expectation of a conflation of roles. This was particularly evident during the whole series of bailouts during the Global Financial Crisis in 2008–2009, across many countries (US/EU) and industries (banks, insurance, mortgage corporations, auto companies and airlines).

In peace time, the expectation of the government to solve all employment issues is a given. Technology advances and disruption have shortened career cycles or even rendered certain jobs redundant. This has obviously made the task of ensuring employment and employability all the more challenging. However, it does not stop the public from thinking that the state can somehow weave some magic; there's always the SOE sector that can absorb unemployed persons.

Example 5.3: De-railing Modernisation Plans

SOEs in many countries are maligned for their bloated bureaucracy, archaic business practices and worst of all, for allowing corruption to fester. Yet ironically, the public frequently would expect these very same SOEs to step up to the plate and perform national service, in times of need. This could run the gamut from imposing subsidies on costs of public goods to providing employment for the masses. So what is a government to do? The Indian government's efforts in addressing the overwhelming response to a recruitment drive by the Indian railway is an example where the government, in trying to balance its conflicting goals, has conflated its roles, thus perpetuating the unfavourable positioning of SOEs in the economy.

In 2018, India's Railway Recruitment Board advertised some 90,000 vacancies for a variety of positions, from engine drivers to technicians to track inspection crews. Within a month, more than 25 million people submitted online applications from around the country.[22]

The recruitment drive coincided with efforts by Prime Minister Narendra Modi who, facing an election the following year, had been voted into power in 2014 on promises to re-ignite growth in the country and create 100 million jobs by 2022. This railway recruitment drive was the largest ever conducted by the government since Mr Modi took office.

---

[22] https://www.straitstimes.com/asia/south-asia/over-25m-apply-for-90000-rail-jobs-in-india, 31 March 2018.

Meanwhile, an estimated one million youths were entering the labour force each month.[23] Reflecting the intensifying challenge, India's jobless rate surged to a 15-month high of 6.1% in February 2018.[24]

The state-run railways organisation, which employed 1.3 million people in total, was already India's biggest employer and was in the midst of a US$130 billion modernisation plan. The jobs it opened to the public in its recruitment drive also included roles related to improving safety. Prior to this massive recruitment exercise, the government-run Indian railways, which are Asia's oldest rail network, had not been recruiting despite its age and related maintenance requirements. Insufficient investment in the railway had gradually led to poorly maintained railways that were not only inefficient but also dangerous.[25]

Moreover, in a landmark policy move, the railways is set to become the first government department to implement the 10 percent quota for the general category poor, providing around 23,000 jobs in the next two years.[26] This motion came around in a move just ahead of the 2019 elections, when the Union approved a 10% reservation in jobs and higher education for the "economically backward" sections in the general category.[27]

This move comes as part of a continued effort by the Indian government to lift its people out of poverty. However, therein lies the problem — the railway would essentially be obliged to reserve jobs and employ people with no skills or experience instead of taking on the appropriate number of skilled personnel. Here, the government is subordinating its role as a shareholder of the railway service to that of its social role of locating employment opportunities for the population.

If the government were to behave solely as a shareholder of the railway service, it would independently decide what headcount is needed to run a proper and efficient service and what skills these people would need. It would not simply take on more than needed, let alone people with no

---

[23] *Ibid.*

[24] *Ibid.*

[25] https://economictimes.indiatimes.com/industry/services/advertising/solutions-to-indias-railway-problem-agam-berry-quantified-commerce/articleshow/64278167.cms?from=mdr, 16 May 2019.

[26] https://economictimes.indiatimes.com/industry/transportation/railways/railways-to-provide-23000-jobs-under-10-quota-for-general-category-poor-in-2-years/articleshow/67660441.cms?from=mdr, 23 January 2019.

[27] https://economictimes.indiatimes.com/news/politics-and-nation/big-move-by-modi-government-ahead-of-polls-announces-10-quota-for-upper-castes-reports/articleshow/67418661.cms?from=mdr, 7 January 2019.

experience at all. It would calibrate its recruitment process to ensure appropriate orientation and training could be provided in a meaningful manner. As one observer put succinctly, "When you take 90,000 people in one shot, you simply don't have the training facilities".[28] The temptation to simply employ these jobless people under the railways, regardless of their ability to contribute to that SOE's operations, in the face of an impending election, was too great to resist.

The Indian railway was already suffering from a myriad of problems, the most pressing one being general inefficiencies. It lags on many parameters — in the previous fiscal period, it missed most of its targets, including electrification, track renewals, bridge works and doubling of tracks. In 2014–2015, projects worth Rs 6.5 lakh crore (US$94 billion) were stuck, including works related to doubling, new lines, gauge conversion, traffic facilities and electrification. This persisted into 2016.[29]

By design, the railways organisation was caught up between making itself a self-sufficient organisation and serving as a transport system for the poor, which meant no rise in passenger fares and new trains and routes being decided on for non-commercial reasons. The Indian railways network could only be self-sufficient if the railway were run as an efficient corporation with a healthy balance sheet that can be leveraged to raise debt.[30] Yet, with the new recruitment drive by the government, there is no telling what the employment of 90,000 new workers, many with no experience, will do to the balance sheet of the railway.

The government's decision to mount the enormous recruitment drive would be to perpetuate the inefficiencies associated with the rail service. There is also the possibility of commuters having to pay higher fares in the future just to cover the costs of this surge in employment without getting a safer and more efficient railway.

Most governments would probably have tried to balance its various ous roles and goals, regrettably usually with limited success When faced with such a situation, the tendency is to conflate its roles and possibly ending up fulfilling none of its goals satisfactorily, if at all. In fact, the government often ends up in a worse situation than before. It would be fair to say that the move by the

---

[28] https://www.straitstimes.com/asia/south-asia/over-25m-apply-for-90000-rail-jobs-in-india, 31 March 2018.

[29] https://www.businesstoday.in/current/policy/5-big-challenges-indian-railways-faces/story/237388.html, 17 September 2016.

[30] *Ibid.*

> *government to mount such a large recruitment effort for the railway was a politically convenient option. It was possibly hoping to kill two birds with one stone — alleviating the unemployment rate of the country and somehow also improving the efficiency and railway safety. Short-term populist politics these days regrettably mean that when the state faces competing goals, the temptation to accede to a social cause with immediate, visible results is a great one. This frequently will lead to the persistence of efficiencies in SOEs which are unfortunately often used as public policy execution means.*

If left unchecked, over time, more and more expectations of the social role the government plays may be layered on. It is not always unreasonable though, as is the case with runaway drug prices in many countries, including the US. The reality is that unless the state were to intervene, the consumer public at large would simply have to be unhappy price-takers. The small man simply has no chance with the big pharma Goliaths.

Example 5.4: Matters of the Heart and Wallet

Healthcare services have always been viewed as a public good. It is, after all, a service crucial to the well-being and welfare of the people. Drug prices have hitherto not attracted their due share of attention given their relatively "small and stable" part of the overall medical bill.[31] *No longer so, that assertion is being robustly challenged. When big pharma corporations continue crimping the public's ability to be well by charging runaway drug prices, the government is obliged to intervene. The state must curb any tendencies on the part of companies to exploit the lack of regulatory attention and profiteer, so as to ensure the well-being of the people remains within affordable reach.*

Medical care is a matter close to every citizen's heart. The reality and expectation is that it is ultimately up to the government to ensure healthcare remains affordable for everyone. The US has attempted to do this,

---

[31] https://www.politico.com/story/2016/07/obamacare-prescription-drugs-pharma-225444, 13 July 2016.

by implementing the Affordable Care Act (ACA), also known as Obamacare, in 2010. It aims to provide affordable healthcare for all, especially the low-income, uninsured and under-insured population. This initiative, however, has been hijacked by politics, with President Trump and the Republicans working hard to repeal it after the former's election in 2016. One thing that had bipartisan support, however, is the immense need to control drug prices. Both Democrats and Republicans agree that something needs to be done to reduce the drastic increases in drug prices.

To put into context, pharma companies tend to price drugs at "what the market would bear".[32] Not surprisingly, drugs are more expensive in America than anywhere else in the world. Take for instance the drug Harvoni, which cures hepatitis C and costs almost twice as much in America as in Switzerland.[33] Prescription drugs are now the fastest growing category of medical costs, with pharma companies charging exorbitant prices for new cures. Novel cancer therapies would cost an arm and a leg, running into hundreds of thousands. It's not just the prices of breakthrough drugs that are soaring — in their wake, prices of older medicines are being escalated at a drastic rate as well. The most audacious has to be that by Turing Pharmaceuticals for an AIDS drug, where prices soared an astounding 5,000% in 2016.[34]

Left Alone by ACA

ACA, for all its worth, had been unable to address this prescription drugs pricing problem. Its primary goal was to slow the rising cost of healthcare by taking steps to provide universal coverage — make health insurance more available and more affordable to those who need it most. One of the ACA objectives was to allow people with pre-existing conditions to afford preventive care, thereby reducing hospital visits and ultimately slowing the rise in healthcare costs. It also aimed to make health insurance more afford-able for those with the lowest incomes by subsidising the cost.[35]

---

[32] https://www.economist.com/leaders/2018/05/19/why-trumps-plan-will-not-cut-drug-prices, 19 May 2018.

[33] *Ibid.*

[34] https://money.cnn.com/2016/08/25/news/economy/daraprim-aids-drug-high-price/index.html, 25 August 2016.

[35] https://www.thebalance.com/what-is-obamacare-the-aca-and-what-you-need-to-know-3306065, 23 January 2020.

However, ACA left a gaping hole — there was no way of reining in the price of prescription drugs, albeit not from lack of trying. In return for a US$90 billion assistance to fund some of the proposed law's wide insurance coverage, the pharmaceutical industry remained largely unregulated.[36] The reason was simple — one of the priorities of the Obama administration then was to make a deal with the pharma lobby in order to secure the passage of ACA.

As of 2019, retail spending on prescription drugs alone in the US had reached an estimated high of US$360 billion, representing a seemingly tame annual rise of just under 5% but a hefty 36% cumulative surge since 2013.[37]

Part of the price surge was perhaps attributable to the design of the ACA. ACA required insurers to cover a wider array of benefits while prohibiting them from denying coverage based on pre-existing conditions, setting new rules regarding how insurers could set premiums. However, the catch was that insurers had to reflect the cost of healthcare in general. At the same time, limits were imposed on how much of a plan's revenue could be used for purposes such as marketing, administration and profits. As a consequence, insurers shifted more of the cost of drugs to patients than they do the cost of hospital or medical care, leading to patients bearing a bigger load of their drugs costs than their other healthcare services.[38]

Results of ACA

Despite this, ACA actually helped reduce healthcare costs for the average American. In 2017 alone, health expenditures were $650 billion lower than projected, translating to under 18 percent of GDP — all while expanding health coverage to more than 20 million previously uninsured Americans. For the average citizen, healthcare spending in 2017 was $2,000 less per person than it was projected to be. Furthermore, for the 176 million Americans who have private employer-sponsored insurance, their lower premiums averaged just under $1,000 per person. The ACA lowered family health insurance premiums as well, saving about $4,000 per family.[39]

---

[36] https://morningconsult.com/2016/03/24/why-prescription-drugs-arent-part-of-obamacare/, 24 March 2016.

[37] https://www.statista.com/statistics/184914/prescription-drug-expenditures-in-the-us-since-1960/, 9 August 2019.

[38] https://morningconsult.com/2016/03/24/why-prescription-drugs-arent-part-of-obamacare/, 24 March 2016.

[39] https://www.statnews.com/2019/03/22/affordable-care-act-controls-costs/, 22 March 2019.

Despite rising drug prices, the ACA did manage to reduce the overall healthcare burden for Americans, and for public spending, to the tune of a staggering US$2.3 trillion between 2010 and 2017.

Repeal of ACA

However, with the election of President Trump in 2016, Republicans claimed that ACA was imposing too much costs and regulations on businesses and needed to be repealed. It should however be noted that since the implementation of ACA, jobs in the healthcare sector rose by at least 9 percent, and 2.6 million jobs could potentially be lost if ACA were repealed.[40] Till today, except for the repeal of the individual's mandate, the insurance market has adjusted and attrition has been manageable.[41]

Since he was elected into office, President Trump has directed cuts in budgets and advertisements, and funding for the "navigator" programme, which trained individuals or organisations to help individuals sign up for insurance through ACA. Perhaps most materially, the Trump administration ended cost-sharing reduction payments. This meant that insurance companies that covered lower income ACA patients no longer would get these payments from the government, which in turn led to an increase in insurance premiums to compensate for the loss.[42] If ACA were successfully repealed altogether, nearly 54 million Americans under age 65 could face coverage limitations.[43]

Shifting Focus to Drug Prices

In the midst of putting the ACA to bed which involved a lengthy legal process, President Trump chose to focus on runaway drug prices instead of healthcare coverage. He sought to alleviate public concerns by campaigning to reduce drug prices, including suggestions to make it easier to import drugs from abroad, and the price regulation of drug companies to lower prices for Americans.

---

[40] https://www.bbc.com/news/world-us-canada-24370967, 29 March 2019.

[41] https://www.vox.com/policy-and-politics/2020/1/6/21052264/obamacare-still-in-effect-mandate-gone-voxcare, 6 January 2020.

[42] https://www.bbc.com/news/world-us-canada-24370967, 29 March 2019.

[43] https://finance.yahoo.com/news/obamacare-is-working-194659034.html, 22 November 2019.

Some of his ideas are welcome, including the proposal to frustrate the attempts of pharmaceutical companies at postponing the arrival of generic versions of their drugs after patents expire. However, some, like the idea of making foreign governments pay more for drugs to reduce the burden on US by extending periods for patents on American-made drugs, would need a lot more persuasion.

Whatever the initiatives, the issue of drug prices is one that merits serious consideration and planning. There was the perennial question of bargaining power with the pharma giants. Medicare, the health scheme for the elderly, is unable to barter directly with drug companies regarding prices and products it has to provide by law. Intermediaries that sit between the makers and takers of drugs, who in theory are supposed to negotiate for lower prices on behalf of insurance companies who will then pass the savings on to consumers, have vested interests. They are blocked by a complex and largely confidential system of rebates on published prices which has driven prices up for patients who pay out of their own pockets and see little of the discounts.[44]

When Obamacare was implemented, it brought about extensive changes to how healthcare insurance was underwritten and services delivered, towards a universal coverage objective. However, it left drug prices alone. When President Trump assumed office, he sought to unravel ACA and tackle runaway drug prices. Without concentrating negotiating power against the powerful pharma lobby, by fiat if necessary, a lot remains to be seen as to how successful his war would be.

At the end of the day, the paying public is the one who suffers the most. With no control over as sensitive and impactful an issue as drug prices that directly impacts their wallets, they have no choice but to look to the government for help. The government has an important role to play in this — not just a social responsibility to ensure citizens get affordable healthcare but also a fiscal responsibility to ensure that all stakeholders can sustain themselves and are not at the losing end of any policy change. Admittedly, this is a tough balance to strike, one that not too many governments are successful at doing.

---

[44] https://www.economist.com/leaders/2018/05/19/why-trumps-plan-will-not-cut-drug-prices, 19 May 2018.

Containing Corruption

Managing overlapping roles requires a consistent, strategic focus for policy formulation which must be accompanied by deft implementation and a huge reservoir of patience and commitment to purpose. In many cases where the conflict is systemic, there is really no other actor but the state to address the challenges. Take corruption in SOEs, a reality which plagues many countries. From Brazil to South Africa to India to China, governments are having to grapple with the dominant role that SOEs play in the economy and the festering corruption that is entrenched within the SOEs and across various ranks of public officials.

Operation Car Wash is perhaps a good illustration of how deep-rooted the problem is in Brazil. When the scandal unfolded in 2015, the unprecedented web of corruption that emerged was mind-boggling.[45] What began as a straightforward investigation into possible money laundering led to the uncovering of an illicit network involving foreign companies dealing with some US$5 billion of illegal payments. More critically, it exposed a culture of systemic graft in Brazilian politics and SOEs, no less the national oil company Petrobras.

China found itself with exactly the same predicament. President Xi Jinping decided that the Chinese government had to act resolutely and what transpired was perhaps the most extensive anti-corruption campaign in living memory.

Example 5.5: China — Getting rid of Tigers and Flies

It is a common phenomenon that state enterprises are the usual culprits of corruption. Corruption takes a long time to fester, but once entrenched, it becomes a systemic challenge. Meanwhile, China continues with her twin battles — eradicating corruption and restructuring the state enterprises.

The Chinese government's anti-corruption efforts since November 2012 are well documented. To put into context, 18 December 1978 marked the beginning of major economic reforms spearheaded by the late leader

---

[45] https://www.theguardian.com/world/2017/jun/01/brazil-operation-car-wash-is-this-the-biggest-corruption-scandal-in-history, 1 June 2017.

Deng Xiaoping.[46] Essentially, China opened up to the international community, established diplomatic relations anew and welcomed foreign investments, albeit in a calibrated fashion. Entrepreneurship and capitalism were in a way legalised, in stark contrast to the decades of suffering as a result of the self-imposed isolation. The result was an impressive eradication of poverty from a high of almost 90% in 1981 to a low of 2% by 2013; in other words, more than 800 million Chinese were lifted out of poverty! Coupled with this exploding prosperity however is the unwitting entrenchment of corruption into all levels of society in the form of bribes to government officials for favours or contracts.

With the SOEs dominating the economy, and therefore the most viable vehicles for perpetuating corrupt practices, the planned economic reforms were soon closely intertwined with the "vast fortunes that a privileged few" had amassed. The blatant inequality soon became untenable, hence the determination by the Chinese Communist Party (CCP) to stamp out corruption. To signal its resolve to minimise corruption, the anti-corruption campaign was formally launched at no less, the 18th National Congress in 2012. President Xi Jinping famously vowed that the authorities would go after "tigers and flies", referring to high-level officials and local public officials, respectively.

Economic Reforms towards a Market Economy

The anti-corruption efforts were being mounted at a time when many important national strategies were being implemented and efforts to reform the SOEs were still underway (since 2003).

In the following year, President Xi Jinping outlined a long-term plan to shift from a command economy to a mixed economy.[47] The economy would slowly transform as to depend less on government spending or SOEs to provide stimulus nor low-cost exports. It would instead intensify efforts at nurturing private investment, entrepreneurial innovation and promoting domestic consumption. Ultimately, the aspiration was towards a "Made in China 2025" plan which necessarily implied that advances in technology, aircraft engineering and green cars would be instrumental.

---

[46] https://qz.com/1498654/the-astonishing-impact-of-chinas-1978-reforms-in-charts/, 18 December 2018.

[47] https://www.thebalance.com/china-economic-reform-3305479, 8 August 2019.

Formation of SASAC a Milestone

There's no denial that the SOEs collectively have been accounting for the bulk of GDP and provide a substantial part of national employment. This brings the reform process of the SOEs to a head, despite commendable efforts at structural and governance reforms since the formation of a high-level State Council body, the State-owned Assets Supervision and Administration Commission (SASAC) in 2003. Amidst the massive formulation of shareholding and governance principles and financial policies, which were gradually rolled out to all cities, provinces and autonomous regions, there was a keen sense of the need to attract and retain talent at the SOEs. This would be a prerequisite before one can hope to see more efficient and effective SOEs.

Market Salaries to Retain Talent

Talent was needed at all levels, particularly at the board and senior management levels. What complicated the challenge was that the government departments and the SOEs were sharing the same pipeline of senior personnel for the longest time. SASAC had the unenviable task of trying to right-size this pipeline to the absolute minimum, comprising only the very top-level professionals who have aspirations beyond SOE leadership, into political roles. Some measure of this was reportedly achieved by the start of this decade.

Not surprisingly, as the private sector booms, the wage disparity between senior management at private companies and the SOEs soon became a yawning gap. This was untenable if SOEs were to hope to retain their own talent. Hence, SASAC had been gingerly moving the compensation packages towards market levels, especially where there were direct comparables.

Nailing Corruption at the Core

The swoop down on errant and corrupt senior guys within the public sector became entangled with rising unhappiness over the salaries of top SOE leaders. As a result, in 2015, some 18 SOE bosses had sizeable pay cuts,[48] bucking the industry trend for the private sector. Leaders at the five biggest

---

[48] https://www.scmp.com/news/china/policies-politics/article/1933836/pay-cuts-some-top-bosses-chinese-state-firms, 5 April 2016.

state-owned banks suffered the same fate. To put in perspective, leaders at some other SOEs actually received bigger pay checks.

Regardless, optics is everything. At a time when the SOEs desperately need to attract and retain talent, publicity on cuts would not be helpful to the cause. Worse still, many attempted to link the cuts to a corruption crackdown. In 2018, the Chinese government clarified that the wage reform for SOEs would be directly linked to operational performance.[49] This can be seen as an attempt to delink the two developments; all said, the ability of SASAC to move towards market-competitive salaries for leaders at the higher profile SOEs will clearly be constrained.

It is purely speculative as to whether the wage cuts at the SOEs were at all related to the anti-corruption drive. Nonetheless, it suffices to say that the anti-corruption drive that the Chinese government was assiduously implementing does embody a strong austerity element. Keeping SOE salaries low may help to cool tempers and reduce criticism of SOEs' performance. It is however uncertain what the derailment effect, on the initiative to make SOE wages competitive through market benchmarks, is. If the impact is one of returning to wage levels that are insufficient for talent retention like before, then the SOEs may continue to be a drag for SASAC.

Protection of the Small Businesses

Occasionally, the conflation of roles changes complexion over time or the developmental cycle. A socio-political norm across many economies is the protection of the small retailer, the mom-and-pop corner shop so to speak. This is undergirded by a fairly sound social and economic basis, if not local politics. Local entrepreneurship does not happen by chance, it has to be carefully nurtured so as to prevent small players from being swallowed up by foreign giants. This has justified some degree of regulatory protection in many markets and India is no different.

---

[49] http://english.www.gov.cn/policies/latest_releases/2018/05/25/content_281476160475444.htm, 25 May 2018.

Example 5.6: India's Passage towards Retail Liberalisation

It is the practice in many developing countries for the government to limit foreign influence in sectors where its local entities may otherwise be overshadowed by larger and better-funded players. Indigenous entrepreneurship may be snuffed out as a consequence. Restraints include rules that make it harder for foreign interests to command a major market share in the industry or regulations that boost local players' efforts to compete with foreign conglomerates. Brick-and-mortar retailing has hitherto been a protected sector in India and had some discernible success at keeping big international retail giants out. With an increasing volume of retailing migrating online, the government in India will accordingly regulate e-commerce along the same principles and with the same fervour.

The Indian e-commerce market is a sizeable one and can be expected to balloon in the next few years. At an estimated US$35 billion currently, growth will accelerate with revenues poised to exceed US$100 billion by 2022. The online retail and travel segments currently account for more than 90 percent share. The upside to such an expansion of the market can be found in the creation of more than one million jobs by 2023.[50]

Despite the numerous regulatory hurdles to playing in the domestic market, the reality is that India is simply too big a market to ignore. Its online market represents a new opportunity that is up for grabs among well-established e-commerce firms. Furthermore, with India opening itself up to foreign investments in retailing in recent years, foreign-owned e-commerce giants Amazon and Flipkart soon commanded the biggest influence in the market, offering products from clothing to electronic items.[51]

In 2018, US firm Walmart paid US$16 billion for a majority stake in Flipkart, an e-commerce website founded in 2007. By then, Amazon, an US e-commerce giant had already invested US$5 billion into the market, with plans for an additional US$2 billion injection into Amazon India.[52]

---

[50] https://www.straitstimes.com/asia/south-asia/new-e-commerce-rules-in-india-may-hit-amazon-and-flipkart, 28 December 2018.

[51] *Ibid.*

[52] https://www.cnbc.com/2019/02/05/amazon-how-india-ecommerce-law-will-affect-the-retailer.html, 4 February 2019.

Together, Amazon and Walmart controlled a substantial 70% of the Indian online shopping market.[53]

It didn't take the government long to put new e-commerce regulations in place in 2018, promptly putting a dent in the companies' influence in the market. This was an attempt by the government to level the e-commerce playing field for smaller, local operators in India.

The new e-commerce rules essentially sought to counter the tyranny of deep pockets and a massive scale of these giants to achieve uncompetitively low pricing levels, to the detriment of viability of the smaller players. Therefore, the rules were meant to curb practices like steep discounts that have been instrumental in helping Amazon dominate the US market and which were already being dished out to good effect in India. The rules prohibit foreign online retailers from making exclusive deals with companies to offer products that are not available elsewhere. They also prevent these platforms from selling products distributed by companies they have invested in, putting paid to Amazon's strategy of acquiring strategic stakes in local suppliers.[54] The government's stance is that these players should act as (neutral) marketplaces connecting buyers and sellers instead of having any equity stakes in companies whose products they sell, in short no captive sellers.

The changes in regulations are clearly aimed at dampening the influence foreign-owned e-commerce giants Amazon and Flipkart had on the Indian market and helping local retailers with a smaller market share. Up to then, these companies often struck exclusive deals with mobile phone companies like One Plus or Xiaomi to launch their products on their online platforms.

Not surprisingly, lobbying on both sides was intense. The Confederation of All India Traders, which reportedly represented more than 70 million local retailers, obviously had politics on its side. The entry of the American giants unnerved thousands of small, local traders, who said the massive discounts these giants often offered were putting them out of business. They also accused the foreign firms of predatory pricing, with the All India Online Vendors Association even filing a complaint with the Competition Commission of India against Amazon and Flipkart in 2018.[55] The new

---

[53] https://edition.cnn.com/2019/01/31/tech/amazon-walmart-india-ecommerce-restrictions/index.html, 1 February 2019.

[54] https://edition.cnn.com/2019/01/31/tech/amazon-walmart-india-ecommerce-restrictions/index.html, 1 February 2019.

[55] https://www.straitstimes.com/asia/south-asia/new-e-commerce-rules-in-india-may-hit-amazon-and-flipkart, 28 December 2018.

policy will give these small retailers the chance to compete fairly with the corporate giants. Customers who had turned to the online retailers for an abundance of variety and massive discounts will once again turn back to the local brick-and-mortar retailers as they will now have lesser options on online platforms with the new regulations.[56]

In contrast, foreign companies like Amazon and Flipkart will now have to look for alternative business models in the absence of leaning on local firms in which they hold an equity stake. The new rules will significantly impact the availability of products on these platforms in the short term as these sellers accounted for a minimum of 45–50% of sales on these platforms. Furthermore, the government denied requests from Amazon and Flipkart to defer the implementation of the new rules to buy the companies more time to comply. More than 400,000 items available on Amazon's site could instantly disappear in strict compliance with the new rules.[57] Amazon and Walmart lost a combined US$50 billion in market capitalisation when the policy came into force, on the back of a projected plunge in online sales of around US$46 billion by 2022.[58]

Ultimately, the overall impact of the new rules is unlikely to make the giants crumble. The new restrictions would affect about a third of the goods Amazon sells in the country; one estimate has the company losing US$250 million in sales. To put in perspective, Amazon is expected to generate US$280 billion in total revenue in 2019 so the loss in the Indian market would translate to only an immaterial 0.1 percent of the total.[59] While the government's intention is not to harm foreign investments in the country, it clearly has accorded higher priority to giving local entities the opportunity to become more active in the e-commerce space. This does not bode well for attracting foreign direct investments in the retail sector or the larger e-commerce space in the future as the regulatory interference has created great uncertainty and exacted a real financial cost.

With the restrictions placed on e-commerce giants, the retail sector at large is ironically likely to suffer. Smaller, local retailers may benefit

---

[56] https://www.mondaq.com/india/Consumer-Protection/775328/Modi39s-New-E-Commerce-Policy-2018-Impact-On-Online-Retail-Giants-Amazon-Flipkart-End-Consumers-And-Benefits-To-The-Local-Retail-Sector, 28 January 2019.

[57] https://www.cnbc.com/2019/02/05/amazon-how-india-ecommerce-law-will-affect-the-retailer.html, 4 February 2019.

[58] https://qz.com/india/1539834/amazon-flipkart-adapt-as-indias-new-e-commerce-rules-kick-in/, 4 February 2019.

[59] https://www.cnbc.com/2019/02/05/amazon-how-india-ecommerce-law-will-affect-the-retailer.html, 4 February 2019.

slightly, but as the provision of cashbacks will also be regulated, the incentive given to customers to shop more often from a said platform will be reduced, affecting the decision of the customer and ultimately resulting in less shopping demand by a majority of customers. The end of exclusive deals will also disadvantage customers. Ultimately, the restrictions placed upon the e-commerce sector might result in the limitation of a variety of goods, inefficiencies and a lack of innovation. Investors will be less likely to invest in entities over which they have no control over, and which do not guarantee profits like the giant corporations do, leading to less investments in the online retail sector.[60]

Amazon and Walmart made investments because of India's large retail market, but with regulation now posing huge risks, it may be difficult to get such giants to invest in the market again.

Perhaps in time to come, a relaxation of restrictions on e-commerce could transpire as the government did in 2012, when it relaxed its mandatory 30% domestic sourcing rule for single-brand companies opting for a majority investment, enabling Swedish furniture and home furnishing retailer IKEA to establish its first fully owned mega store covering 400,000 sq. ft. at Hyderabad. Even then, it was a long, laborious process but one with a beautiful opening day record of 40,000 customers in August 2018.[61] More importantly, it demonstrated the government's commitment to liberalise the retail sector.

The tightening of restrictions for the retail sector by the Indian government has its merits and deserves credit for protecting the local retail industry from being overshadowed by foreign corporate giants. However, such protection would also mean an inadvertent exclusion of foreign investment and the attendant improvement in the variety of goods and innovation in the industry. Perhaps, the Indian government could continue to explore a middle-of-the-road strategy so that foreign retail giants would not be turned away permanently.

---

[60] https://www.mondaq.com/india/Consumer-Protection/775328/Modi39s-New-E-Commerce-Policy-2018-Impact-On-Online-Retail-Giants-Amazon-Flipkart-End-Consumers-And-Benefits-To-The-Local-Retail-Sector, 28 January 2019.

[61] https://www.businesstoday.in/current/corporate/around-40000-people-visit-ikea-hyderabad-store-on-first-day-twitter-reacts/story/281216.html, 10 August 2018.

Shifting Expectations

A government may wilfully over-reach across its different roles to serve the larger good or for short-term populist reasons. In this regard, nothing is however more challenging and complicated than shifting expectations, especially of the public. Regrettably, under such circumstances, political instincts tend to gravitate towards immediate gratification. As a consequence, longer term goals may be sacrificed as politicians realistically have to live for the here and now; in other words, kick the can down the road and let somebody else worry about the future.

Every government managing the economy is like steering a big ship. Even for smaller economies, it can be extremely difficult to turn around or shift position overnight especially if it involves changes to the regulatory or competition framework or subsidy policy positions. In contrast, it doesn't take very much for the public to change its preferences. The Singapore government's public housing programme provides a striking example of the shifting expectations of the public whose heads it is seeking to provide a roof over.

Example 5.7: Housing the Masses in Differentiated Ways

What's public housing? If it's for the minority of low-income citizens who would not be able to afford their own homes for the foreseeable future, would basic units be sufficient? If it's for the masses, especially in cities with runaway property prices, then the challenge becomes increasingly complex and requires a long-term policy strategy.

By all accounts, Singapore's Housing & Development Board (HDB) is doing a good job of catering to the housing needs of around 80% of her resident population, with more than one million flats completed across 24 towns and three estates.

What's HDB's original mandate? Back in February 1960 when HDB was established, it was simply "to provide sanitary living conditions" to replace the then prevalent unhygienic slums and crowded squatter settlements.[62] To cope with the severe housing shortage as only 9% lived in

---

[62] https://www.straitstimes.com/singapore/housing/evolution-of-hdb-designs, 3 February 2020.

government flats,[63] the flats built then were predominantly simple basic units lined along a common corridor, forming long slab blocks. And lifts stopped only at intermediate floors.

Expectation of Better Quality Flats

Recount this mandate to any resident millennial today and you'll probably get quizzical looks as surely Singaporeans deserve better than that. Today, the variety of public housing options is, to put it mildly, impressive. It runs the gamut from smaller rental units to the full range of three-, four- and five-room flats, elderly friendly two-room Flexi units, as well as 3Gen flats that cater to multi-generational families. Through the 1970s and 1980s, rising affluence raised expectations of the quality of living spaces.

Expectations of Conducive Living Environment

Through the 1990s, expectations extended beyond individual flats to the larger living environment, that of town identity. Children's playgrounds, fitness corners and open spaces for community events became commonplace.

Gone are the slab blocks; the public was expecting more distinctive features for each new housing estate. They wanted a unique character to be associated with their estates. Soon, estates took the form of a harmony of low- and high-rise profiles and every new housing estate was conceptualised with a distinctive character, such as sloped roofs or heritage features, where relevant.

Partnership with Private Sector Operators

To the credit of HDB, through the decades, it has been proactively assessing the shifts in preferences and planning for living spaces that would best meet current, if not future needs. This was evident on several fronts — more creativity in design and taking cognisance of the desirability of privacy. HDB has boldly explored taller apartment blocks and incorporating creative features like a sky garden atop these developments or rooftop gardens above multi-storey carparks. Childcare and eldercare centres were added to take into account the routines of young families or multi-generational families. Likewise, greenery and spaces for community

---

[63] https://www.hdb.gov.sg/cs/infoweb/about-us/history, accessed 9 February 2020.

interaction were provided for offering relief from an otherwise "concrete jungle" ambience. In fact, community gardens promoting urban farming and, indirectly, neighbourly interaction sit well with aspirations towards sustainable food supply.

Another conscious policy was to enlist the participation of private sector architects and developers for the Executive Condominium (EC) Housing Scheme and the Design, Build and Sell Scheme (DBSS), introduced in 1995 and 2005, respectively. ECs are private housing introduced to meet the housing needs of citizens who aspire to own private properties but find them beyond their means. They offer similar design features and facilities as other private developments but come with initial eligibility and ownership restrictions similar to those for public housing, to make them affordable. On the contrary, DBSS flats are a type of public housing that are designed, built and sold by private sector developers, for those who prefer alternative options in design and finishes.

Meeting Social Aspirations

HDB has through the years centred its efforts squarely at meeting the housing aspirations of its target segment, which at more than 80%, ironically will be the masses, by most definition. It aims to do this in as timely a manner as possible. The shifts in expectations can sometimes outpace even the best of planning efforts, as was evident during the General Election of 2011.

This is often best described as work in progress as expectations frequently take on a different complexion as social norms change. To keep pace with these changing aspirations and ensure that different needs are met, HDB reviews its policies and schemes so that they remain relevant. For instance, extended families that wish to live with or near one another can benefit from the various mutual care and support policies and schemes that HDB offers, such as the Married Child Priority Scheme and the Proximity Housing Grant.

Commentators on the protests in Hong Kong over many issues, including the cost of housing, have pointed to the success of the Singaporean model. Were it so simple! Ramping up the scale of coverage itself would take time as unlike in Singapore, most of the land parcels, where construction of mass housing estates can proceed smoothly, are not in public hands. Reviewing the eligibility criteria to cover more people, determining the different flat types and pricing (assuming not just rental units) are individually non-trivial issues. It has taken Singapore decades for public housing to evolve to where it is, and one which promises to continue to present challenges.

> *Attempting to meet rising or shifting expectations in public housing requires long-term efforts and a commitment towards the mission. Often, the shifts can outpace what's realistically possible for the government to provide a viable, meaningful response. In such circumstances, trust in what the relevant housing authorities stand for or are mandated to do, becomes important. Consistency in public policy formulation and execution would also be essential towards quelling any unhappiness or even unrest.*

Nationalisation vs Privatisation

Another hot topic that routinely crops up in discussions within business circles is centred on the dominance of the government in business, specifically as SOEs. Arguments for and against both privatisation and nationalisation are well documented. They tend to come and go in seasons too. In good times whenever the public feels that money-grabbing private sector operators are getting away scot-free at their expense, there will be strong lobbies for nationalisation. Never mind the attendant inefficiencies and solve the immediate pricing issues first by the state regaining control.

Example 5.8: The Right Train of Thought

> *Railway services in the EU can be a contentious issue. Some countries seem to have mastered the ability of providing a good standard of service to passengers while keeping costs in check. Yet some others are constantly struggling to provide an acceptable rail service. Overall, it seems hard for the public at large to agree on the best modus operandi for public railway services, with opinion split between privatising railway services and nationalising the responsibility.*

A few countries in the EU, such as Switzerland and France, have not opened their railways to private operators. Most are in the process of doing so, while Britain's railway operations are largely privatised through a franchising system, albeit to franchises run by the Department of Transport.

A Difficult Journey in the UK

However, with escalating fare prices, track incidents and train delays, passenger dissatisfaction has been running high as there is no meaningful alternative, leading to calls to renationalise the British Rail. Formerly a nationalised industry, privatisation over several years from 1995 saw the industry broken up into 100 separate companies, leading to a complex contractual web of operation transactions between them. Spearheaded by Prime Minister John Major then, the privatisation was expected to ensure "greater responsiveness to the customer, and a higher quality of service and better value for money".[64]

The franchise model the British Rail operates on is basically dysfunctional. Passenger train operating companies are awarded on a franchise basis, with operators paying the highest premium to the government to win the right to operate train services on specific routes. The bid they place is based on the revenue each company projects they can earn from passengers after paying their premium. The issue is these operating companies would often overbid on the most optimistic assumptions in order to win a franchise but can walk away before their contract is up, because the penalties for failing to deliver are too low. Furthermore, this costly and time-consuming refranchising process is repeated every seven or eight years, preventing long-term planning and wasting precious resources. Renationalisation would end the operational and structural inconsistencies designed into the industry.[65]

A key concern for British passengers is that even though privatisation of the rail was supposed to lead to lower fares for passengers, prices have done just the opposite — they have been increasing ever since. Only 36% of fare revenue is regulated by the British government, and even then, fare increases are pegged to the higher retail price index (RPI) measure of inflation and not the lower consumer price index. Across all operators, standard-class unregulated fares have increased by nearly 30% in real terms since privatisation.[66] The onslaught of fare increases from an unforgiving formula served only to incense the British public further as they were already

---

[64] https://theconversation.com/nationalising-britains-railways-is-the-only-way-to-fix-chronic-problems-heres-why-88591, 17 January 2018.
[65] *Ibid.*
[66] *Ibid.*

paying the highest ticket prices in Europe for overcrowded and under-staffed trains.[67] Furthermore, direct government support was being given to private sector train operators if their revenues fell below expectations, meaning state subsidies remain high, along with fare prices.[68]

A key reason for this phenomenon is that several operators have the same parent companies behind them,[69] leading to reduced market competition and little of the increased quality of service and reduced fare prices privatisation of the British Rail had hoped to bring about.

Not surprisingly, the British public had been dissatisfied with the state of virtually nil competition and calling for renationalisation of the rail-ways — already 60% of Britons support renationalisation of the railways in a poll in January 2018. This came in the wake of timetabling issues over the past year, resulting in 43% of trains being delayed or cancelled each day by one operator.[70] Renationalisation would enable the state to aim at providing better service standards and regain control that government maintenance of the rail would bring about.[71]

Mixed Views across EU

Some countries in the EU support the idea of letting their railways remain nationalised as well, agreeing that it was still possible to have good rail services without liberalisation. For example, the French railway service has consistently remained one of the best in the EU even though it is not priva-tised. In support of remaining state owned, strikes have been carried out as railway workers protest against a planned liberalisation.[72]

Meanwhile, the new EU rules (the "fourth railway package")[73] will force state rail firms to open their tracks to private operators, in a bid to

---

[67] https://www.independent.co.uk/news/uk/home-news/trains-uk-railways-renationalise-countries-operators-companies-a9058961.html, 14 August 2019.

[68] https://theconversation.com/nationalising-britains-railways-is-the-only-way-to-fix-chronic-problems-heres-why-88591, 17 January 2018.

[69] https://www.independent.co.uk/news/uk/home-news/trains-uk-railways-renationalise-countries-operators-companies-a9058961.html, 14 August 2019.

[70] https://www.economist.com/leaders/2018/06/30/why-europes-train-network-needs-more-not-less-competition, 30 June 2018.

[71] https://theconversation.com/nationalising-britains-railways-is-the-only-way-to-fix-chronic-problems-heres-why-88591, 17 January 2018.

[72] *Ibid.*

[73] https://www.consilium.europa.eu/en/policies/4th-railway-package/, 1 September 2017.

create a single European rail area. Such an attempt would include structural and technical reforms. Liberalisation has worked for some countries where fare prices have fallen drastically. On lines in Austria, the Czech Republic and Italy where there is genuine competition between operators, fare wars have broken out, resulting in massive fare reductions since state rail firms lost their monopoly.[74] Austria was also ranked tier one in the 2017 European Railway Performance Index.[75]

Besides fare incentives, it is also believed that privatisation would lead to better services. Between 1996 and 2016, rail passenger-kilometres grew fastest in European countries with the most liberalisation. Costs of operating trains also fell by 10% in the decade after deregulation due to competing firms battling it out.[76]

Many governments have been experimenting with different models, including the ideal degree of state ownership or control. Sweden appears to have found a nice balance between some reasonable control via a quasi-autonomous government agency to counter the politicisation of rail fares. Meanwhile, half of the trains are run by "open access" operators that can compete against the government franchises for passengers, thus providing an effective check against monopolistic tendencies.[77] It is state owned but operates on fully commercial conditions as if it were a private company.[78]

> *Countries in the EU are split in their stance on the effectiveness of liberalising the railway system. Some countries with no competitive railway system seem to be coping fine though the unhappiness of the British public over a failed privatisation effort is a reminder that liberalising the national railway is not always the best option. There exist countries with a privatised railway system that have succeeded in reaping the benefits of having a truly competitive system. At the end of the day, the split in opinion comes from the different conditions and systems the respective railways are rooted in. There are important policy issues of separation of track and trains as well.*

---

[74] https://www.economist.com/leaders/2018/06/30/why-europes-train-network-needs-more-not-less-competition, 30 June 2018.

[75] https://www.bcg.com/en-sea/publications/2017/transportation-travel-tourism-2017-european-railway-performance-index.aspx, 18 April 2017.

[76] https://www.economist.com/leaders/2018/06/30/why-europes-train-network-needs-more-not-less-competition, 30 June 2018.

[77] *Ibid.*

[78] http://www.ejrcf.or.jp/jrtr/jrtr08/f22_lun.html, September 1996.

> *Finally, the politics of the day would probably have the largest influence — how fares should be adjusted and should fares be regulated, and whether rail-related jobs need to be protected. Any model that ignores this reality can only expect to fail. The public will have their own views and their sentiments may shift drastically from privatisation to nationalisation. However, ultimately it is up to the government to plan for such heavy capex infrastructure investments for the long-term benefit and implement the best sustainable model without pandering to fickle public opinion.*

Challenges of Divestment

Ironically, a course of action at one point in time can be regarded as completely flawed at another. This is particularly true for privatisation efforts — it's almost a no-win situation for most governments. Making a public offer via a listing on a stock exchange is commonly employed as a means of divestment. When an offer is priced too high, the public would decry the state efforts as opportunistic and not a genuine attempt to distribute to or share national assets fairly with the public. There would accordingly be blame for under-performance post the public offer. Conversely, if the offer is priced too low, the government would be blamed for short-changing state coffers or even accused of favouring new private shareholders.

Example 5.9: Selling Family Silver at the Right Price

Each time a government decides to float one of the larger SOEs, expectations of a gift for the man in the street would start building up. It is inordinately complicated a process, one which will require ample conceptualisation and preparation. Politics unfortunately would serve only to compound the challenges.

Compelling Case for Privatisation

Some may say that the writing is on the wall. Others would agree that privatising the Royal Mail, one of the last few UK state enterprise bastions standing, was an open-and-shut case. By the time the decision was taken by the government in 2013, the number of letters sent daily was already a massive 30% fewer at 58 million than a decade ago. Meanwhile, with the advent of online shopping, parcel volumes were galloping away. In short, the Royal Mail business was transforming rapidly.

Add to this is the inability of public coffers to invest further to accommodate this business transformation. Besides, the government had already invested some £3 billion into modernising the Post Office's 11,500 branches. This transformation was, and still is, occurring against a backdrop of public sector spending cuts.[79]

The participation of private capital would also provide a much-needed barrier for the government against the troublesome workers' union, deemed a political plus. There was also a private wish that many people would be grateful to the government for the discounted shares, since the last series of privatisations was so long ago.

Privatisation, in whole or in part (around 60% in this case), was the obvious solution. Conventional wisdom had it that a stockmarket listing would help ensure sufficient investment over the longer term. Moreover, there were successful precedents — the postal service in Belgium which returned to profitability soon after, and enhancements in operating performance at both Austria Post and Deutsche Post.

On a Bumpy Ride

Royal Mail was accordingly floated in October 2013 at 330p. On the first day of trading, it jumped to 475p. Investors must be overjoyed when the shares peaked in May 2018 at above 600p, albeit after a short-lived rally.[80] Unfortunately, poor fundamentals and looming union problems had triggered a bumpy decline since then. In January 2019, it recorded what was then considered a record low of 270p on the back of a combination of continued decline in physical letters and business uncertainty.[81] Little did investors know that the bumpy ride was just beginning. About a year later, the shares sank to another low, below 170p or about half of the initial offer price. Meanwhile, the Communication Workers Union continued to threaten industrial action.

---

[79] https://www.economist.com/the-economist-explains/2013/10/10/why-is-the-royal-mail-being-privatised, 11 October 2013.

[80] https://www.londonstockexchange.com/exchange/prices-and-markets/stocks/summary/company-summary/GB00BDVZYZ77GBGBXSTMM.html, accessed 21 February 2020.

[81] https://www.theguardian.com/business/2019/jan/29/royal-mail-shares-letters-profit-parcels, 29 January 2019.

Retail investors who had subscribed to the float were probably elated for quite a while and happy at the government's decision to share Royal Mail with them. Those who did not argued that the government sold family silver too cheaply. Unfortunately for the ones who had clung onto their Royal Mail allocation faithfully, the prognosis now looks decidedly poor. The gratitude is probably all but gone.

Same Narrative in Japan

The privatisation of Japan Post in 2015 followed the same script — where questions of under-pricing emerged following an exuberant share rally on the first few days of trading.[82] The Japanese government sold its 11% stake in Japan Post and two newly listed subsidiaries in a deal which had been labelled as "a low-priced gift to the Japanese public". The same polarisation of views as seen in the UK government's experience was in play in Japan too.

Different Experiences

The Austrian Post posted a strong debut upon partial privatisation of 49% in May 2006. Pricing was determined via a book-building process, to best match supply and demand, which hopefully would mitigate against share price volatility upon trading. The offer was eight times oversubscribed which led to the pricing being fixed at the top end of the range at 19€.[83] Prior to the flotation, the government had undertaken a number of restructuring and cost-cutting steps. Since then, the transformation of its businesses towards logistics has strengthened its fundamentals but the macro conditions have continued to be challenging.

Beyond the difficult decision on whether to privatise, and how much to divest the state's interest in a state-owned enterprise, selecting the means to fulfilling this objective can be an equally challenging one. Listing on the stockmarket is especially tricky. Priced too low, non-subscribing taxpayers will cry foul at the big sell-off of family silver. Priced too high, pensioners and long-term holders would accuse the government of not being sincere about wealth sharing.

---

[82] https://www.ft.com/content/08d5d9ea-843d-11e5-8e80-1574112844fd, 6 November 2015.
[83] https://postandparcel.info/14998/news/austrian-post-ipo-stock-gains-100-percent/, 31 May 2006.

> *Governments will do well to have a strategic plan for divestment, especially of large chunks of stocks, to include timing, pricing mechanism, size of tranche(s) and ability of enterprise to sustain itself for a while without needing a cash call for the medium term. Equally pertinent is the preparation of the SOE prior to the divestment which could include unpopular measures like restructuring and cost-cutting. Kicking the can down the road could have serious consequences, including the tanking of the share price and the ensuing unhappiness of subscribers to flotation.*

Timing any privatisation effort right is in itself a challenge. A greater complication lies in the mood of the day and the shift in sentiments over time, sometimes triggered by unrelated developments. What was deemed entirely superfluous to government requirements, and therefore a perfect target for privatisation, could later be considered a policy mistake, a flawed decision. This was the spot that the Singapore government found itself in when it encountered engineering issues for its mass rapid transit system.

Example 5.10: Engineers — Now You Need Them, Back Then You Didn't

> *Unlike a small enterprise that can respond nimbly to changing market needs, public sector expertise takes time to assemble and the right habits to form, especially after a devolution of such competency. The Singapore government divested its engineering capabilities when downscaling its infrastructure-building programme, only to require the same pool of expertise years later.*

It never rains but it pours — this must have an unpleasant ring of truth to the over-worked engineers at Singapore's Mass Rapid Transit ("SMRT"), the dominant operator of the mass rapid transit services, at the end of 2011. In the words of the Transport Minister, "the incidents of 15 and 17 December were unprecedented in terms of severity and scale of disruption in the history of running the MRT system".[84] Some

---

[84] https://www.mot.gov.sg/news/Key%20Points%20of%20Ministerial%20Statement.pdf, 9 January 2012.

127,000 and 94,000 commuters, respectively, were inconvenienced; the cause — a misalignment between current collector shoes and the power/third rail.

A Committee of Inquiry concluded that the disruptions could have been prevented if adequate maintenance measures and checks had been carried out. This is probably a short form for a whole host of problems — flaws in original design, lack of life cycle renewal and replacement plans, absence of back-up and operational redundancies, inadequate maintenance given the long operating schedules, and most critically of all, a lack of a strong sense of ownership of transport services which was aggravated by insufficient engineering resources.

And it literally poured — heavy rains flooded a tunnel at Bishan MRT and disabled the backbone North–South line for more than 20 hours in October 2017. Public frustration and loss of confidence were understandable even as the Transport Minister took pains to provide a diagnosis of the disruption. It boiled down to "poor maintenance and neglect of duties".[85] This is most probably short form again. In his opinion, the tunnel flooding incident was preventable. Questions were raised then over whether such work lapses were a systemic problem at SMRT, if there was sufficient expertise to deal with such lapses and the accountability of senior management for them.

Meanwhile, in between these major incidents, the Singapore government was diligently replacing and trialing a signalling system for the North–South line, a rather complex exercise which entailed some train delays. SMRT undertook a multi-year Sleeper Replacement Project to improve journey times and a smoother ride.[86] There were also several other incidents of disruption from a variety of causes — broken steel cables, fire from short circuit, power shutdown, damaged devices and track and signalling faults.

Separately, a technical advisory panel[87] of local and international experts, formed in 2013, underscored a need for more maintenance and upgrading rigour. It was noted that there was virtually no room for error as there were no redundant networks or parallel lines. Back in 2012, the Transport Minister conceded that as regulator, the Land Transport Authority ("LTA") had to shoulder its share of responsibility. Apart from

---

[85] https://www.channelnewsasia.com/news/singapore/are-work-lapses-a-systemic-problem-at-smrt-analysts-weigh-in-9384340, 7 November 2017.

[86] https://www.smrt.com.sg/Portals/0/InvestorRelations/SMRT-Group-Review-2018-2019.pdf, 2 February 2020.

[87] https://news.nestia.com/detail/-/130956, 22 September 2017.

the more material causes around design, life cycle management and sense of ownership, the more obvious hole to plug was the lack of engineering expertise at both the LTA and SMRT. To develop a sustainable pipeline of engineering professionals, SMRT launched the Trains Engineering Programme in 2015. Between 2013 and now, SMRT has tripled its engineering complement then of 170 to around 600 professionals. Having the necessary headcount is not good enough; imbibing a strong sense of (collective) ownership in employees over the provision of public transport services such that there's a wish to continuously improve, ranks as a top priority, hence the Kaizen initiative.[88]

Government Once had Engineering Expertise in Operations

Rewind a mere decade back — the government ironically had a sizeable pool of competent and experienced engineers then before it took a major public sector-wide decision in April 1999 to corporatise the Public Works Department ("PWD"). This was to "progressively devolve non-regulatory functions".[89] PWD Corp, which was formed as far back as 1833, was transferred to Temasek Holdings and would provide engineering and architectural consultancy services, estate management services and cater to the development of building projects for Ministries and departments. The unhappiness among the private sector players then was palpable — with its past track record and moratorium of public sector projects through the transition, many alleged that the government ownership created an uneven playing field. Eventually, the Minister for Finance reported in his Budget Statement of 2004 that Temasek Holdings had successfully divested in April 2003[90] its full interest in PWD Corp, also known as CPG Corp since 2002.

The acquirer was the Australian Downer Group which in turn transferred ownership to the China Architecture Design and Research Group, now known as China Construction Technology Consulting Company subsequently in 2012. CPG has built on its Singapore legacy and currently has a footprint covering more than 25 countries.[91]

---

[88] https://www.kaizen.com/what-is-kaizen.html, 3 February 2020.

[89] https://www.clc.gov.sg/docs/default-source/urban-systems-studies/uss-built-by-singapore.pdf, Page 11, Para 2.6, 2015.

[90] https://www.singaporebudget.gov.sg/archives/budget_2004/FY2004_Budget_Statement.pdf, Para 2.37–2.39, February 2004.

[91] https://www.cpgcorp.com.sg/images/brochure%2FCPG_Corporation_Corporate_Brochure_(English).pdf, 2 February 2020.

> *Singapore appears to have come a full circle — what was unacceptable then in terms of competition from a government-linked company led to a complete divestment. Years later, the state gets questioned as to why it never kept a pool of experienced engineers, "Why did the government ever divest PWD Corp?" It is difficult to settle on a solution around a dynamic resource pool and the reality is that public expectations do change over time. The challenge is that these expectations tend to shift faster than the state can realistically respond to in a satisfactory manner.*

When arguments for privatisation and expectations of a speedy divestment exercise are raging, there would be substantial pressure on the government of the day to launch headlong into compiling a list of SOEs to be rid of. The ensuing irrational exuberance in response to public unhappiness over corrupt or over-dominant SOEs may sometimes be just as undesirable as lethargy towards doing anything.

Example 5.11: Cranking up the Privatisation Engine

> *Privatisation of SOEs is often welcome news. For fast-growing economies where SOEs dominate, the opportunity for private investors to participate in the underlying growth through a partial or complete divestment of the state's interest will be very much sought after. That said, many governments have found to their grief that it is often easier said than done. Translating privatisation intentions into the final desired outcomes can often be a frustrating, if not futile, exercise.*

It is perhaps not from a lack of trying but the Vietnamese government had sought to undertake its own brand of privatisation, to be preceded by "equitisation" to convert the SOEs into companies with shares first, as far back as the early 1990s.[92] However, the intentions have been thwarted by a combination of setbacks, leading to disappointment among both foreign investors and bankers eager for a slice of the action.

---

[92] https://www.reuters.com/article/us-vietnam-privatisation-analysis/after-years-of-delays-vietnams-privatization-plans-move-up-a-gear-idUSKBN1E20QG, 8 December 2017.

Key Reasons for Poor Response

Owing to the state's tight control over foreign ownership of specific sectors like banking, telecommunications and mining, foreign strategic investors are often having to resign themselves to being a passive, financial investor with no influence whatsoever over management. As such, the equitisation of otherwise-promising SOEs like Vietnamese insurer Bao Viet in 2007 ended on a humdrum.[93]

It was also opined that unrealistic valuations and the prescriptive valuation methodologies in use contributed to the less than enthusiastic response. There was also the introduction of stricter regulations, including the requirement to audit projects of investment valued above 1.7 trillion Vietnamese dong (US$73 million) and the complex land use rights.[94] Yet others felt that there was poor transparency and corporate governance in the SOEs to be equitised and then privatised. In fact, some leaders were themselves frustrating the efforts of equitisation. In sum, it was widely felt that there was a need to change the thinking of both the state and SOEs towards a proper shareholders' perspective instead of retaining "administrative authority".

In August 2019, the government renewed its efforts at equitisation again — the revised goal was to equitise 93 SOEs by 2020,[95] largely the major and strategic players for which the state was expecting to retain between 50 and 65 percent of the capital.

To recap, since 2016, 162 SOEs have undergone the programme with a total value of US$8.8 billion,[96] a far cry from the 4,400 targeted for the period 2016–2020. For 2019 itself, only 35 out of a planned 127 were successfully equitised.

Plugging the Fiscal Gap

The urgency is understandable, given the deteriorating fiscal position from servicing a growing public debt and funds needed for infrastructural

---

[93] https://www.allens.com.au/globalassets/pdfs/insights/asia/vietnamequitisation_soe_2017.pdf, March 2017.

[94] https://vietnamnews.vn/economy/524166/govt-plans-to-equitise-93-soes-through-2020.html#cO494DHiwk7XKXvV.97, 17 August 2019.

[95] *Ibid.*

[96] https://www.vietnam-briefing.com/news/vietnams-equitization-opportunities-and-challenges.html/, 18 October 2019.

development.[97] Taking cognisance of foreign investors' reservations, the government made some attempt at assuaging these by indicating willingness to dispose of majority stakes and as easing of restrictions on strategic partners. It remains to be seen if these revisions would convince more to participate in the Vietnamese economy.

Same Fate in Italy

Like Vietnam, Italy found its privatisation process tough going. Motivated by the objective of reducing its debt, the Italian government embarked on an ambitious privatisation programme for 2019 in a bid to raise 18 billion euros (US$19.6 billion).

From several accounts, the plan was a rushed job, drawn up to avoid a disciplinary procedure by the European Commission over public finances. It was also deemed to be overly ambitious, just like previous over-estimations. Attempts were made to raise funds through the sale of real estate as well.

It didn't help that the new coalition government had reservations over the fund-raising potential of such a privatisation plan, which was scaled back.[98] The new government preferred to rely on the 'dividends from the big, efficient and strategic national companies which play a major role in industrial policy'.

> *Privatisation is no trivial matter and should be pursued only after examining some of the following factors: the state of the capital market, both in terms of the cycle and the ability to absorb sizeable demands on capital, and the preferences of foreign investors with regard to effective control. A careful calibration of the pace and scale of privatisation is often helpful to whet up appetite as well as sustain private, especially foreign interest. Finally, consistency in policy positions on foreign ownership limits, capital controls, where applicable, and competition framework for SOEs is extremely essential.*

---

[97] https://www.reuters.com/article/us-vietnam-privatisation-analysis/after-years-of-delays-vietnams-privatization-plans-move-up-a-gear-idUSKBN1E20QG, 8 December 2017.

[98] https://www.reuters.com/article/italy-debt-privatisation/italy-scales-back-privatisation-plans-after-dismal-2019-effort-idUSL5N26M2RZ, 1 October 2019.

Bloated State Enterprises

Aside from the shift in public sentiment over the role of SOEs in the economy, admittedly, sometimes even high-flying SOEs can fall heavily. More so for such situations, governments would feel compelled to act so as to placate an increasingly unhappy public. Once negativism has been triggered, the pace would quicken and public pressure, mount. When fiscal budgets tighten to the extent that massive cropping of labour is unavoidable, the fault-finding and call for accountability will intensify.

Example 5.12: The Bloating of a Broadcasting Corporation

It is undeniable that the British Broadcasting Corporation occupies a fairly respectable position outside of Great Britain, not least due to its popular World News Service. Yet at home, while many, especially the elderly, have hitherto relied on its broadcast services for their daily news diet, increasingly, it now bears the brunt of sharp criticism. Nothing seems to be right about it — it's bloated with an unwieldy bureaucracy, fat salaries of top management and archaic business models. Most challenging of it all, it faces the threat of being eaten by a "giant blob".

A display of public anger[99] at the British Broadcasting Corporation ("BBC") is increasingly common, as some media publishers would have us believe or respond accordingly. The BBC, once the grand doyenne of broadcasting, faces a confluence of challenges — the fierce competition for audience for its traditional services, the slow but surely unhealthy bloating over time and the vicious cycle of a successive series of reduction in public funding from the decline in viewership.

Nothing annoys the British public more than when the BBC announced in June 2019 about its abolition of free TV licences for the over-75s, in a bid to save its finances.[100] Many have countered that the BBC could have

---

[99] https://www.thesun.co.uk/news/10809324/bbc-must-face-investigation-abuse-public-money/, 23 January 2020.

[100] https://www.dailymail.co.uk/news/article-7130127/British-Bloated-Corporation.html, 11 June 2019.

tried hosting advertising like its competitors did instead. Or make a serious attempt at reducing regional overlaps in output.

The displeasure with the bloated entitlement at the BBC is not new. Back during the Global Financial Crisis, the Conservatives failed to freeze the BBC's licence fee for one year. The defence trotted out then — any interference with the multi-year funding agreements would undermine the editorial independence of the Corporation.[101] Then, while many would concede that much of the broadcasting is first-rate, the reservations remained over senior management pay, size of bureaucracy and the unfair competitive position it enjoyed. As recently as in 2017, the Government demanded that the BBC reveal details of its stars' pay, again in a bid to reduce the inflated salaries. The public believes that senior BBC managers enjoy pay packets far in excess of what is typical for the public sector. In any case, the current plan includes 450 job cuts, out of 6,000, as part of an £80 million savings drive for its news service.[102]

What a contrast this makes for those of us outside of the UK who grew up listening to the crisp British accent of the news reader, savouring every word of the BBC World News as gospel truth or at least, delivered with authority. BBC detractors would be quick to point out that this wielding of "soft power" comes at a price, a hefty £268 million in 2018, one which the taxpayers could no longer sustain.

More critically, the BBC is simply not catering adequately for the "younger, non-linear audience"[103] whose diet is clearly not around papers, radio or television. BBC faces the threat of being eaten by a giant blob and a more centralised story-led model without distinction.

Whereas in the past the BBC has invoked pride outside of Great Britain, it now is at the receiving end of sharp criticism. This criticism is not unlike that levied at many large SOEs, especially those performing a critical strategic role like broadcasting. Currently, the battle against fake news takes on an even more strategic degree of importance that realistically speaking, one that only the BBC can discharge fully.

---

[101] https://www.independent.co.uk/voices/editorials/leading-article-bloated-entitlement-at-the-bbc-1688470.html, 21 May 2009.

[102] https://www.ft.com/content/825db83c-42a7-11ea-a43a-c4b328d9061c, 30 January 2020.

[103] https://www.ft.com/content/b64b692e-4387-11ea-abea-0c7a29cd66fe, 30 January 2020.

> *Reducing public spending is only but a start for such strategically important state enterprises. There should be at the very least be sustained efforts at streamlining for productivity and cost control, over the medium term. The very question of business strategy, especially in a domain that's fast being disrupted by technology, is a lot trickier. This is clearly an existential question, one to be discussed at length.*

Reflections

Governments must always endeavour to guard against both witting and unwitting conflation of roles towards political ends. When that happens, the public will resign in wariness while the foreign investor dollar will vote with its feet. Once repeated too often, the much-needed foreign direct investments would avoid that destination for good.

In the same vein, it pays to be clear about the economic or social goals that may prove unpopular or biased towards certain beneficiaries. In this regard, consistency, or no flip-flopping of underlying principles, is everything. This should be matched by a readiness and ability to respond in a dynamic fashion to changes in the economic environment or shifts in expectations.

In short, many governments would need to start rebuilding confidence in the political centre and take responsibility to ensure a sustainable future. To quote Senior Minister Tharman Shanmugaratnam of Singapore, "Take responsibility … rather than obfuscate, postpone action and impose harsher burdens on our children and future generations".[104]

Governments will do well to regularly review their extent of involvement in the economy, particularly as a capital provider. Where feasible or relevant, they should chart a medium- to long-term plan for partial or complete divestment. They should however resist short-term populism to devise any over-ambitious divestment plans. Likewise, the same discipline should be exercised against public pressure to nationalise certain businesses purely on account of social goals.

---

[104]"Rebuilding confidence in the political centre by Tharman Shanmugaratnam" *Straits Times*, 29 December 2019.

The best guiding principle remains that of the market failure test. It's always tempting for politicians to settle for short-term gains and easy wins in order to remain in power. This would invariably come at the expense of longer term goals which may be for the greater good of the public. Worse still, there are many roles and responsibilities that only the government can accomplish or would have the moral courage to undertake. Such responsibilities would be sacrificed in the quest for immediate gains.

Nothing brings reality home as ably as the prevailing Covid-19 pandemic crisis. In peacetime, healthy robust debates over the extent of state involvement and guarding against populist tendencies are par for the course. However, when a crisis as wide-ranging and severe as that triggered by the Covid-19 pandemic occurs, political leaders would be compelled to think on their feet and rely on their innate instincts, for better or for worse.

Where politicians live and die by the ballot box, one term at a time, populism would take on starker forms. Populism would be made manifest over several hot topics like class inequality, stamping out immigration to preserve jobs for locals, and even extend to hitherto subtler issues like priority to healthcare services. For political parties that are more attuned to planning for the long-term good of society, this crisis would still pose serious challenges to identifying massive resources and balancing trade-offs between short-term relief and sustainable stimulus for the economy.

Nonetheless, post Covid-19, life goes on. Chapter 6 discusses some of the essential pillars that an economy and society would still need that only the government can build — blueprint for the type of infrastructure and large-scale urban masterplan, security and strategic investments, war against terrorism and cyberattacks, social systems for an ageing population. As life goes on, so will the list.

CHAPTER 6
ADDRESSING MARKET FAILURE

Chapter 6

Addressing Market Failure

It is indisputable that there remain many responsibilities that only the government can undertake. Where heavy capital expenditure is required or where there is a long gestation period before any social or economic payback can be realised or where a public good needs to be provided at affordable rates or where new ambitions require long-term investment and efforts, there would be the classic market failure. As infrastructural development is germane, if not critical, to realising any economic growth potential, the government has to front major transport projects like highways, high speed rail, airports and sea-ports. Often overlooked, infrastructure once built, has to be regularly maintained to keep them shipshape. Unfortunately, the sight of crumbling highways or dilapidated underground tunnels is commonplace even in the developed economies.

Conventional wisdom is that before infrastructural development can proceed, some degree of master planning has to happen, be it for the country as a whole or for something as important as building the capital city. Many governments realise the importance of master planning, occasionally belatedly and to their grief when land use gets unwieldy or transport systems become a nightmare.

Of increasing prominence is the preoccupation with the implications of climate change, particularly with global warming and its impact on rising sea levels vis-à-vis low lying areas. Likewise, the momentum towards renewable sources, especially solar energy, continues unabated.

Finally, there is the plain old traditional economic restructuring that only the government of the day can address. This typically accompanies a radical change in government where reform promises are made as part of the campaign. From India's example, it can be seen why most governments ultimately settle on incremental changes simply because they are easier to push through.

The exception is obviously the economic havoc created by the Covid-19 pandemic. With every government saddled with very real healthcare and economic crises, globalisation is being upended. Protectionism is now the instinct. Domestically, severe hardships for smaller enterprises and the spike in unemployment have collectively led to an unwitting major restructuring of the economy.

Driving Infrastructural Development

For any economy to grow and sustain momentum, the availability of appropriate and adequate infrastructure is a necessary condition. Yet transforming an idea to reality would require a whole spectrum of carefully planned actions, from conceptualisation to securing finances to smooth execution post-completion. Numerous challenges exist at each stage requiring the different stakeholders to constantly find ways of mitigating the overall risk.

Infrastructure development provides the perfect example of market failure — business economics hardly exist as payback is seldom within sight and ticket sizes are well beyond what are ordinarily the norm. Add to this the complication that the politics of the day would bring and it's hardly a surprise that many participants shy away from public sector projects. This underscores the observation made in Chapter 2, of the crucial role in infrastructural development that ultimately a government needs to play in order to realise meaningful economic expansion.

The Politics of Infrastructure

Politics have infiltrated every aspect of society — the hallmark of successful leadership can be found in the many campaign statements of a promise to provide reliable economic and social infrastructure. Delivery is often fraught with huge financing and conceptualisation problems, often leading to mis-steps. Many others are mired in corruption and the links to opportunistic politicians.

Increasingly, poorly maintained infrastructure such as rickety train tracks, decaying tunnels or collapsing road bridges are coming back to haunt politicians as well. This takes the form of a twin challenge — build new and maintain old. Unfortunately, such undertakings require loads of funding as the US and UK governments are more than aware of.

Example 6.1: Functioning Infrastructure — Indispensable to Growth

Infrastructure is the cornerstone of development and growth in any country. An investment in infrastructure will have the biggest multiplier effect on the economy compared to any other fiscal boost. Infrastructure catalyses economic activity through the access and linkages it provides. It enables social communities to flourish through the very same linkages. Hence, the rate of return to infrastructure investment is significant in both tangible and intangible ways, and can lead to a large increase in productivity in the long run as well by boosting public capital stock.[1]

By extension, neglecting to upkeep the standard of existing infrastructure would have severe consequences for the country's economic potential and quality of life. Some countries are coming to grips with this and are trying to locate public funds for maintenance. Others, however, are still being crippled by debates around budgetary concerns and allocations.

America's ageing infrastructure has long been a much-debated topic, but it came into focus when it became a key point in President Trump's election promise in his 2016 campaign. He promised to "breathe new life into your very rundown highways, railways and waterways, we'll transform our roads and bridges … to a source of absolutely incredible pride" on a US$1.5 trillion budget. With the nation's infrastructure in a dire state, from both neglect and a lack of funds available for maintenance, both Republicans and Democrats have agreed on the pressing need to upgrade America's decaying infrastructure, mindful that the growth of the economy will be crimped by its current state. However, reflecting how challenging and huge a task it is, not much has been done since President Trump took office. No concrete implementation plans have been outlined and the underinvestment in infrastructure has prevailed.[2]

Key sectors in the US economy rely heavily on infrastructure to sustain its growth, yet infrastructure is rapidly deteriorating, with insufficient funding available to upgrade it. The Congressional Budget Office reckoned that the equivalent of a low 2.3% of the US GDP or around US$441 billion was spent on infrastructure by the federal, state and local authorities in aggregate in 2017. Most of the country's major infrastructure projects were completed in the 1960s, when the population was half of what it is today. The lack of proper maintenance of the ageing infrastructure over the years has compounded the problem of serious deterioration of the infrastructure.

---

[1] https://www.epi.org/publication/the-potential-macroeconomic-benefits-from-increasing-infrastructure-investment/, 18 July 2017.

[2] https://budget.house.gov/publications/report/strong-infrastructure-and-healthy-economy-require-federal-investment, 22 October 2019.

This resulted in a poor report card by the American Society of Civil Engineers, for bridges, a grade of "C+", on account of structurally deficient bridges; highways received an even poorer grade of "D", with one out of every five miles of highway exhibiting potholes. The funding gap is a yawning one; no increase in gas or other taxes would be forthcoming and public–private partnerships (PPPs) are not likely to be the solution either.[3] In short, the US is likely to continue to suffer from the twin problem of fast deteriorating existing infrastructure and the absence of any meaningful investment in new projects.

Many arguments for investing in infrastructure are sound — pivotal to growing the economy, increasing productivity and providing immediate job opportunities, reducing unemployment in the country. However, spending by the US federal government has bucked the required level of resources, declining from 1% to 0.5% of GDP over the past 35 years, pushing more of the burden to the state and local governments to bear.[4] The knock-on effects on industry make for poor operating conditions, from logistics players to manufacturers to services. Equally badly off are citizens who have to put up with poor commuting options or deficient access to services.

On a Different Orbit

In contrast, China and India are keenly aware of the importance to economic growth infrastructure has; both economies have been intensifying infrastructure building plans.

Long before plans were made for the Belt and Road Initiative to improve connectivity with other countries, China had already been ramping up its domestic infrastructure building programme. China spends 9% of GDP every year on infrastructure, as compared to America's 2.5% of GDP.[5] China built its first highway only in 1988, and after 23 years, the length of its network exceeded that of the US' interstate highway system, becoming the world's largest network. China has not stopped there — since then, it has continued adding at least 10,000 km to the network yearly.

Given her aggressive and heavy investment in transportation building programme, China is now leading the rest of the world and aims for her infrastructure quality to be on par with that of a high-income country.

---

[3] https://www.straitstimes.com/world/united-states/americas-ageing-infrastructure, 9 April 2018.

[4] https://www.cbpp.org/research/state-budget-and-tax/its-time-for-states-to-invest-in-infra-structure, 19 March 2019.

[5] https://www.straitstimes.com/asia/chinas-binge-indias-boom, 10 April 2018.

Investment in rural roads between 2001 and 2004 increased by an impressive 51% yearly, and China is currently home to the world's longest high-speed rail network of 31,000 km. There is no doubt its investment in infrastructure has underpinned the healthy economic growth momentum. However, given the huge geography, the government has to keep investing, no mean feat against a global slowdown, in the wake of a full-blown trade war with the US. This would help mitigate against the slowing economy, which recorded just over 6% last year, its slowest pace in 30 years.[6]

China is not alone in realising the catalytic value of investment in infrastructure — India is also aspiring towards a high quality of infrastructure. The newly built Eastern Peripheral Expressway, a new addition to the series of projects Prime Minister Modi has embarked on, is expected to reduce traffic jams and waiting time by diverting 200,000 vehicles daily.[7] In 2018, the last Indian village was connected to the power grid, and now has access to electricity.[8] India has increased its federal budget allocation for infrastructure in 2018 to roughly US$86 billion, in an attempt to support its growth targets. It clocked an extremely robust 7.5% in 2019. In the last two decades,[9] India's greater emphasis on developing infrastructure has borne fruits and the multiplier effects on the economy are evident. In October 2019, Union Steel Minister Dharmendra Pradhan elaborated on the sustained building, where US$1.4 trillion would be dedicated to infrastructure over the next five years.[10]

> *While many governments understand the importance of infrastructure to economic growth, few are able to realise their ambition of providing greater access or better connectivity for business and society. There are several challenges, the foremost of which is a lack of funding, given the huge capital outlays required for transport infrastructure. Even those who have successfully built a commendable road network system earlier on struggle with*

---

[6] https://www.investasian.com/2015/10/20/china-infrastructure-investment/, 10 October 2019.

[7] https://www.straitstimes.com/asia/chinas-binge-indias-boom, 10 April 2018.

[8] https://www.straitstimes.com/asia/south-asia/last-indian-village-now-hooked-up-to-power-grid-says-govt, 30 April 2018.

[9] https://www.straitstimes.com/asia/chinas-binge-indias-boom, 10 April 2018.

[10] https://economictimes.indiatimes.com/news/economy/infrastructure/india-to-spend-usd-1-4-trillion-over-5-yrs-to-develop-infrastructure-pradhan/articleshow/71776099.cms?from=mdr, 26 October 2019.

> *maintenance issues. Here, financial deficit is again the hurdle. Once left for too long, it would become an almost impossible task to upkeep these facilities to an acceptable standard, let alone make new investments.*
>
> *In the context of the ginormous burden, the reality is that infrastructure building presents an almost perfect example of market failure. Even if PPP solutions were successfully structured, it would still not be sufficient. Therefore, it is unavoidable that governments will have to proactively plan for infrastructure. The relatively large demands on capital would mean that revenue streams to fund such development expenditure would have to be planned for, however unpopular tax increases may be.*

Playing the Long Game

Planning for the future involves a detailed analysis of underlying needs and an articulation of aspirations against a realistic assessment of resources and capabilities. What lessons can we draw from experiences around the world? Many governments have built swanky airports but with little regard to the location attributes. Or as many deep-water ports in a bid to capture a bigger market share as the shoreline would allow.

Many governments frequently find their master-planning efforts hampered by financing challenges. Ensuring that major infrastructure projects are bankable is one challenge — ultimately, it boils down to an ability to reliably service any debt taken out on projects. What are the key drivers of financing decisions, especially that of big-ticket projects? Would there be sufficient cashflow generated to cover interest payments? Are projected revenues secure? Is there sovereign or political risk? Is operator of good repute? The list goes on.

Not surprisingly, financing large infrastructure projects is often a joint effort: governments, the private sector and supranational organisations. They can develop synergies ranging from the pooling of financial resources to multi-party efforts in mitigating and sharing risks. Capital markets can provide the necessary liquidity for fiscally tight governments and investors as well as create more business opportunities. To achieve these, governments need proper structuring of projects and acceptable standards of governance and implementation processes. Regulators can help to develop and oversee the appropriate framework to maintain integrity.

The observation has been that attention to the somewhat mundane aspects of infrastructure project planning is often lacking. Before financing can be secured, or even if availability of funding were not an issue, the government would do well to define the objectives, scope and scale of a project diligently. What are some of the pitfalls? How does one plan right-size projects?

Many governments have had to grapple with more than just financing availability. Many are increasingly bogged down by environmental considerations and the consequential long delays to realising their airport dreams.

Example 6.2: Preventing a Crash-landing of Airport Ambition

Expanding or building an airport is no easy feat for any government. There are many issues to factor into consideration, including but not limited to funding, land and environmental concerns. Governments around the world are facing repeated delays and issues with their projects — to build a new airport or expand existing ones. Occasionally, some would immediately reach full capacity or conversely, wind up being a white elephant after a tedious period of construction. In particular, the role of the government in expanding airports cannot be overstated, with the state needing to take the lead in such developments since this is an area which the private sector is manifestly unable to single-handedly handle successfully.

At 98% capacity, the Heathrow Airport expansion project is well justified. However, the initial plans to build a third runway by 2026 would now be delayed by at least two to three years. This comes after the Civil Aviation Authority (CAA) denied requests to raise spending limits from £650 million to £2.4 billion before Heathrow even obtained planning consent, with the CAA citing concerns about passengers needing to shoulder sunk costs if the project does not get the requisite permission to proceed.[11] The compromise was reached at a limit of £1.6 billion for early construction costs.

---

[11] https://www.bbc.com/news/uk-england-london-50861132, 20 December 2019.

Another reason for the delay is due to the British Court of Appeal ruling the project as non-compliant due to possible violations of the UK's legally binding agreement to the Paris Agreement on climate change.[12] The completion of the third runway in Heathrow would jack capacity up by 740,000 flights a year, or 700 more planes per day,[13] raising carbon emissions by a significant amount and breaching UK's legal limits on noise pollution.[14]

The expansion project has been a long work-in-progress, with first proposals submitted as far back as in 1971.[15] Besides potentially creating up to 114,000 local jobs by 2030,[16] it was proposed to allow greater number of connecting flights with other UK airports and meet demand for new, direct flights, especially to fast-growing markets like Russia, India and China which will be crucial to economic growth. This is especially important at a time when Heathrow, Britain's only hub airport, is bursting at the seams, running virtually at full capacity.[17] However, key concerns surrounding the project include funding and environmental issues, with opposition coming from politicians, local residents and environmentalists.[18]

The plan had been to split construction works into four phases to keep costs at a reasonable level, and alleviate worries about noise and pollution, with the final completion date planned for 2050.[19] Plans to reduce damage to the environment include "diverting rivers, moving roads and re-routing [a motorway]", as well as a new low-emission zone for the airport, meaning extra fees for driving a more polluting vehicle to the airport,[20] on top of

---

[12] https://www.straitstimes.com/world/europe/court-ruling-against-heathrow-expansion-finds-climate-pact-binding, 29 February 2020.

[13] https://www.thesun.co.uk/news/2043601/heathrow-third-runway-expansion-pros-cons/, 26 June 2018.

[14] https://www.bbc.com/news/business-48668001, 18 June 2019.

[15] https://www.thesun.co.uk/news/2043601/heathrow-third-runway-expansion-pros-cons/, 26 June 2018.

[16] https://www.businesstimes.com.sg/transport/johnson-under-pressure-to-scrap-third-runway, 24 February 2020.

[17] https://www.thesun.co.uk/news/2043601/heathrow-third-runway-expansion-pros-cons/, 26 June 2018.

[18] https://www.ft.com/content/15c12364-a426-11e9-974c-ad1c6ab5efd1, 12 July 2019.

[19] *Ibid.*

[20] https://www.bbc.com/news/business-48668001, 18 June 2019.

a possible congestion charge to reduce traffic to the airport.[21] At least 750 homes will be demolished to pave the way for expansion, with almost a million people affected by noise.[22] Heathrow is willing to pay "the full market price plus 25 percent for properties in its compulsory purchase zone, as well as for some houses in the surrounding areas".[23] Environmentalists believe the new runway will violate noise pollution legal limits in the UK, something which the government was prepared to set aside £700 million to fund noise insulation measures for remaining residents.[24]

Elsewhere in the Philippines, the New Manila International Airport project at Bulacan also faced delays pending a review of its terms by the Department of Finance, even though the proposal was approved in 2018.[25] Aimed at easing congestion at the main airport in Manila, the new airport was planned to accommodate 100 million passengers annually, with four parallel runways and a toll road linking the airport to the motorway.[26] The new airport facility is estimated to amount to US$14 billion, under a "build-operate-transfer" program[27] with a PPP with San Miguel Corporation (SMC).[28] Works include reclamation of land and expansion of the current small airport, with SMC pledging that the project would be built at no cost to the government.[29]

An extreme case of the importance of government supervision exists in Berlin, where the Berlin Brandenburg Airport, expected to open in June 2012, has remained closed for eight years due to "technical issues". In a country known for its engineering expertise, it is an unthinkable situation

---

[21] https://www.thesun.co.uk/news/2043601/heathrow-third-runway-expansion-pros-cons/, 26 June 2018.

[22] *Ibid.*

[23] https://www.bbc.com/news/business-48668001, 18 June 2019.

[24] https://www.thesun.co.uk/news/2043601/heathrow third runway-expansion-pros-cons/, 26 June 2018.

[25] https://business.inquirer.net/284643/15-b-bulacan-airport-project-faces-delay, 3 December 2019.

[26] https://www.airport-technology.com/news/philippines-airport-consortium-cccc/, 18 December 2019.

[27] https://news.abs-cbn.com/business/09/18/19/san-miguel-dotr-sign-deal-to-build-new-bulacan-airport, 18 September 2019.

[28] https://news.abs-cbn.com/business/08/09/19/look-new-manila-international-airport-in-bulacan-proposed-design-released, 9 August 2019.

[29] https://www.pinsentmasons.com/out-law/news/philippines-approves-plan-to-build-new-manila-international-airport, 13 August 2019.

to be in. A faulty fire-protection system design seems to be the main culprit, but there are several other problems as well, such as overheating of wiring, escalators that were not the right length, and serious structural faults in the ceiling. With so much construction work found to have fallen short of regulatory requirements, many components had to be rebuilt.

Compounding the technical difficulties are allegations of corruption and legal issues around the financing of the project, which were complicated by political and bureaucratic obstacles.[30] Besides technical issues, a more severe issue lay in the lack of a central management to oversee and monitor the project. A lack of clear leadership, fuelled by two different German federal states in this project, added on to the burden of the project. Approximately US$7 billion has already been invested in the airport, but nearly a decade later the airport remains a white elephant.[31]

These and other experiences are useful cautionary tales for the Singapore government when it began planning for a fifth terminal at Changi East, as part of an air-hub master plan a few decades ago. Singapore's total air passenger traffic and aviation-related jobs will more than double in 20 years, increasing the aviation industry's contribution to GDP to S$88 billion by 2035. Once completed, Changi Airport's annual capacity will top 150 million passengers, compared to the current 82 million. The long-term planning by the government underscores the importance of the airport facilities to Singapore's transportation hub status. Approval for plans for more land to be reclaimed for airport development was already secured in 1989, before Terminal 2 (T2) even opened, paving the way for the construction of T5.[32]

The new terminal will also include green features, such as the use of renewable energy, with plans to "[integrate] photovoltaic cells into the building facade" besides the conventional solar panels. Rainwater harvesting is also another avenue being looked at to make T5 a sustainable development, by draining the water into a canal and treating it for another round of usage.[33]

---

[30] https://edition.cnn.com/travel/article/berlin-brandenburg-airport-debacle/index.html, 5 December 2017.

[31] https://edition.cnn.com/travel/article/berlin-brandenburg-airport-debacle/index.html, 5 December 2017.

[32] https://www.straitstimes.com/singapore/transport/decades-of-groundwork-for-t5-to-take-flight, 3 December 2017.

[33] https://www.channelnewsasia.com/news/cnainsider/singapore-changi-airport-terminal-5-t5-sia-aviation-9940744, 10 February 2018.

> *Expanding and building a new airport is a costly and multi-faceted challenge that only the government is able to handle. Besides the massive costs involved, there are also environmental concerns that affect a large neighbourhood or even the whole country (as in Singapore's case). Often, these are accompanied by social issues such as possible resettlement of residents and the location of the airport itself.*
>
> *Not all suitable locations for new airport facilities allow for land alienation or reclamation. The locations of Heathrow in London or the New Manila Airport, being close to built-up areas, can be particularly troublesome as residents will be affected by the building and development of the airport. This could lead to public and political problems, which are issues only the government can deal with. It is certainly nearly impossible for private corporations to attempt to take on such a project by themselves. Regardless of the financial model, the government has to drive the project and address regulatory, planning and political issues.*

Making Difficult Choices

Even the best laid plans can fail during execution. This is more pronounced for infrastructure projects which typically will take many years to materialise and involve multiple foreign capital providers. Changes in political leadership will render trophy and even well-intentioned projects vulnerable to abandonment. Further, geopolitical sensitivity, arising from foreign investors' participation, may not surface until long after project development is underway. As long as there is foreign capital, sovereignty issues are bound to crop up routinely, in sync with political changes to government.

Example 6.3: Sri Lanka Port Development — Sailing into Choppy Waters

> *It was a compelling proposition founded on the sound advice of Dutch economist Albert Winsemius[34] — to capitalise on*

---

[34] Credit to inputs from former Prime Minister Ranil Wickremesinghe 14 April 2020.

> *Sri Lanka's strategic location where key shipping routes traverse, between the Malacca Straits to Singapore and the Suez Canal from Jebel Ali. As many as 36,000 ships pass through this stretch*[35]. *Prior to 2002 when the idea of a new Hambantota Seaport was mooted by the then Prime Minister Ranil Wickremesinghe, the only major port in Sri Lanka, the Port of Colombo, catered only to container handling and was losing ground owing to ageing facilities and limited capacity. It was felt then that the strategic location of Sri Lanka was not fully exploited. The proposed Hambantota Seaport could offer bunkering services, ship repair and replenishment of food, water and medical supplies. The list goes on.*

Winsemius' prediction proved correct. Today the Indian Ocean accounts for 50% of the global oil shipments. South Asia is indeed becoming the next growth region.

Back in 2015 when former Prime Minister Ranil Wickremesinghe re-assumed power, to fulfil the aspiration of becoming an upper-middle income economy, his government conceived the initiative to develop a shipping and major player in transhipment cargo. Instrumental to realising this vision was the development of three ports, of Colombo, Trincomalee and Hambantota.

Supporting Infrastructure

Secure connectivity between the three ports was also regarded as a pre-condition for its success. The extension of the Southern Highway from Colombo to Hambantota was given funding by the Government and eventually completed in 2019. The Asian Development Bank (ADB) prepared the Eastern Economic Corridor Report on utilising the economic potential of the Colombo–Trincomalee Road. There were reportedly also discussions with the Indian Government on the construction of a new highway connecting Trincomalee to Vavuniya that will be linked to the A9 Highway between Colombo and Jaffna.[36] The proposed Central Highway will strengthen the connectivity between Colombo and the key city of Kandy and enable the establishment of further Investment Zones.

---

[35] https://web.archive.org/web/20100224055824/http://www.sundayobserver.lk/2010/02/21/fea20.asp, 21 February 2010.

[36] https://www.livemint.com/Politics/pr8OLuER1jMo3DFIq81svO/India-to-develop-road-infrastructure-in-Sri-Lankas-Jaffna.html, 26 April 2017.

Revision of Policy Framework

Emanating from these physical infrastructure plans was a need to develop a new policy framework to encompass shipping practices. Discussions were commenced with all relevant parties on formulating new strategies on shipping, trade as well as financial incentives. By the time the former government left in November 2019, this groundwork had been substantially completed. Development of the individual ports meanwhile entailed longer term planning, patient capital and consistent politics.

Progress of Individual Port Development Slow

Colombo Port
Sri Lanka's principal port, the Colombo Port, will maintain its historical status as a major transhipment hub for the region. It was envisaged that in 20 years' time, the current expansion of the South Port would be insufficient. Assistance by the ADB[37] in the form of a US$300 million loan for a public–private partnership (PPP) arrangement was already sought for the planned South Port expansion.

Trincomalee Port
The naturally-endowed and historical harbour of Trincomalee, home to major navy bases, was charged with long-term prospects alongside the anticipated rapid economic development of the Bay of Bengal economy. It was targeted at the bulk and break-bulk cargo business, related industrial and global logistics activities. The ultimate aim, with added emphasis on tourism and agriculture, was a metropolis growth centre. The Indians and Japanese have reportedly stepped in to help develop the port. Singapore-based Surbana Jurong prepared the master plan and handed it over to the Government of Sri Lanka[38].

Hambantota Port
The strategy to develop the Hambantota Seaport in phases cannot be faulted. The first phase, costing US$361 million, was completed ahead of schedule in November 2010, thanks to excellent collaboration between the Sri Lankan engineers and their Chinese counterparts from China Harbour Engineering Company and Sinohydro Corporation. The EXIM Bank

---

[37] https://www.adb.org/projects/39431-013/main#project-pds, accessed 1 May 2020.

[38] https://surbanajurong.com/sector/trincomalee-district-master-plan/, accessed 12 May 2020, http://apex-group.asia/maritime-infrastructure/sri-lanka-launched-the-development-of-trincomalee-port-with-a-singapore-infrastructure-company/, 11 July 2018.

of China provided 85% of the funding and SLPA, the rest. The physical attributes of the port site were ideal — a draft of 22 metres versus 15.5 metres at the Port of Colombo, and sufficient land parcels to establish a proper bunkering facility with 14 tanks, warehousing and offshore services, the full works. Most noteworthy, local employment would be created, numbering a non-trivial 50,000 jobs.

The masterplan envisaged a second port project, including a container terminal, costing some US$750 million for completion in 2014, and a third project, a Dockyard. When fully completed, the Hambantota Harbour would be the largest in South Asia, boasting 4,000 parcels of land with the ability to accommodate 33 vessels at any given time. Not only that, shippers would be able to witness peacock and deer roaming freely as part of the plan to safeguard the environment.

Owing to a variety of reasons, many of the proposals beyond the port were rejected. The port struggled to service its huge debt as it was barely operationally breaking even. Overall, it was chalking up losses to the tune of US$147 million a year.[39]

In 2015, when Prime Minister Ranil Wickremesinghe assumed power, he approached China to invest US$1 billion for a 80 percent stake. By 2016, the Sri Lankan government had reportedly already spent US$1.2 billion building and sustaining the port. Eventually in July 2017, after extensive discussions over not just the financial issues but also geopolitical/sovereign concerns, a state-run Chinese company, China Merchants Port Holdings, agreed to inject US$1.1 billion for the control and development of the southern deep-sea port of Hambantota, in the form of a 99-year lease on the port and 15,000 acres nearby for an industrial zone.[40]

Leasing of Hambantota Port to the Joint Venture between China Merchants and the Sri Lanka Ports Authority (SLPA) settled pressing issues concerning the level of government debt more than the financial viability of the Hambantota Port. One reason for the latter was the lack of an industrial hinterland to support the Port. The Joint Venture planned to invest in ship repair and warehousing facilities for transhipment as well as to promote investment for an oil refinery. China Merchants planned to make Hambantota a transhipment point for other ports and a Special Economic Zone in the Indian Ocean, established with Chinese assistance. Towards this end, the China Harbour Company came in with a request for land to build a large Special Economic Zone in the locality.

---

[39] https://economynext.com/sri-lankas-hambantota-port-loses-rs18-8bn-a-year-6236/, 11 November 2016.

[40] https://www.bbc.com/news/world-asia-40761732, 29 July 2017.

This triggered unhappiness as thousands of villagers had to be evicted for the new developmental plan. Regional trade rivals India and Japan feared the start of Sino colonisation. There was a strong political response, not surprisingly from the Rajapaksa camp as well. Separately, to assuage local concerns, the government then gave assurances that China will run only commercial operations from the port and that there would be no military presence.

As is the nature of such a mammoth undertaking, long-term planning is a prerequisite and must necessarily involve difficult discussions over project ownership, land titles, financing and operational arrangements. Although this would qualify as a textbook case of *market failure*, it however did not quite square with the short-term nature of Sri Lankan politics, as is the case in many other countries.

National Strategies Call for more Private Investments

In parallel, plans to expand the Queen Elizabeth Quay at the Port of Colombo were undertaken as well, which involved other multilateral development banks namely the IFC/World Bank, Asian Development Bank and the Commonwealth Development Corporation committing in aggregate the bulk of the US$240 million.[41]

In September 2017, the government released under the auspices of the economic development strategy Vision 2025, how it would transform Sri Lanka into a leading trans-shipment and logistics hub. These plans involve heavy capital expenditure, which given the underperformance of the state-owned enterprises involved in the transportation activities, would severely limit the ability of the government to finance. Consequently, the emphasis falls on PPP as an important financing mechanism.[42]

> *Mapping long-term strategies, such as for major economic infrastructure like seaports or airports, are chequered with multiple challenges, from conceptualisation to sources of financing to extent of private or foreign investor involvement. Nonetheless, it is clearly something that only the government can and should do. The Sri Lankan example here also highlights the difference that the politics of the day can make. Regardless of who's in charge,*

---

[41] https://www.esc-pau.fr/ppp/documents/featured_projects/sri_lanka.pdf.

[42] https://oxfordbusinessgroup.com/overview/charting-development-national-strategies-increase-private-investment-across-sector, accessed 8 February 2020.

> *sovereignty issues would regularly emerge as fresh concerns, given the extent of foreign investor participation.*

Infrastructure development can obviously be risky. Even carefully planned projects can run into execution, operation, coordination and various other problems, some of which can stem from unforeseeable political missteps. What is often ignored or overlooked is preparation for a mechanism for resolving disputes. A well-planned resolution approach ahead of time can help parties involved to use pre-agreed mechanisms to solve problems and avoid a creating a vicious cycle.

Master Planning for Resource Optimisation

Master planning holds special meaning for countries of limited land mass like Singapore. Scarce land resources would need to be properly allocated to the different uses and be ideally, perfectly compatible with the overall economic vision. The converse is however not true; countries with a large land expanse in reality have a tougher time deciding on what sort of activity to promote and where to locate the concomitant economic development. Such decisions could easily play right into the hands of local politicians, and invariably end up being politicised. The difference lies in strong political leadership, one that is willing to mediate between competing needs for real assets or between feuding factions, and assert discipline in execution.

Example 6.4: Making a Difference — Oman's Master Planning

> *Recognising the need to diversify Oman's economy so as to achieve sustainable development, the late Majesty Sultan Qaboos Bin Said saw it fit to establish the Supreme Council for Planning (SCP) back in May 2012.[43] The SCP was personally chaired by His Majesty and comprised seven Cabinet Ministers. His vision*

---

[43] https://www.thebusinessyear.com/oman-2018/future-plans/interview, 2018.

was for the long term, encompassing a comprehensive plan to prescribe new or revise the necessary regulations "to give effect to such strategies and policies" and to optimise the utilisation of available natural and human resources. Such is the extraordinary farsightedness of His Majesty then, setting an all-important tone from the very top.

Oman currently has a population of 4.2 million, comprising 2.3 million Omanis and the rest expatriates, and is categorised as a "high income economy". Incorporated at the same time was the National Centre for Statistics and Information (NCSI).

Given the relatively weak but nonetheless significant private sector presence, the government rightfully should drive specific action plans and transformation of the economy principles. In essence, the government aims to apply its resources judiciously so as to achieve diversification and ultimately to enhance the competitiveness of its economy. Oman does have a number of other natural resources such as natural gas, copper, asbestos, marble, limestone, gypsum and frankincense, which she hopes to build on. Likewise, agriculture and fishing are also traditional staples with potential for expansion.

The basic themes of the vision are around the development of human resources, upping the game in technical development while responding ably to the ever-changing conditions. It is also about the creation of a stable holistic economic climate, with the active and increasing participation of a responsible private sector, over time. The importance of the role a viable private sector can play cannot be overstated; Oman seeks to build national competitiveness through an active private sector which will continue to provide employment for a significant portion of the Nationals. The vision also speaks of the need to design incentives towards economic excellence and sustainability. And what good is a master or grand plan if there are no express social goals? Exhortations of reduction in income inequality and a national uplifting of every household, which can be measured using the usual metrics, have also been included.

The SCP has worked hard to define a framework for guiding the development of the Oman National Spatial Strategy (ONSS), including the regional strategies of the governorates till 2040, to ensure sustainable high quality urban and rural development Sultanate-wide. This is not mere highfalutin stuff but a resolve that is drilled down to the bolts and nuts; it means the provision of basic infrastructure like roads, water supply and electricity grid. It also means the spreading out of economic concentration around the capital Muscat, for a more even distribution of human capital and economic opportunities. More importantly, it calls for the creation of multiple (new) urban centres in the numerous unique rural landscapes.

Connectivity would figure prominently in such a master plan; hence, a long-term transportation strategy would complement the various economic and social initiatives. To this end, a range of field surveys to build an Oman National Transport Model (ONTM) would be logical. Apart from defining new network needs or enhancements, the ONTM would serve to inform decisions around the impact of transport to the living environment. The survey findings on travel patterns and transport needs would of course be only as useful as the quality of the inputs of all stakeholders. This importance is not lost on leaders tasked with this aspiration.

All in all, it is envisaged that a well-developed spatial strategy, supported by a sound transportation strategy, would in turn convince investors of opportunities to help build a diversified economy.

While effort was clearly expended in spelling out in detail the Vision and Mission statements, the test remains one of translating plans into outcomes. This challenge is not unique to Oman but one that every government seeking economic transformation can expect to face. Ultimately, there must be active participation of society; what is implied is therefore the building of a sense of ownership of the national vision and moving in concert towards executing the mission. Towards this end, The National Program for Enhancing Economic Diversification (TANFEEDH) was instituted, with the aim of bringing to fruition all the key pillars of the master plan as envisaged by the SCP.

Perplexing Questions

Economic transformation is obviously a form of "market failure" that only the government can address, plan for and execute in a meaningful fashion. Where there is insignificant private sector presence to speak of, efforts at attracting private sector investment must necessarily include foreign sources. Apart from having to compete for the attention of foreign investors, there would also be cultural issues in terms of how the public sector and the economy at large will interact with these newcomers.

An alternative would be to privatise or partially divest some of the state enterprises to jump-start home-grown private sector players. This is not without its challenges: firstly, pools of domestic capital have to be identified; next, talent to take over state enterprises; and finally, the potential social issues arising from any large-scale retrenchment. A hybrid approach of a partial privatisation of state enterprises to build indigenous capabilities while attracting foreign direct investments (FDIs) for new, promising areas could also be considered.

> *Regardless of the challenges, it is abundantly clear that for something as strategic as economic diversification such as Oman's vision, only the government is in a position to do so. The trade-off between offering incentives to entice would-be private investors and foregoing value upon success must be managed carefully. Equally poignant are cultural issues around the need for public officials or ex-employees of state enterprises to adapt to a private-sector commercial discipline.*

Locating the Capital

Many a debate have taken place over where the capital city of a country should be located or what components its master plan should have. As master planning would comprise both economic and social elements, no single or cluster of private sector interest(s) would be able to undertake this responsibility. Sure, there are many architectural outfits or planners competent enough to help guide and draw up plans. However, there is no denying that financial investors of a new capital city, a massive and diverse mandate, are virtually non-existent. Aggravating this inherent market failure is the political factor in many situations.

Example 6.5: Defining the Centre

> *Good master planning is the crux of the success of any new capital city. After all, determining the best location for a capital city is no easy feat and one that the government has to take many factors into consideration. Besides planning the development of the critical infrastructure and stipulating the expected timeline for the project, the government, most importantly, needs to ensure that the new capital will be able to attract businesses, tourists and its own citizens into the city. Without the hub effect, the new self-declared capital would just be a costly white elephant.*

Some have criticised Naypyidaw as an example where the government seemed to have failed at building up a robust capital city. In fact, this capital sits "in the middle of nowhere", surrounded by rice paddies and sugarcane fields. Officials explained that the move was due to congestion and over-crowding in Yangon, but that has failed to quell rumours and speculations surrounding the real reason for the capital's move in Myanmar.[44]

Completed in November 2005, Naypyidaw is seven times the size of Singapore, with highways that are 20 lanes wide, reliable electricity and fast wi-fi, something that the rest of the country lacks. It has golf courses, a zoo and water parks. The total price tag? A rumoured US$4 billion to construct, dwarfing the country's ordinary budget expenditure items. Despite the spanking new facilities, the government has been unable to attract people to relocate there. Its population is approximately one million, according to official statistics, which does not square with witness accounts of empty roads and shopping malls. Most strikingly, foreign aid workers would rather take the five-hour car ride to and from Yangon, rather than relocate to Naypyidaw.[45]

This was a massive project which the Myanmar government undertook somewhat in secret to the rest of the world, de-populating the areas around Naypyidaw and enlisting hundreds of villagers to help build the capital.[46] Yet it would appear that more planning could have gone into this city. Given its distance from all the other established cities like Yangon and Mandalay, anchoring hub-like business activity at Naypyidaw was a tall order. The relocation of one of the government's investment agencies back to Yangon[47] admittedly lends weight to questions over the ability of Naypyidaw to succeed as a capital. Or perhaps, it just needs more time.

Caught up in Politics

The termination of the development of Amaravati city of Andhra Pradesh serves as a reminder of why government master planning is so crucial to the success of any capital. In 2019, following the change in political leadership, the government of Andhra Pradesh decided to shut down the Amaravati

---

[44] https://www.theguardian.com/cities/2015/mar/19/burmas-capital-naypyidaw-post-apocalypse-suburbia-highways-wifi, 19 March 2015.

[45] *Ibid.*

[46] *Ibid.*

[47] *Ibid.*

Capital City Start-Up Area project, and terminate the partnership with Singapore to build the new capital city.[48]

The government had sought Singapore's assistance back in 2014 when Chief Minister Naidu was still in power. They signed with the Singapore consortium a memorandum of understanding for the development of a global city[49] over a period of 15 years. However, following his election defeat to Mr. Reddy in 2019, the new government decided to stop the new capital project and focus on other priorities instead. Furthermore, the project itself would have been nearly impossible to execute. The land meant for the building of the capital was in an ecological–legal mess where no development activity was allowed. Moreover, farmers in 29 villages were made to give up their land for this ambitious project. Mr. Naidu's government had tried to alter the city's master plan to allow it to proceed, but with land belonging to various organisations and corporations, it was practically impossible to change it, and hence the project would not even have been able to get started.

The importance of the role of the government in master planning for any new capital city cannot be overstated. It is a challenging task, with many imponderables in terms of predictions and estimations. Conversely, if no conscientious master planning were carried out, and tested for pragmatism, as seemed to be the case of Amaravati city, it would just be akin to throwing money down the drain, with little to no returns for an investment as large as the new capital cities.

Escalating Climate Change Concerns

Climate change is fast becoming a weighty issue on many national agenda, and for good reasons. While it is difficult for governments, especially of smaller economies, to grapple with the amount of carbon dioxide emissions that they are contributing to, at the conceptual level, many can

---

[48] https://www.straitstimes.com/singapore/amaravati-city-joint-project-officially-terminated-mti, 12 November 2019.

[49] https://www.livemint.com/news/india/tdp-caught-on-back-foot-over-capital-decentralisation-row-in-andhra-pradesh-11578221958486.html, 5 January 2020.

readily understand the impact of global warming and rising sea levels. It represents an existential challenge for countries with low-lying areas which may have no bearing to the amount of emissions contributed by these countries. With the projected acceleration in the rise of sea levels by 1–4 feet by 2100,[50] the urgency for action is being keenly felt by these countries.

Example 6.6: Shoring up the Coast

Climate change is a phenomenon that can no longer be ignored by nations around the world. As the effects are increasingly being felt in our day-to-day lives, governments have been turning their attention to dealing with the impact climate change will have on the environment, and what they can do to help mitigate against it. The Paris Agreement represents the collective commitment countries are putting in to slow down climate change, with "commitments from all major emitting countries to cut their climate-altering pollution and to strengthen those commitments over time".[51] Singapore is one such party to the Paris Agreement, with the country contributing 0.11% to global emissions,[52] and she has committed to ramping up efforts to halve the 2030 peak by 2050 and thereafter to achieve net-zero emissions.

Despite being a relatively small contributor to global carbon dioxide emissions, Singapore is experiencing a disproportionately large impact of global warming and rising sea levels as large areas of Singapore are low-lying. Underscoring the severity of this threat, the government has committed at least S$100 billion on a long-term plan to protect Singapore from rising sea levels. Efforts to protect infrastructure include a requirement for new structures to be built at least 4 m above sea level, and even higher for more critical installations. On top of this, coastal defences are also necessary to protect the city from flooding. Existing developments include

---

[50] https://climate.nasa.gov/effects/, 12 March 2020.

[51] https://www.nrdc.org/stories/paris-climate-agreement-everything-you-need-know, 12 December 2018.

[52] https://www.straitstimes.com/singapore/environment/spores-2050-target-halve-emissions-from-2030-peak, 29 February 2020.

Marina Reservoir and Marina Barrage, where a pump lies to drain water from the reservoir.[53] However, this alone is not enough.

One solution the Singapore government is looking into is a larger-scale mitigation plan — the Dutch polder concept. With a long history of devastating flooding, the Dutch have developed the polder strategy where low lying land was being protected by dykes. In order to create a polder, three things are needed — "a dyke around the land area, pumps to get rid of the excess rainfall and to drain the sea water and storage space to retain the excess rainwater before it is removed".[54] As a result of this innovation, no Dutch has been killed by flooding since 1953.[55] Singapore considers this plan a "serious option", with a small polder already being piloted at Pulau Tekong, with plans for the new land to be used by the Singapore Armed Forces (SAF) for training.[56]

Commitment to Paris Agreement

Being at the receiving end of climate change impact, it is no wonder the Singapore government is staying committed to the Paris Agreement. In fact, it has even updated the pledge it made in 2015, which was to "reduce its emissions intensity by 36 percent from 2005 levels and to peak by around 2030". In 2020, Singapore assigned an absolute figure of its maximum level of emissions in 2030 at 65 million tonnes of carbon dioxide. Furthermore, Singapore also hopes to reduce the amount of emissions produced from this 2030 peak by half by 2050, a tough challenge since she has limited access to renewable energy alternatives.[57]

To achieve this stretched goal, the government has developed a three-pronged climate change strategy: (a) transformation of its industry, economy and society by tapping alternative energy sources; (b) investment in research into low-carbon and storage technologies, and (c) collaborating

---

[53] https://www.channelnewsasia.com/news/singapore/ndr-2019-singapore-climate-change-costs-rising-sea-levels-11819402, 19 August 2019.

[54] https://www.todayonline.com/singapore/explainer-what-are-polders-and-how-does-govt-plan-use-them-defend-spore-against-climate, 15 September 2019.

[55] https://www.straitstimes.com/opinion/can-the-dutch-save-the-world-from-rising-sea-levels, 31 January 2020.

[56] https://www.channelnewsasia.com/news/singapore/ndr-2019-singapore-climate-change-costs-rising-sea-levels-11819402, 19 August 2019.

[57] https://www.straitstimes.com/singapore/environment/spores-2050-target-halve-emissions-from-2030-peak, 29 February 2020.

with other countries to develop regional power grids to tap on renewable energy sources it does not have access to currently.

It plans to increase the intensity of its renewable energy program to capture more solar energy and has plans in place to cut out internal combustion engine vehicles by 2040. The formation of a well-regulated carbon market will allow Singapore to purchase carbon credits to counterbalance its emissions.[58]

Singapore will undertake several initiatives in a bid to reduce the emission of greenhouse gases across different industries and including households. The government will implement a S$24.8 million Climate-Friendly Household Package, and one- to three-room Housing Board flats will receive a S$150 voucher to purchase more energy-saving refrigerator models. Schemes to "train and certify technicians to handle refrigerants properly, and mandating the proper recovery, reclamation and destruction of spent refrigerants" will also be available from 2021. Furthermore, the national water agency PUB's five water treatment plants will run only on renewable energy once the floating solar photovoltaic system at Tengeh Reservoir is built.[59]

> *Planning for the future and allocating resources efficiently and effectively to safeguard the country against climate change effects, as well as reducing adverse environmental impact, are priorities that the government has to invest heavily in. However, it is a long, arduous process. From defining the problem areas to formulating a strategy and generating funding, and finally building a timeline while minimising social impact, this is a process whereby benefits are not immediately evident to the business community. Companies these days are expected to conduct their businesses around a sustainable strategy. However, their time frame and runway are understandably short term, and limited to the spheres of their influence. It remains therefore the government's responsibility to ensure that the long-term well-being of its citizens is intact.*

---

[58] https://www.straitstimes.com/singapore/environment/spores-2050-target-halve-emissions-from-2030-peak, 29 February 2020.

[59] https://www.straitstimes.com/politics/spore-to-take-steps-against-shock-waves-of-climate-change?xtor=CS3-18&utm_source=STiPhone&utm_medium=share&utm_term=2020-03-05%2012%3A03%3A13, 5 March 2020.

Market failure is most evident in the domain of renewable energy. Take solar energy. In order for an entrepreneur to be prepared to start manufacturing solar panels, he has several imponderables — would the economics make sense, which may relate to a minimum scale of production before cost of panels was worth the while switching to; how does one ensure a consistent flow of solar energy during non-production hours which will relate to storage; and how does one relate to the grid which plugs the deficit or sells the excess of solar energy generated?

Many governments have been plugging away at making solar power generation viable for the private-sector investors.

Example 6.7: Make Energy While the Sun Shines

Climate change is now preoccupying many a government's long-term agenda as the implications are real and severe in most cases. One of the better-defined measures is that of harnessing renewable energy instead of generating from traditional fossil fuel sources. Using renewable energy sources not only is a good way of sustaining economic growth while reaping environmental benefits but also is more cost-effective. Given the historical practice of regulating different parts of the value chain of what is considered a public good, the government clearly has a large part to play in both the formulation of appropriate green policies and their successful implementation.

In Singapore, the government understands this responsibility very well and has adopted a multi-prong strategy to drive the transition from traditional sources of energy to renewable sources. At the national level, the theme revolves around "Transforming Energy — Invest, Innovate, Integrate".[60] In this regard, it was observed in 2018 that globally, renewables had been recording a healthy 8.3% growth annually on the back of better technology and lower costs. Consequently, the share of renewables in the overall mix has been rising.

---

[60] https://www.ema.gov.sg/speech.aspx?news_sid=201902185bayeDOdvGb9, 30 October 2018.

The 4 Switches Plan

Singapore has been a part of the green movement for the past 50 years, most significantly moving from oil to natural gas for cleaner power generation. The transition is almost complete as currently, about 95% of the electricity is generated using natural gas. However, it is now looking to better sources of energy to sustain not only its rate of growth but also its future generation.

The government is doing so through its "4 Switches" plan, the first switch being diversifying its power sources and increasing efficiency of its energy sources. Similar to how Singapore has diversified its water supply, it is looking to do the same to its energy sources to ensure resilience and reduce dependence on a single power source.[61]

The second switch is promoting an aggressive adoption of solar energy to reach a target of 350,000 households, representing about 4% of total electricity demand. This implies the adoption rate of solar energy has to be multiplied by eight times from today's capacity. In aggregate, this would be supplied by a solar target of 350 megawatts-peak by 2020, escalating to a capacity of 2 gigawatt-peak by 2030. This calls for an all-out plan to maximise available spaces such as rooftops, reservoirs and offshore spaces to install as many solar panels as possible.

As solar power can be rather intermittent in supply for a variety of reasons including unpredictable weather conditions, energy storage becomes key to stabilising the quality of electricity supply and ensuring grid resilience.[62] The ability to harness solar energy successfully will go a long way towards increasing Singapore's clean energy supply, as well as enhancing control and security over its own power generation since Singapore can rely less on other foreign sources. The potential of energy storage technology itself is limitless and justifies the investment of huge R&D dollars.

The third switch in the plan centres around tapping into regional power grids. Singapore is looking to access cost-competitive energy generated elsewhere via bilateral or regional arrangements.

Lastly, the fourth switch is about investing in emerging technologies in low-carbon alternatives to reduce Singapore's carbon footprint.[63]

---

[61] https://www.straitstimes.com/singapore/environment/solar-energy-to-meet-4-of-singapores-energy-demand-by-2030-up-from-less-than-1, 29 October 2019.

[62] *Ibid.*

[63] *Ibid.*

Improving energy efficiency will not only reduce costs of production for corporations but also give them a competitive advantage over less cost-efficient companies. They will stand to benefit from lower carbon tax liabilities, as compared to other organisations.[64]

Besides these four switches, the government is also looking into implementing policies such as increased R&D, grant schemes and upskilling its workforce to remain relevant in an ever-changing energy climate. For example, it is implementing an upgraded set of Industry Energy Efficient grant schemes to encourage industrial facilities, including those of small and medium-sized enterprises[65] who often struggle to have the capacity to be energy efficient, to adopt energy-saving behaviours.

> *From the measures Singapore has undertaken, it is on the right track to building a more sustainable future. However, all this was only made possible through the conscious and direct intervention by the government. A structured framework with clear guidelines and policies to keep corporations in check, as well as to shape future development, anchors the state's role. Reflecting the high priority accorded to achieving sustainable energy practices, a significant amount of the national budget will be set aside for investment in energy infrastructure. Such an infrastructure will only serve to aid future development and growth of the country while reducing its carbon footprint. Hence, it is imperative governments start planning long term, and early, setting clear boundaries for its industries and country to follow to ensure renewable sources of energy are being adopted and eventually, the mainstay.*

Restructuring the Economy

Policy formulation is a challenging enough task these days, given the increasing globalisation of the market place and the repeated technological disruptions that have thrown assumptions askew. Even more demanding are the shifts in or revisions to policy positions as a response to the

---

[64] https://www.ema.gov.sg/speech.aspx?news_sid=201902185bayeDOdvGb9, 30 October 2018.

[65] *Ibid.*

dynamics that affect sectors unevenly. Correspondingly, stakeholders would be impacted differently and unevenly. Formulating refinements will essentially entail a re-balancing of the costs and benefits among the different stakeholder groups and often winds up as a political exercise. A radical reform or restructuring of the economy would have a magnified array of challenges and difficulties. Even when viewed as necessary by all and sundry, for example, away from brick-and-mortar towards online retailing, it would still require a vast amount of political capital. This unfortunately is increasingly scarce and even for those with a landslide electoral victory, there might not be enough to see the tedious process through.

Example 6.8: India — Restructuring Pains

Many governments live or die by the economic restructuring sword. Many policies for growth typically involve huge invest-ment outlays with a long lead time, such investment of which may be constrained by revenue collections or competing demands on expenditure. Expansion of a country's economy is thus never an easy task because it would require striking a delicate balance between conflicting goals such as reduced allocations to social spending. This may be unpopular among the public and may even elicit anger from them in the form of protests. All said, no single private-sector body would be able to strategise for and execute an economic expansion plan. Only the government can do so as it has to deal with the accompanying social issues. India's plan to expand its economy is one such example where it is clear that any well-intended development will have its fair share of challenges.

India has big plans to grow its economy and realise the full potential the country has to offer. Known for being open to foreign investments, Prime Minister Modi has now embarked on his latest, and probably most ambitious project to date — making India a US$10 trillion economy and third largest in the world by 2032.[66] And it is not an easy one, with the economy left in policy paralysis and worsening corruption from the

---

[66] https://www.financialexpress.com/economy/modis-10-trillion-dream-commit-to-make-india-worlds-third-largest-economy-by-2032-says-bjp-manifesto/1541466/, 8 April 2019.

previous government, with high inflation and a widening current account deficit.[67] As of 2019, unemployment was at a 45-year record high of reportedly 6.1%, despite the youthful labour force India has,[68] and India's GDP stood only at $2.6 trillion. It is a hard task, but not an impossible one, with India already being the sixth largest economy in the world.[69]

The government's 2019 plan to expand India's economy involves a relaxation of tax policies, lowering of GST rates, a US$1.5 trillion investment in infrastructure by 2024 as well as developing India into a global manufacturing hub. Investment in infrastructure will help India achieve its goal of its economy built on the basis of investment-driven growth. New industrial policies to enhance competitiveness of manufacturing and services will be introduced, and schemes to provide collateral-free credit at a limit of US$5 million to entrepreneurs, underpinning Modi's "Make in India" initiative.[70]

Already, India is seeing results. Post liberalisation, the country would record an average growth of 7.4% and an inflation rate of less than 4.5% between 2014 and 2019, the highest rate of growth and lowest rate of inflation recorded during any government's term of office.[71]

Since independence, the government has been trying to revive the small-scale industry by allocating items for it to manufacture exclusively. The policy remains the backbone of the Indian economy, with major contributions to exports as well as private-sector employment. However, "overall value addition, product innovation and technology adoption remains dismal" and the industry relies heavily on government aid. With the liberalisation of India's economy, the list of reserved items was significantly reduced and their products are in constant competition with cheaper

---

[67] https://www.businesstoday.in/current/economy-politics/pm-modi-sees-india-as-10-trillion-economy-says-change-is-visible/story/321536.html, 23 February 2019.

[68] https://time.com/5595923/modi-india-economic-reform/, 23 May 2019.

[69] https://www.financialexpress.com/economy/modis-10-trillion-dream-commit-to-make-india-worlds-third-largest-economy-by-2032-says-bjp-manifesto/1541466/, 8 April 2019.

[70] https://www.jll.com.mo/en/trends-and-insights/investor/economic-reforms-and-strong-fundamentals, 12 February 2020, https://www.bloombergquint.com/economy-finance/narendra-modi-government-planning-collateral-free-entrepreneur-loans-says-president-in-parliament-speech, 20 June 2019.

[71] https://economictimes.indiatimes.com/news/politics-and-nation/pm-modi-sees-india-as-usd-10-trillion-economy-with-countless-startups/articleshow/68123627.cms?from=mdr, 23 February 2019.

imports from countries such as China, threatening the existence of these local firms.[72]

This aside, Modi's reforms have been met with strong resistance and protests from the people. In 2015, plans to relax stringent labour laws resulted in nearly 150 million workers backed by 10 major unions staying away from work. Unions say such reforms to give companies greater freedom in employment of its workers will put jobs at risk.[73] This plan was put on hold until 2019, when Modi finally attempted to overhaul labour laws again by allowing companies to hire workers on fixed-term contracts so as to attract investments and make it easier to do business in India.[74] Furthermore, the Code on Wages which only requires minimum wage revision at least once in five years and replaces the labour inspector with an "inspector-cum-facilitator", was passed in Parliament in 2019, eliciting more anger from unions who demand that revisions should be made annually. More protests across the country resulted.[75]

Labour reforms are instrumental to the rehabilitation of India's economy so as to provide real employment opportunities to the one million youths entering the labour market each month. Restrictive labour regulation was linked to the 35% increase in companies' labour costs, and India's consequential ranking of 103 out of 141 countries on the competitiveness of its labour market in 2019. Hitherto, fears of union backlash and protests have been a major hindrance to key labour reforms.[76] In January 2020, 10 central unions, claiming 250 million members between them, demonstrated against what they called Modi's government's "pro-corporate" and

---

[72] https://www.insightsonindia.com/2014/12/14/effects-liberalization-indian-economy-society/, 14 December 2014.

[73] https://www.reuters.com/article/us-india-reforms-protests/millions-strike-in-india-to-protest-against-modis-labor-reforms-idUSKCN0R21ZG20150902, 3 September 2015.

[74] https://economictimes.indiatimes.com/news/economy/policy/modis-labour-reform-push-may-remove-key-hurdle-for-investors/articleshow/72234136.cms?from=mdr, 26 November 2019.

[75] http://www.industriall-union.org/indian-unions-hold-nationwide-protest-against-anti-worker-labour-law-reforms, 8 August 2019.

[76] https://economictimes.indiatimes.com/news/economy/policy/modis-labour-reform-push-may-remove-key-hurdle-for-investors/articleshow/72234136.cms?from=mdr, 26 November 2019.

"anti-people" policies.[77,78] Apart from the militant union action, the government has its plate full of challenges with onerous land acquisition laws as well.

> *India is a classic example of regardless of how perfect or imperfect a country's macro strategy seems to be, the government remains the only body able to implement it. On such a large scale, especially for economies like India, restructuring entails a long gestation period before benefits are evident while social problems would present themselves immediately. There must ultimately be sufficient political capital to see the reforms through.*

Reflections

Where there is long lead time required or lengthy cycles are part and parcel of development, or where heavy capital expenditure is required to build a meaningful scale for infrastructure or where a long-term vision has to contend with the short-termism of politics, market failure becomes a real challenge. For these increasingly common combinations, not only are these strictly the very responsibilities that any elected government can be expected to shoulder but also are challenges that only the government can hope to address. No single private sector entity can do this or will have the economic motivation to be able to do this satisfactorily.

Notwithstanding the lack of a consensus at the recent United Nations Climate Change Conference, the reality of climate change, be it weather upheavals or flooding over low-lying areas, is looming large. It is clearly the responsibility of the government of the day to define priorities, map out a long-term plan and lead in the efforts, along with the private-sector players who are appropriately incentivised.

Economic restructuring efforts, particularly with a view towards making domestic players more globally competitive, again belong to the state.

---

[77] https://caravanmagazine.in/policy/trade-unions-against-modi-labour-policies, 6 January 2019.

[78] https://www.trtworld.com/asia/millions-strike-in-india-to-protest-modi-s-labour-policies-unions-32794, 8 January 2020.

Likewise, efforts to eradicate corruption can only succeed with the single-mindedness of the government.

However, an extraneous cause, like the Covid-19 crisis, can upend the best of efforts and intentions of any government to address market failure for sustainable growth. The wide-ranging damaging impact of lockdowns has caused many political leaders to turn inwards, somewhat as a defensive response. To be fair, there are real domestic challenges to be addressed — those of healthcare and unemployment. Fear of the virulent spread of the deadly disease has severely dented trade flows just as travel restrictions have killed off tourism activity. In short, the more immediate challenges of an urgent rescue of the economy, while saving lives, mean that building infrastructure or nurturing global champions or climate change initiatives can wait.

Nonetheless, beyond these fundamental roles, the government, and only the government, must constantly maintain vigilance over any threat to national security. This can be direct threats to physical security or the creeping geopolitical influence through investments. Likewise, the government remains the only potent force capable of protecting or furthering the national or strategic interests of her people. The next chapter discusses the competing priorities that a responsible government needs to take a keen interest in.

CHAPTER 7
SECURITY AND STRATEGIC CONSIDERATIONS

Chapter 7

Security and Strategic Considerations

When it comes to market failure, the state is expected to address and bridge the gap as a regulator, promoter or market participant. Where issues of security or national strategic importance are concerned, the government has to decide if it should intervene, and if so, how. What are the legal bases for such intervention? This dilemma frequently manifests itself whenever an attempt is made by a foreign investor, commonly state-owned, to acquire specific capabilities which are key to a security activity. Or the target could be the single largest producer of an important raw food material. Many intended acquisitions by foreign interests have been frustrated, if not foiled by non-trade barriers, such as the need for foreign investment approvals.

Where the government is most enthusiastic about its involvement tends to be that of a promoter of enterprise. Here, many governments are prepared to devote meaningful resources and energy to supporting start-ups. The other cluster of activities that the government may be active in, albeit often reluctantly, belongs in those with social implications such as healthcare, pre-school education and caring for an ageing population.

However much a government would rather not go down the path of intervention, occasionally they have no choice but to justify their decisions (either way) when public expectations are that they should intervene. This could run the gamut of rescuing a failing business in the provision of some public good or pulling the plug on a growing social ill.

Nowhere is this more evident than the current unfolding of the Covid-19 pandemic. Governments are expected to be sharper in their responses towards any challenge to national security via an investment by a foreign investor, or heightening healthcare concerns or economic well-being of citizens.

Protection of National Security and Strategic Interests

The *raison d'être* of any government must be to preserve and protect national security and strategic interests to the best of its endeavour. That's easy enough a philosophical justification to understand. The challenge however presents itself as a question of the extent to which a government must discharge such responsibilities. A related conundrum revolves around what constitutes "security interests" and on an even more controversial note, "strategic interests". Are such interests circumscribed by geography or scope of impact which may straddle borders?

Increasing globalisation of the marketplace, accelerated by technological advancement, has heightened the sense of urgency in the discharge of such responsibilities. Meanwhile, the "interests" definitional issues remain unresolved, often giving rise to debates over geopolitical influence, especially among the major economic powers or owners of critical resources.

Foreign direct investments (FDI), the life-source of many an emerging economy in the past, are now increasingly scrutinised for the potential threat of de-stabilising certain key sectors of a domestic economy. Shades of geopolitical influence are often alluded to as well.

The measures employed by many governments tend to revolve around an arduous approval process for foreign investments in particular strategic or security sectors, or increasingly often, in any sector. Some, such as the EU, have articulated this as a matter of policy, purportedly to promote "cooperation, information sharing and a minimum level of transparency regarding FDI control between the European Commission and member states".[1] Earlier on in 2017, the EU moved to disallow Chinese companies to "cherry-pick their way through the best and most promising European enterprises".[2] Chinese FDI in Europe had been surging, peaking at €37 billion in 2016 but subsequently declined.

Japan meanwhile has tightened the restrictions on FDIs effective May 2020, requiring foreign investors to notify the government before acquiring a stake of 1% or more in listed companies in national security-related

---

[1] https://www.pinsentmasons.com/out-law/guides/the-eus-foreign-investment-regime, 23 October 2019.

[2] https://www.straitstimes.com/world/europe/europe-plans-to-regulate-foreign-takeover-bids, 17 August 2017.

fields such as semiconductors and nuclear energy. This threshold was previously set at 10%.[3] Many investors have viewed this move as retrogressive, away from good corporate governance and shareholder engagement.

In practice, many would-be foreign investors found that the decision is ultimately an outright "No" on many occasions.

Example 7.1: Many Ways of Saying "No"

Many governments try to embrace free market practices as far as possible, facilitating the movement of both capital and human resources across borders. Others may choose to organise themselves into trading blocs or economic free trade areas for mutual cooperation and benefit, but among members only. Regardless of any pronouncement of a commitment to free trade under the auspices of the World Trade Organization (WTO), the more mature economies tend to admit FDIs selectively.

For the capital-hungry emerging economies, foreign investors are frequently welcomed with a red carpet, even into sectors of national security or strategic importance. This can give rise to geopolitical implications should any foreign investor group dominate economic activity.

The list is a familiar one.

In May 2018, following a comprehensive multi-step national security review process, the Canadian government directed CCC International of China not to proceed with its US$1.2 billion acquisition of Aecon, a construction business.[4] Despite the creation of jobs by foreign investment, national security took priority.

This somewhat paled in comparison to the series of blocked acquisitions across the US border. The list included a US$117 billion bid by Chinese-owned Broadcom for rival chip manufacturer Qualcomm, albeit a hostile move; the US$1.2 billion deal between Alibaba's affiliate Ant Financial with MoneyGram and attempts at taking control of several US semiconductor manufacturers.[5] The common thread running through many of these rejections is that of technology, well understood within the context

---

[3] https://www.japantimes.co.jp/news/2019/12/25/business/financial-markets/japan-foreign-investment-rules/#.Xl5aMS2Q0Sc, 25 December 2019.

[4] https://www.ft.com/content/2d60f25c-5f07-11e8-9334-2218e7146b04, 24 May 2018.

[5] *Ibid.*

of the technology-related trade war being waged between the US and China.

Again, on the grounds of national security and enacting revised rules on foreign investment effective from 2017, the German government intended to reject the attempted takeover by the Chinese company Yantai Taihai of Leifeld, a company specialising in manufacturing for Germany's aerospace and nuclear industries in 2018.[6] The bid did not materialise as it was bound to fail. Concerns were raised over the security risk presented by such a union, given that Yantai has extensive interests in China's nuclear power sector.

This veto came in the wake of another move by the German government to thwart the State Grid Corporation of China's attempt to secure a stake in a local power distributing company, 50Hertz.[7]

Back in 2013, shortly after a pledge to be "open for business", the Australian government bowed to pressure from the local growers' lobby and vetoed the US$2.55 billion takeover of GrainCorp by US agribusiness giant Archer Daniels Midland (ADM). Again, the rejection of the proposed acquisition of the largest grain handler was justified on national interest grounds, taking into account the reservations expressed by the local growers over unfettered access to grain storage with the entry of a huge (foreign) player.[8]

Not surprisingly, some governments are wary of foreign investors wielding too much influence in particular sectors by virtue of their capital participation. Important pillars like the banking systems are historically governed tightly with many regimes imposing myriad foreign or single shareholding limits. From time to time, these limits may be revised to reflect the economic conditions of the day, the state of the banking ecosystem and the desire to allow greater influence in certain spheres.

Late December 2016, the Financial Services Authority (Otoritas Jasa Keuangan or OJK) issued a slew of changes regarding ownership of shares in Commercial Banks, comprising both conventional and sharia banks and non-bank financial institutions. The essence of the changes was to focus the spotlight on relationship between shareholders and to accord preference by the type of shareholder, with the highest limit for financial institutions

---

[6] https://www.bbc.com/news/world-europe-45030537, 1 August 2018.

[7] https://www.dw.com/en/chinese-takeover-of-leifeld-collapses-ahead-of-expected-german-veto/a-44906055, 1 August 2018.

[8] https://www.reuters.com/article/us-graincorp-adm/australia-surprises-with-rejection-of-2-55-billion-graincorp-takeover-by-adm-idUSBRE9AR0SG20131128, 29 November 2013.

(of 40%). The revision defines the circumstances involving related parties and how they would be treated for the determination of such limits. Exemptions as well as additional restrictions on foreign shareholders have been clearly spelt out too.[9] Perhaps what's challenging, arising from these revisions, are the divestment obligations within a 5-year timeframe.

Acquisition targets themselves may well welcome the participation of a foreign investor who brings capital, domain expertise and global networks. At the end of the day, it remains a political call, whatever rules are in place. Rejecting a potential FDI on grounds of national security interests when championing free trade can present awkward situations. Moreover, when it is the same investor group that keeps getting rebuffed, the allegations of being unfriendly can be difficult to defend.

> *To minimise misunderstanding, governments should state upfront the list of industries of security or strategic national interests that would require specific assessment for foreign participation or have ownership limits imposed. The foreign investment review process should be made as transparent as possible. Suffice it to say that it is the prerogative of a government to decide how it wants to be the national gatekeeper, credibility around the process and decision-making will always be important.*

Disallowing a foreign investor to take control of a major market player in a potentially sensitive sector, through an onerous foreign investment approval process, is one of the oldest playbook. The examples discussed earlier amply illustrate the instincts of most states — when in doubt, use the system of approvals to forestall a proposed transaction by a foreign investor. In other words, skilfully apply a commonly accepted non-trade barrier. This should be differentiated from the clearly articulated, and fairly standard, foreign ownership limits commonly imposed on systemically important institutions like banks and the like.

On other occasions, other impediments might take the form of conditions such as a need for local content or safeguards against geopolitical influence. Whatever the reasons, it is often not difficult for the public to see what the real reservations are.

---

[9] https://zico.group/blog/new-regulation-shares-ownership-indonesian-commercial-banks/, 29 March 2017.

Example 7.2: The Link to Nowhere

The burden of building and safeguarding a country's infrastructure often falls on the state and this is a role that most governments take seriously. To deliver on public expectations, the government has to conceive appropriately, settle on the necessary financial model, decide if it has the requisite knowhow to execute and plan how best to balance public–private relations, including foreign partnerships. At times, when the national security interest box does not check, the state would have to make unpopular decisions. This was alluded to in the aborted plan to build the Vegas–Nevada–LA high-speed rail link.

Plans for a Vegas–Nevada–LA high-speed rail have been in the works for more than a decade. Since 2005, XpressWest, the private company led by Marnell Companies, had been conceiving plans for a 370-km Southwest Rail Network, with stations in Las Vegas connected to the Metrolink services to Los Angeles, via towns in between.[10] Such a high-speed rail would make perfect sense, providing a useful, convenient and more environmentally friendly linkage that slashes commuting time to a fraction of that by car. It can potentially catalyse development of land around stops in between too.

In September 2015, XpressWest announced a partnership with China Railway International (CRI) USA, a consortium led by the China Railway Group, to undertake the entire suite of developing, financing and building the high-speed line. There was an option of the joint venture company operating the line as well. The CRI was to provide US$100 million in initial capital[11] for an estimated total project value of US$7 billion, with construction targeted to commence in September 2016 after the completion of the environmental impact assessment.[12]

However, in June 2016, barely nine months after the partnership had been launched, the deal with CRI was called off, mainly because of

---

[10] https://www.railwaygazette.com/high-speed/las-vegas-high-speed-line-promoter-drops-chinese-partner/42631.article, 10 June 2016.

[11] https://www.latimes.com/world/asia/la-fg-xpresswest-rail-line-20160608-snap-story.html, 8 June 2016.

[12] https://economictimes.indiatimes.com/news/international/world-news/china-threatens-usa-after-chinese-consortium-denied-rail-contract-on-vegas-nevada-la-line/articleshow/52703861.cms?from=mdr, 11 June 2016.

"difficulties associated with timely performance and CRI's challenges in obtaining authority to proceed with required development activities". XpressWest recounted that its biggest hurdle in executing the project was a federal government law that the high-speed trains had to be manufactured in the US, for which no such activity existed then. Lamenting that this requirement was too inflexible and that allowing trains from countries with the requisite experience in safe high-speed rail development was necessary to kick-start the industry in the US, XpressWest said it would be looking into other partnerships to implement the project.[13]

Reacting to news of the contract termination, China labelled it a "mistake" and CRI warned of possible legal action against XpressWest for its unilateral cancellation of the partnership.[14] This was a setback for Chinese companies who were looking to export their high-speed rail technology and experience, and the now-aborted Vegas–Nevada–LA project would have been the first of such contracts in the US.[15] China, which began building its extensive high-speed network in 2007, had already topped 12,000 miles at that time.

Though controversial, the US government's federal law to have high-speed trains manufactured domestically is not unreasonable. This is to ensure that there is local domain expertise should the government decide to build a high-speed network. The snag then was that there was no such manufacturing capability. Something has to give, implying the US government has to make the painful decision of deciding the form of foreign partnership that would satisfy its security and strategic interests. The reality stacked against it is the heavy capital outlay required of a meaningful network, one that would cause a noticeable dent to fiscal budgets. Financing from foreign sources might be inevitable.

---

[13] https://www.hongkongfp.com/2016/06/10/us-firm-scraps-plan-china-build-la-vegas-rail-line/, 10 June 2016.

[14] https://economictimes.indiatimes.com/news/international/world-news/china-threatens-usa-after-chinese-consortium-denied-rail-contract-on-vegas-nevada-la-line/articleshow/52703861.cms?from=mdr, 11 June 2016.

[15] https://www.latimes.com/world/asia/la-fg-xpresswest-rail-line-20160608-snap-story.html, 8 June 2016.

Retaliatory Tariffs

Retaliatory tariffs represent another form of counter-action against national interests. The wave of retaliatory tariffs has intensified beyond the US–China trade war. Justifying it as an anti-dumping move, governments have not been shy about imposing retaliatory and often debilitating tariffs on imports to level the field. This is usually the result of lobbying by the aggrieved locally owned operator(s) alleging unfair competition.

Example 7.3: Imposing No-Fly-Zone on Trade

Retaliatory tariffs spiralling into a full-blown trade war is a very real concern governments face. In protecting the country's own national, security or economic interests, governments occasionally have little choice but to combat actions by other countries. A case in example would be the Airbus and Boeing feud, with neither side relenting even after 16 years, leading to the implementation of tariffs.

Until Airbus entered the scene in 1970, Boeing had been enjoying a monopoly in aviation for more than five decades. Airbus and Boeing have been arch-rivals in the aircraft industry since the 1990s when Airbus launched competing products to Boeing's staples. The key bone of contention underlining their competition is the accusation both parties have thrown at each other about illegal subsidies by their respective governments. These have led to appeals and counter-appeals to the WTO in a seemingly never-ending battle. The duopoly is clearly an uncomfortable relationship, with Airbus slowly eating away at Boeing's pie.

The feud started around 2004, with the US government alleging that Airbus had received unfair EU state support, leading to the EU counter-filing a complaint on illegal US state aid for Boeing as well. The WTO later ruled that Airbus had received US$18 billion in illegal subsidies over four decades,[16] while 80% of the US$23 billion subsidies received by Boeing were found to be fair.[17] In 2018, the WTO ruled that the EU had failed to halt unlawful assistance to Airbus, leading to a nod to the US' decision to

---

[16] https://www.straitstimes.com/world/united-states/us-to-impose-103b-in-tariffs-on-eu-goods-over-airbus-row, 4 October 2019.

[17] https://www.aerospace-technology.com/features/airbus-vs-boeing/, 31 January 2020.

impose tariffs on EU goods, not just aircraft or aircraft parts, to the tune of US$7.5 billion in October 2019.[18] To put into context, this represented only about 1.5% of the total EU imports into the US.

In between in 2017, the US moved to slap correctional tariffs of 292% on Bombardier,[19] another aircraft company that Airbus had acquired majority stake in the C Series Aircraft Limited Partnership with.[20] This came after Boeing had complained to US authorities that the C-series aircraft were being sold to US airline Delta below production costs after receiving unlawful subsidies from the UK and Canadian governments. However, in 2018, the US International Trade Commission (ITC) voted in favour of Bombardier, halting the imposition of tariffs on Bombardier's aircrafts.[21] The tariff would otherwise more than triple the cost of a C-Series aircraft sold in the US.[22] The UK government heaved a sigh of relief as thousands of jobs at Bombardier's site in Belfast, Northern Ireland, have been spared.

This feud, however, has continued on, with the US imposing WTO-approved tariffs on US$7.5 billion of European goods in 2019. With these tariffs of 10% on aircraft and 25% on industrial and agricultural products,[23] the US hoped that the threat would pressure the EU into negotiating an agreement to lower tariffs, as well as eliminate illegal subsidies to Airbus, so as to allow the two companies to "compete on a level playing field".[24] After all, the imposition of US tariffs on European goods could very well spiral into a trade war. The EU responded by publishing a list of US$20 billion of American imports it could in turn impose tariffs on in retaliation

---

[18] https://www.reuters.com/article/us-wto-aircraft-timeline/timeline-highlights-of-the-15-year-airbus-boeing-trade-war-idUSKBN1WH198, 2 October 2019.

[19] https://www.theguardian.com/business/2018/jan/26/bombardier-us-tariffs-imports-uk-trump-jobs-belfast, 26 January 2018.

[20] https://www.airbus.com/newsroom/press-releases/en/2017/10/airbus-bombardier-cseries-agreement.html, 16 October 2017.

[21] https://www.theguardian.com/business/2018/jan/26/bombardier-us-tariffs-imports-uk-trump-jobs-belfast, 26 January 2018.

[22] https://www.theguardian.com/business/2017/sep/27/punitive-export-tariff-placed-on-planes-made-in-northern-ireland, 27 September 2017.

[23] https://www.straitstimes.com/world/united-states/us-to-impose-103b-in-tariffs-on-eu-goods-over-airbus-row, 4 October 2019.

[24] https://www.ft.com/content/dab6ba96-1512-11ea-9ee4-11f260415385, 3 December 2019.

for Boeing's subsidies[25] and is awaiting WTO ruling on whether the EU will be allowed to impose tariffs on US.[26]

> *The long-running feud, now into its sixteenth year, shows no signs of abating, but understandably so, with the government of each country/bloc needing to protect their own security and national interests. The aircraft industry is a major one, with countries needing aircraft for military or civilian purposes and national airlines needing them for commercial reasons. This ongoing saga reinforces the reality that when it comes to the crunch for matters of strategic or security importance, only the government can and has to step up to the plate to defend a market position on behalf of a private sector player, regardless of whether it is state owned.*

Threat to National Security

Terrorism is indisputably a top priority that many governments are currently seized with. The potent combination of technology and terrorism explains the huge amount of resources that are being devoted to combatting all forms of terrorism acts and cybercrime.

Current efforts of many governments are centred on both the early detection of potential attacks, physical or cyber, so as to enable preventive steps to be taken, and the actual moves to counter terrorism or cyberattacks. Technology plays a huge part in such efforts as much as it has been pivotal to fertilising terrorism or cybercrimes. For the latter, technology has facilitated the spread of terrorism to the extent of self-radicalisation in places far away from centres of terrorism activity. Social media networks have been instrumental in this regard. Technology has also been used towards iniquitous ends, commonly in the form of cyberattacks on public systems.

---

[25] https://www.straitstimes.com/world/united-states/us-to-impose-103b-in-tariffs-on-eu-goods-over-airbus-row, 4 October 2019.

[26] https://www.ft.com/content/dab6ba96-1512-11ea-9ee4-11f260415385, 3 December 2019.

Example 7.4: Striking Out Terrorism and Cyberattacks

It is indisputable that any government worth its salt will assume responsibility for tackling any form of threat to national security. For the last few decades, terrorism has dominated the agenda. This overlaps with the onslaught of cyberattacks which have come fast and furious. Combatting terrorism and cybercrimes will now be where any government can be expected to invest more time and effort in to protect its people. From partnering with companies to develop the latest, most efficient technology to investing in infrastructure and enforcing regulations on organisations, the government plays a vital role in keeping its citizens and increasingly, their personal data safe.

Bane of Cyberattacks

Cybersecurity is acknowledged as one of the biggest threats to businesses, with the global value at risk estimated at US$5.2 trillion over the next five years.[27] Establishing a secure defence in cyberspace is hence critical not just to protect citizens' and governmental data but also to protect the future of the country's economy.[28]

Britain alone suffered from 658 cyberattacks in 2018, a large majority of the total 1800 cyberattacks recorded since the National Cyber Security Centre was founded in 2016.[29] Research also found that the average cost a business has to bear after a cyberattack has increased by more than £1,000 since 2018 to £4,180. The UK government subsequently approved a £36 million scheme in 2019 to protect businesses from cyberattacks by partnering with prominent tech firms such as ARM. It also funded the development of more resilient networks and techniques to identify future threats and alleviate their impacts through partnerships with research firms and universities.[30] This is building

---

[27] https://www.accenture.com/us-en/insights/security/cost-cybercrime-study/, 6 March 2019.

[28] https://www.gov.uk/government/news/britains-cyber-security-bolstered-by-world-class-strategy, 1 November 2016.

[29] https://metro.co.uk/2019/10/23/uk-targeted-600-cyber-attacks-last-year-10967419/, 23 October 2019.

[30] https://www.techradar.com/uk/news/uk-government-reveals-major-cybersecurity-investment, 18 October 2019.

on the UK's National Cyber Security Strategy launched in 2016 to protect the UK economy and the privacy of British citizens through three key areas of defence, deterrence and development.[31]

Singapore has also had serious breaches in cybersecurity in recent years, from the SingHealth data breach in 2018 to the online leak of HIV-positive Singaporeans' personal information and the personal information of blood donors exposed online from mishandling in 2019.[32] In response, the Singapore government will invest S$1 billion over three years to boost its cyber and data security systems, which is of increasing importance as Singapore moves towards becoming a smart nation and governmental agencies look to adopt technologies such as Artificial Intelligence (AI) and Internet of Things (IoT).[33] Such enhancements to security capabilities would protect critical information infrastructures and citizen data. Moreover, financial institutions can access a S$30 million grant to fund up to 50% of their expenses in efforts to enhance their cybersecurity operations. This is part of the government's effort to increase government–industry partnerships to strengthen national cyber resilience.[34]

Pervasive Use of CCTVs

Besides cyber defence, the use of surveillance closed-circuit television (CCTV) cameras is also an essential part of preventing crime and terrorism. Though initially the source of public scrutiny over privacy concerns, CCTVs now are ubiquitous, if not indispensable, in all major cities. Whatever the misgivings, the usefulness of video surveillance to combat crime has been fast gaining support. In all, 54 terrorist attacks have been thwarted because of information collected by surveillance programmes,[35] and a notable breakthrough was the identification of suspects in the Boston Marathon bombing in 2013 through video images captured in the city's cameras. There is a whole range of cost–benefit analyses on the use of

---

[31] https://www.gov.uk/government/news/britains-cyber-security-bolstered-by-world-class-strategy, 1 November 2016.

[32] https://www.channelnewsasia.com/news/singapore/government-improve-data-security-contact-public-report-breaches-12130700, 27 November 2019.

[33] https://www.zdnet.com/article/singapore-to-spend-719m-beefing-up-governments-cyber-data-security-systems/, 18 February 2020.

[34] https://www.zdnet.com/article/singapore-banks-offered-21m-in-funds-to-boost-cybersecurity-capabilities/, 3 December 2018.

[35] https://www.tandfonline.com/doi/full/10.1080/01972243.2017.1414721, 8 March 2018.

CCTVs for crime prevention; in the US, a recent analysis pointed to a saving of over $4 otherwise lost to crime for every dollar spent on technology.[36] Though every analysis is likely to throw up different effects, the conclusion is nonetheless directionally clear, hence the proliferation of CCTVs in all countries, especially major cities.

Singapore too recognises the potential of such technology and has been expanding its network of CCTVs significantly, covering all 10,000 public housing blocks. Over the last few years, an additional 11,000 cameras have been installed on top of the 65,000 police cameras already in place.

Hardening of Security

Developers of large-scale projects and building owners have been asked to include security plans at the design stage according to a live document "Enhancing Building Security".[37] The Singapore Home Affairs Minister reasoned thus, "Terrorist attacks in other places have focused on soft targets because there was little or no security protection".[38] The government also reached out to the public at large; crowdsourcing platforms have been set up for the public to send videos to the police to be part of the nation's security defence.

Counter-terrorism is fast figuring prominently in many government budgets, given the increasing number of terrorism activities over the years. That for the US has been steadily increasing over the past two decades since the September 11 terrorist attacks, by US$360 billion annually, and reaching an estimated total of US$2.8 trillion since then to 2018.[39]

Countering terrorism has taken on more urgency in the EU as well, following terrorist attacks in 2015 in Paris and Copenhagen and 2016 in Brussels.[40] The European Counter-Terrorism Centre was quickly established in 2016 following these attacks, and significant efforts have been

---

[36] https://www.ifsecglobal.com/video-surveillance/role-cctv-cameras-public-privacy-protection/, 1 January 2014.

[37] https://www.accenture.com/us-en/insights/security/cost-cybercrime-study/, accessed 8 March 2020.

[38] https://www.straitstimes.com/singapore/more-surveillance-cameras-as-deterrent, 19 March 2016.

[39] https://www.accenture.com/us-en/insights/security/cost-cybercrime-study/, 17 May 2018.

[40] https://www.europeansources.info/record/counter-terrorism-funding-in-the-eu-budget/, April 2016.

made to establish a strategy to take on terrorism.[41] A Counter-Terrorism Register was also established in 2019 to compile information from EU countries on "ongoing investigations, prosecutions and convictions of militants, including foreign fighters that joined terrorist groups abroad". This would help courts to more effectively connect cases across different member states and ensure criminals are properly punished.[42] Broader EU spending on "Security and Citizenship", including counter-terrorism efforts, continued to escalate, almost doubling from €2.5 billion in 2015 to €4.1 billion in 2016.[43]

> *Preserving a country's national security interests has become increasingly complex, especially with new and different types of threats emerging rapidly. More than funding technology and research, and hardening infrastructure to counter such attacks, the government needs to unite the country psychologically. It also has to drive these initiatives together with the private sector not just towards developing solutions but also to ensure that additional regulatory compliance is manageable. To do this competently, a government cannot just react to attacks in a knee-jerk fashion; instead it has to plan ahead and proactively set up defences in place to counter future threats.*

Taking Cyber Threats Seriously

There is no doubt that many states are taking cyberthreats very seriously; the simple act of hacking can bring many systems to their knees and daily lives to a halt. Smaller economies tend to be more vulnerable, given the constraints to building proprietary resilience. With increasing sophistication of cyberattacks, larger countries aren't spared either. Many governments readily collaborate across borders, as they do on physical security matters, in recognition of the advantage of a consolidation of efforts. Bigger economies such as the U.S. and China obviously have more resources to devise their own customised, national responses.

---

[41] *Ibid.*

[42] https://www.euractiv.com/section/justice-home-affairs/news/eu-launches-new-counter-terrorism-database/, 9 September 2019.

[43] https://www.europeansources.info/record/counter-terrorism-funding-in-the-eu-budget/, April 2016.

Example 7.5: China Operating its Own Home-Grown Systems

Security considerations these days reign supreme especially in the pervasive role that technology plays. China is blest with scale and financial resources. Together with the ample talent she has, creating her own operating systems becomes quite simply a question of when.

The quest towards self-sufficiency for myriad reasons has preoccupied China for the past few decades. In December 2019, there was much fanfare as the two biggest Operating System ("OS") makers jointly announced a collaboration towards building a new "domestic operating system".[44] China Standard Software (CS2C) and Tianjin Kylin Information (TKC), established local OS players, will symbolise their merger with a common Chinese mythical beast, the *qilin*.

The Kylin OS has a long history, having been created in 2001 by academics in the National University of Defense Technology. Since then, several variants have evolved including some used to power the Tianhe-1 and Tianhe-2 super computers and others for community use. Meanwhile, CS2C created and developed the NeoKylin OS that gave TKC a run for its money.

In 2014, arising from a strategic decision by the Beijing government to replace foreign OS, both CS2C and TKC collectively secured a dominant 90% share of the public sector. A second push to be rid of reliance on foreign technology is underway. By 2022, all public sector units have to replace foreign-made hardware and software with Chinese alternatives, known as the "3-5-2" directive.[45] The replacement goal is 30% for 2020, 50% for 2021 and the remaining 20% in 2022. Harmonisation and integration of the different OS could still pose problems, but the overriding goal is clear.

OS Independence for Smartphones

In the same vein, in a bid to break the monopoly of US tech giants Google and Apple, China developed and unveiled its own mobile platform, the

---

[44] https://www.zdnet.com/article/two-of-chinas-largest-tech-firms-are-uniting-to-create-a-new-domestic-os/, 12 December 2019.

[45] https://www.zdnet.com/article/chinese-government-to-replace-foreign-hardware-and-software-within-three-years/, 9 December 2019.

China Operating System ("COS") in 2014.[46] COS was developed by the Institute of Software at the Chinese Academy of Sciences and the Shanghai Liantong Network Communications Technology, mainly to compete with Apple's iOS and Android. Linux-based, COS serves as an operating platform for *inter alia*, PCs and smartphones. Security and safety concerns meant that it could not be an open source system.

Meanwhile, Android and iOS continue to dominate smartphones in China, with a market share of 83% and 16%, respectively, as at the end of 2019.[47] Separately, Huawei announced in August 2019 that its Harmony OS could potentially replace Android in its smartphones, smartwatches and other devices.[48] This would bring about a material change as Huawei has grown to be one of the largest smartphone companies in the world. The current US–China trade war will however continue to have implications for Huawei's market fate, especially with regard to its 5G role. But clearly, there's no stopping the China-centric efforts at eradicating her reliance on foreign technology.

> *The US–China trade war has heightened the need for many countries to re-examine their reliance on certain suppliers for both hardware and software. Security considerations now rank at the very top given how real cyber misdeeds have crystallised, with the potential of striking at the very core of politics and government. It behoves every government to explore all options, from establishing one's own system where it's absolutely critical and ideally where there's sufficient scale and resources, to collaboration with friendly partners.*

Strategic and Social Considerations

While security interests may be more straightforward in terms of definition, strategic interests are harder to identify as they may morph over time as an economy matures or in response to a fast-changing global marketplace.

---

[46] https://www.zdnet.com/article/china-reveals-own-mobile-operating-system/, 17 January 2014.

[47] https://gs.statcounter.com/os-market-share/mobile/china, December 2019.

[48] https://www.zdnet.com/article/huaweis-new-smartphone-operating-system-is-completely-different-from-android-and-ios/, 9 August 2019.

Social considerations on the contrary contain too many imponderables; the reality is that they tend to make or break politicians.

Seeding Sustainable Growth

Long before the notion of "sustainability" becomes common vocabulary, many governments have already been seeking to cultivate and nurture their own indigenous pool of enterprise. The hard truth about FDI is that there is seldom loyalty to the host country; understandably, it's all about the dollars and cents. There is therefore no permanence in the economic activity that they generate. Home-grown enterprises, on the contrary, are usually fiercely loyal and sentimental especially if they have received state support in their growth journey.

Where market failure figures prominently, all the more the state has to be proactive in nurturing the innovative, entrepreneurial spirit. This support usually takes the form of an ecosystem to both help lighten overheads burden and foster business development.

Example 7.6: Giving Start-ups a Leg-up

Entrepreneurship in a country is important for many reasons, namely, to drive economic growth and increase the country's indigenous productive capacity. It helps to drive innovation while providing more job opportunities for the labour force, ultimately raising the standard of living. However, launching and sustaining a start-up in a market of finite size like Singapore requires substantial capital, an amount that not all aspiring entrepreneurs can afford. Hence, in order to encourage local entrepreneurship, a government would need to provide some form of assistance to help nurture these start-ups to enable them to survive for a meaningful period.

Singapore is one of several countries that recognises the need to provide support to local entrepreneurs as part of a holistic strategy to sustain economic growth. She established Enterprise Singapore (ESG) in 2018, a merger of International Enterprise, which was the lead agency in assisting Singapore companies to expand overseas, and Spring Singapore, which hitherto had helped grow small- and medium-sized businesses. ESG provides specialised programmes and assistance for companies tailored to their specific needs.[49] It is a one-stop business development agency that serves as a liaison for companies of various sizes and supports "upgrading, innovation and business model transformation to capture new revenue streams". It also has a focus on adopting new forms of technology to aid productivity and encourage overseas expansion. One example would be the Productivity Solutions Grant which subsidies up to 70% of a company's IT solutions and equipment purchases to improve productivity.[50]

In its pioneer year, ESG helped about 76,000 companies in Singapore, and more than 1,000 start-ups were helped through the Start-up SG Programmes and partners,[51] which provides Singapore-based start-ups access to funding and mentorship.[52] ESG has also supported the set-up of NSG BioLabs, a privately owned co-working space for biotech start-ups which will provide access to funding, advice and equipment worth millions of dollars to these start-ups. Companies will be able to rent these spaces at an affordable price, targeted at small start-ups ranging from one to two researchers to those with 20–30 people.[53] Hitherto, the lack of a suitable ecosystem to help develop products has hindered progress of the biotech industry. The establishment of this co-working laboratory and office space will go a long way towards enabling start-ups to validate their products and in turn attract more investors, ultimately accelerating the company's development.[54]

Indonesia is another country that is allocating more resources to support start-ups in the country. Home to thousands of start-ups and four unicorns[55] (privately held companies valued at over US$1 billion), there

---

[49] https://www.businesstimes.com.sg/government-economy/enterprise-singapore-assisted-76000-companies-in-2018, 14 March 2019.

[50] https://www.singtel.com/business/articles/sme/how-enterprise-singapore-help-sme, 1 March 2019.

[51] https://www.businesstimes.com.sg/government-economy/enterprise-singapore-assisted-76000-companies-in-2018, 14 March 2019.

[52] https://www.startupdecisions.com.sg/singapore/incentives/startup-funding-sources/, accessed 2 March 2020.

[53] https://www.straitstimes.com/business/co-working-space-for-biotech-start-ups-in-spore-to-be-launched-next-month, 10 October 2019.

[54] https://kr-asia.com/nsg-biolabs-launches-biotech-focussed-co-working-lab-and-office-space, 3 October 2019.

[55] https://kr-asia.com/what-to-expect-from-indonesian-startup-landscape-in-2019, 7 January 2019.

were 2,000 local start-ups in Indonesia in 2016, the highest number in Southeast Asia. This is projected to spike to 13,000 by 2020.[56]

The Indonesian government is sparing no efforts in helping to cultivate the start-up culture and is set to remove the requirement for foreign workers in start-ups to obtain written permits. This comes as a move by the government to reduce bureaucratic inefficiency and encourage more foreign workers to reduce the country's digital talent gap and import knowledge and skills into the country.[57] The government is also partnering with Venture Capital Association for Indonesian Start-ups (Amvesindo) and Ernst & Young to link up local start-ups with global investors by providing funding for them to develop their product offerings.[58]

To house start-ups, the Jakarta government launched a co-working space in 2017 called "Jakarta Smart City Hive". While not funding the start-ups themselves, the government will work with venture capitalists to procure funding for the start-ups and collaborate with the private sector to operate the co-working space. This initiative will allow the government to better understand the needs of the start-ups, and in turn link them with mentors from more experienced companies. Rental amounts of an affordable $25 per month[59] provide a conducive environment for start-ups to grow and be mentored. The set-up of a co-working space by the government is timely, given the surge in demand for co-working spaces in Jakarta and amidst the increase in supply of the number of serviced offices and coworking spaces by 60% in 2018.[60] Co-working offices are popular for not just good internet connectivity but also the opportunity to network and connect with other start-ups. Professionals can also seek advice and explore other job opportunities.

Elsewhere in Europe, Lithuania already has a flourishing start-up ecosystem with a value of S$156 million. Lithuania's appeal lies in the start-up ecosystem for both entrepreneurs and investors, given her low-cost access to talent from local universities and the strategic location of the country in Central Europe, with access to both the Russian and European markets.

---

[56] https://www.thejakartapost.com/news/2017/07/06/coworking-space-a-melting-pot-digital-nomads.html, 6 July 2017.

[57] https://www.thejakartapost.com/news/2020/02/20/no-permits-required-by-foreigners-in-start-ups.html, 20 February 2020.

[58] https://jakartaglobe.id/business/govt-creates-special-directorate-for-1000-startups, 16 November 2019.

[59] https://govinsider.asia/innovation/jakarta-to-launch-its-own-hive-co-working-space/, 14 March 2017.

[60] https://www.thejakartapost.com/news/2019/06/27/thriving-start-ups-drive-strong-growth-for-coworking-spaces.html, 28 June 2019.

Its local organisations are also supportive of local start-ups. For example, The Bank of Lithuania offers a Fintech regulatory sandbox that allows start-ups access to 34 countries through the CENTROlink system and is one of the reasons why Lithuania saw a 45% jump in Fintech companies incorporated in 2018. However, more than the attractive start-up climate is the continued effort by the government to support entrepreneurship in the country where it takes just three days to register a business.[61]

Enterprise Lithuania is a governmental institution with the express mandate to support start-ups in the country and collaborates with organisations like *Startup Lithuania*, a one-stop destination for businesses, providing access to a large network and educating and consulting start-ups. Lithuania's Funding Growth Index was ranked 9 out of 10 in 2019, "showing large growth in total start-up creation, calculated on an annualised growth rate".[62] Lithuania continues to push for more changes to aid the development of start-ups in the country, one such example being the reduction in processing time for issuing a start-up visa from the maximum of 30 days to 15 days, and the maximum period for holding the visa increased from 2–3 years, giving foreign entrepreneurs more time to develop their business in Lithuania.[63] Furthermore, the Lithuanian government set up Go Vilnius back in 1996/7, the official development agency of Vilnius, in the capital of Lithuania. It provides entrepreneurs with not just advice but also co-working spaces needed to develop their business.[64]

As seen in the three countries above, government support is a crucial part of cultivating a friendly, sustainable climate for start-ups and businesses. Besides setting up agencies and offering consultation and advice, helping entrepreneurs with real estate overheads either through the availability of co-working space or financial support is a concrete investment the government can make towards nurturing indigenous entrepreneurship. This is in recognition of the reality that real estate and labour costs tend to dominate viability concerns for start-ups.

---

[61] https://startupgenome.com/blog/lithuania-startup-ecosystem-fintech-mobility, 18 November 2019.

[62] *Ibid.*

[63] https://china-cee.eu/2019/08/06/lithuania-economy-briefing-lithuania-increases-efforts-to-boost-the-fintech-startup-ecosystem-by-improving-the-startup-visa-program/, 6 August 2019.

[64] http://www.govilnius.lt/about-us/, 2 March 2020

Healthcare for Rising Affluence and Longevity

Social needs are another kettle of fish. Despite public goods like education and healthcare being the perennial favourites for politicisation for the longest of time, many countries are still grappling with these challenges. What has compounded the challenge is the shift in expectations of such public goods. Rising affluence is the main driver of rising expectations of treatment, quality of hospital care and what's considered as acceptable minimal standards of healthcare. Not surprisingly, the campaign agenda for any election these days is dominated by the prevailing healthcare challenges.

Example 7.7: Headache over Healthcare

Healthcare is deemed a basic commodity, and access to affordable, efficient healthcare services is something many governments around the world have pledged to provide for their people. From subsidies for services to efficient hospitals, healthcare is a public good that only the government is in a position to effectively provide at affordable levels to all its citizens. If left to the free market, although effective cures and efficiency can no doubt be delivered, they will be priced accordingly. Profitability will be the number one priority of private corporations. Given that runaway healthcare costs will never be tenable for the society at large, the government can and has to play an important role in meeting public healthcare needs. This means ensuring the availability of affordable healthcare services of acceptable quality for the masses, a simple calling but a tall order.

Satisfactory public healthcare is not an easy thing to deliver on, as exemplified by the woes of the struggling British National Health Service (NHS). First established in 1948, the NHS remains in a crisis, facing financial and efficiency issues after a series of reorganisation every so often. One of the major reforms in 1990 led to a separation of the NHS into two parts, one responsible for buying services from hospitals and the other running hospitals, in a bid to create an "internal market" to engender competition. This paved the way for the subsequent labour government to step up the creation of even more opportunities for competition and enable private hospitals to provide NHS treatment. Wittingly or otherwise, this bifurcation led to a shift away from treating acute healthcare problems to long-term conditions.[65]

Unsustainable Model

The budget for NHS had escalated by about 3.7% annually since its inception but is expected to decelerate to 0.9% for the decade ending 2021. As of 2014–2015, this translated into a sizeable 7.3% of GDP, or about £134 billion, and will fall to 6.6% by 2021, lower than for most of its peers. Against continued rising demand, NHS is poised to countenance a shortfall of £20 billion imminently.

Financial distress is evident — several hospital divisions already face closure, and virtually all of the hospital trusts ended 2015 in deficit. Though suggestions for replacing the taxpayer-funded model with health insurance, widely in use in Europe, have been mooted, most officials believe the cost of migrating to social insurance would overshadow its benefits.[66] Many rationally argued that attention should be focused on raising efficiency and getting more bang for the buck in NHS spending.

Dealing with Inefficiency

Inefficiency is another big problem that the NHS faces. One glaring example is the so-called bed-blockers conundrum. In 2016, 6000 patients in hospitals, or a hefty 50% more than the previous year's, were ready to go home, but were not yet discharged for a variety of reasons, costing the NHS hundreds of millions of pounds per year and preventing others from receiving medical care.

Aggravating the understaffing situation at hospitals was the lack of discipline or knowledge around costs and outcomes. Equally unhelpful was how hospitals were being paid, a system that favoured repeat activity over innovation. It needs to instead start reducing demand for expensive hospital treatments to reduce the burden on the NHS system.[67]

Meanwhile, the UK population has grown dramatically and is ageing, thereby placing more pressure on the NHS. Spending on manpower accounts for more than two-thirds of the hospital budget, and Britain

---

[65] https://www.economist.com/britain/2016/09/10/accident-and-emergency, 10 September 2016.

[66] *Ibid.*

[67] *Ibid.*

suffers from more shortages of hospital staff than any other rich country.[68] This results in longer waiting times — in 2016, 4.2 million people were waiting for consultant-led, non-urgent hospital treatment, and 3000 of whom had been waiting for over a year.[69] Attention has to be paid to the role of the General Practitioners' (GPs) network as well, particularly as gatekeepers.

Confronting the Same Challenges

The Hong Kong healthcare system faces rather similar issues. To its credit, its healthcare system has done well, placing first in the Bloomberg Health Care Efficiency Index in 2018, on an absolute cost of US$2,222. The Hong Kong government has also catered to changing population needs, increasing its budget for healthcare by 7% over the past decade.[70]

However, like its British counterpart, the Hong Kong public healthcare system is grossly overworked and overburdened. It's the norm for doctors to work for 12 hours straight, and during winter, non-urgent patients have to wait for up to 8 hours at some emergency units. Hospitals are grossly understaffed, with the number of doctors not proportionate to the increasing number of patients. In a span of 10 years, the Hong Kong population increased by 7%, with a significantly higher percentage of people aged 65 or above. The Hospital Authority expects a constant shortage of 300 doctors, while the Food and Health Bureau has predicted a higher deficit of 500 doctors in 2020. To counter the shortage, suggestions have been made to allow foreign doctors into the market to ease the burden on local doctors.[71] This recommendation has been contentious, and many have argued that the top priority should really be to improve the working conditions for doctors.

Once again, the spotlight had been shone on the role of the GPs in Hong Kong. It has been assessed that GPs are quite capable of handling half of the public hospital admissions. Yet, Hong Kong residents continue to favour public hospitals even for minor ailments.

---

[68] *Ibid.*

[69] https://www.theguardian.com/society/2018/jul/02/is-the-nhs-the-worlds-best-healthcare-system, 2 July 2018.

[70] https://hongkongbusiness.hk/healthcare/news/hong-kongs-healthcare-system-beats-singapore-worlds-most-efficient-bloomberg, 26 September 2018.

[71] https://www.scmp.com/news/hong-kong/health-environment/article/2187630/hong-kongs-health-care-system-teetering-brink, 26 February 2019.

Towards Striking a Balance

Over the years, the Singapore government has been trying to strike a nice balance between good quality and affordable services. In November 2015, it introduced a compulsory nation-wide insurance, a scheme named MediShield Life, for all 3.9 million Singaporeans and Permanent Residents. This replaced the old, optional MediShield scheme which only covered citizens up till the age of 92 and excluded some people with certain pre-existing conditions. MediShield Life on the contrary has no age or lifetime claim limit and even covers those with pre-existing conditions, though those with serious conditions will have to pay extra premiums. If citizens are unable to pay the normal premium even after initial government subsidy, they will be able to apply for additional ones. The government is even paying 40–60% of premiums for Singaporeans aged 65 or older.[72] This way, the government ensures that its people have access to affordable healthcare delivered by the entire ecosystem, from GPs to polyclinics and hospitals.

Nationalised healthcare schemes, it seems, can go two ways, depending on the extent of government intervention in the industry. Intervention is usually aimed at lowering healthcare costs for the masses with access to minimum acceptable standards of healthcare across the country. This is of course predicated on the ability of the government to plan and allocate financial and healthcare resources effectively.

The role of the government cannot be overstated in this instance. Being price-takers, the public has no choice but to look to the government for assurance of affordable and efficient healthcare. The government plays a key role in setting up the relevant policies, providing sufficient budget and overseeing the long-term planning for the healthcare industry. It needs to be able to project the population's needs in the future, predominantly ageing implications, decide on the operating model, including the merits of national healthcare insurance and allocate resources accordingly. Many public healthcare systems suffer from legacy issues. In order to bring about real change, it is often incumbent upon the

---

[72] https://www.straitstimes.com/singapore/health/all-will-be-able-to-afford-medishield-life-premiums-gan-kim-yong, 1 November 2015.

> *government of the day to consider radical reforms against the practicality of execution. Usually, this calls for political will that regrettably current-day populist politics and short-termism would not allow.*

It doesn't help that many countries are running grossly under-funded national pension plans. While the day of reckoning may be the problem of another batch of politicians, essentially the public is seized with the fear of falling critically ill during their old age and not being able to afford the necessary medical care. Designing a national healthcare scheme requires great effort, mastery of actuarial projections and fiscal discipline to ensure funding.

Population Growth Pains

Equally daunting is the task of ensuring that the population continue to be able to replace itself. Many modern cities face the real challenge of not reproducing themselves. Over the past many decades, immigration has been successful at plugging this gap. The immigration solution however is fast disappearing as a viable solution as xenophobia takes over many societies who are resentful at losing employment opportunities and fair salaries to these newcomers.

Meanwhile, many governments continue to crack their heads, trying their best to devise as many ways as possible to encourage family formation. This challenge has long been the preoccupation of the Singapore government as far back as the 1980s, with innovative but socially untenable schemes like the Graduate Mother Scheme which accorded school priority to children of graduate mothers. Undeterred, the government continues trying.

With dual-income families increasingly the norm, flexible work arrangements understandably rank high on the wish-list. Given the pervasive availability of technology and shifting work cultures in parallel with the development of the gig economy, employers are now obliged to ensure that there is meaningful flexibility, particularly for working mothers. Again, this is something that the government, by both public policy and setting a good example as an employer, has to take leadership.

Example 7.8: A Good Head Start is Everything

How does a government raise flagging birth rates? Does it exhaust any and every avenue possible to encourage young couples to consider starting a family, or better still, having as many children as they can afford to? How far should such efforts go? Where regulations aren't sufficient or incentives unattractive or inefficiently dished out, market intervention becomes a real alternative.

An analysis into the reasons for the declining birth-rate in Singapore throws up a variety of causes. Double-income families are increasingly the norm, implying having more children, if any at all, takes second place to staying employed or career progression. Another aspiration is to be able to secure permanent housing before starting a family, invariably accentuating the trend of later marriages. Added to this, perhaps the greatest determinant of family size, is the concern over the high cost of bringing up a child. There's a perceived lack of good, affordable education, or literally a poor head start, for a young couple contemplating starting a family. While formal schooling expenses have been kept affordable in most countries including Singapore, pre-school fees have been running away. Intervention is therefore justified in many scenarios.

Prior to 2012, the Singapore had been resisting the call to "nationalise pre-school education" to counter rising kindergarten and childcare fees. Affluence obviously has a big part to play towards whetting up the appetite for yet more sophisticated pre-school programmes, from basic 3Rs to faith-based not-for-profit to Montessori and the like at the higher, expensive end. The ballooning cost of pre-school arrangements was inevitable. Taking baby steps then, *inter alia*, the Singapore Ministry of Education (MOE) initiated three underpinnings — establishing an autonomous agency to oversee the regulation and development of kindergarten and child/infant care programmes, piloting its own kindergartens at five schools and enhancing, and ensuring access to sufficient places for lower- and middle-income families. The initial lukewarm response comprising a small crowd of 250 toddlers to the MOE pilot kindergarten programme beginning in 2014 was misleading, to say the least. Few had attached value to the priority admission to the same primary school where the preschool is sited.

Since that timid start, enrolment has galloped to 3,841 across 24 pre-schools as at July 2019. The target then was to enlarge availability to 43 by

2022.[73] The February 2020 Budget announcement held even bigger plans — to raise the total to 60 by 2025,[74] on the back of a doubling of the S$1 billion expenditure to S$2 billion over the next 5 years on the early childhood sector. This would include collaborations with existing partners and is aimed at increasing the share of government-supported pre-school places from around half in 2020 to a dominant 80% by 2025.[75]

The conscious decision by the Singapore government to intervene in a sector which hitherto had been supplied by private operators is not a trivial one. Against a lack-lustre birth trend, the pre-school market had been a crowded but sustainable one, with prices driven by relatively healthy competition. Till 2012, MOE regulated standards and licenced operators but did not "compete" as an operator. Various price-points were established and the variety was acceptable to young parents. With the entry of the government into the fray, backed by ample resources, the field can rightly be described as tilting away. The smaller, faith-based not-for-profit kindergartens or run-of-the-mill outfits in older housing estates obviously are feeling the squeeze. It would not be surprising if many would eventually find declining enrolments unsustainable economics.

Whenever the state decides to intervene and consciously conflate its roles of a regulator and an operator, it must assume responsibility for addressing the uneven playing field that results. To begin with, such a decision must be predicated on the achievement of a much larger social goal, such as an improved reproduction rate, that would otherwise not be possible under the status quo. Perhaps, it may be argued that the smaller, less distinctive pre-schools would have died a natural death over time with declining birth rates. This will remain debatable.

Ageing Population Implications

The flip-side to a declining birth-rate is an ageing population. With better living conditions and affluence on the back of sustained economic

---

[73] https://www.todayonline.com/singapore/parents-fight-keep-non-profit-preschools-alive-popularity-moe-kindergartens-grows, 14 July 2019.

[74] https://beta.moe.gov.sg/preschool/moe-kindergarten/overview/, 24 February 2020.

[75] https://www.straitstimes.com/singapore/more-help-to-give-every-singaporean-child-a-good-start-in-life, 19 February 2020.

expansion, the resulting longer life expectancy accentuates the challenges of managing ageing. This covers the entire spectrum from employment to emotional, financial and physical well-being.

Example 7.9: Growing Old Gracefully, and Happily

An ageing population is a phenomenon most cities will face as life expectancies increase and fertility rates drop, representing a multi-faceted challenge confronting many developed countries. With this development comes several socio-economic issues the government will have to address in order to ensure the well-being of not just the elderly but also future generations who will be supporting them, and the economy in turn. Japan and Singapore are two such countries facing this challenge full on, albeit at different stages of the ageing cycle.

Japan is probably feeling the heat the most as she continually attempts to come up with an array of solutions to alleviate the burdens of an ageing society. It is a real concern the country has been living with for several decades already, with the country having the longest life expectancy of 84 years and the highest share of elderly in her population (ages 65 and above) at 27%. A key issue is the inversion of the pyramid in the labour force as more adults reach retirement age with fewer children to replace them. This impacts not just economic markets but also financial markets through a drop in savings accumulated and investment levels. Not only that, the quality of goods and services will also be affected with a smaller working force.[76]

Beyond a Shrinking Workforce

A disproportionally large elderly population has led to new problems for the government. Healthcare expenditure will continue to figure prominently and remain a major withdrawal from savings, as can be seen from Japan's expenditure of a hefty 10.7%, the sixth-highest percentage among all countries, of her GDP on healthcare. Beyond the bulging healthcare budget from the sheer combination of a greater variety of treatments for a bigger range of age-related ailments is the social burden of ensuring sufficient numbers of care-givers. Promoting elderly well-being is really

---

[76] https://voxeu.org/article/japan-s-age-wave-challenges-and-solutions, 3 December 2018.

the only sustainable response. Apart from preventive healthcare efforts, deferring the retirement age has myriad advantages, although most elderly persons would baulk at the very thought of not being able to retire. Older persons who continue working beyond the prescribed retirement age, which incidentally was set when life expectancy was shorter, tend to enjoy better mental, emotional and physical health. Moreover, working longer has the added benefit of additional financial assurance.

Japan is already experiencing fiscal stress through its pay-as-you-go National Pension Program as the number of adults under the programme is accelerating. Its social security payments nearly doubled between 1990 and 2017 as a share to total budget, outpacing contributions. Besides fiscal concerns, social challenges are another important part to keep in mind. As dependency ratio increases in Japan, working adults will be burdened with the cost of supporting the elderly not merely through monetary burdens but also productive time that could be spent on other activities.[77]

A Multi-Pronged Approach

Japan has already worked on integrating complementary measures to alleviate the burden on society, specifically future generations. Policies aimed at raising fertility rates include reducing educational costs, improving housing and allocating funds to childcare facilities to relieve the burden on working parents. To boost labour force numbers so as to sustain growth, measures include incentivising female workforce participation and allowing foreigners by relaxing immigration restrictions. Raising retirement age and pension eligibility remains the most effective policy solution as this would help to enlarge the productive workforce years and reduce fiscal burden for pension obligations.[78]

Singapore — Adapting from Japan's Experience

Singapore has taken a leaf from the experiences of other countries with an ageing population, particularly from Japan. Although the current dependency ratio, at 20.4[79] residents aged 65+ years per 100 aged 15–64, is not as

---

[77] *Ibid.*

[78] *Ibid.*

[79] https://www.statista.com/statistics/966808/old-age-dependency-ratio-singapore/, 29 February 2020.

severe as Japan's ratio of 50,[80] the almost doubling of this ratio since 2010, has serious implications on many fronts. Certainly, time is not on the government's side. The hard truth is that this ratio would climb to 25 by 2030.[81]

Different Retirement Financial Sufficiency

Having had the benefit of seeing how the mismatch in traditional pay-as-you-go schemes can be accentuated by an ageing trend, the Singapore government introduced the individually capitalised pension plan back in the 1950s. Essentially a forced-savings plan for old-age purposes, it operates on the principle of compounding and self-funding. Hence, it is not vulnerable to politically motivated changes to pension benefits rules or in the worst-case scenario, a bankrupt scheme arising from a complete mismatch between withdrawals by disproportionally large elderly pensioners.

It is not enough to persuade residents to work longer. Given the fast-changing economy, Singapore has been focussing on ensuring the elderly will remain active members of society, by providing life-long learning programmes to equip them with the necessary skills to stay relevant. Schemes such as *SkillsFuture* and Intergenerational Learning Programme and institutes like National Silver Academy provide seniors with the opportunity to learn new skills such as IT or even social media, music and the like.

Social interaction between generations towards better mutual understanding is encouraged through the sharing of knowledge and bonding over time. Projects to connect seniors with the community are also abundant, such as the Community Befriending Programme and Silver Volunteer Fund, to ensure that seniors do not feel ostracised but instead feel included in the community. The government also works hard at providing affordable long-term care for the aged.[82]

Many different approaches to addressing ageing issues have been rolled out globally, each tailored to the needs of each society. However, the common theme is one where the government has to

---

[80] https://www.oecd.org/japan/working-better-with-age-japan-9789264201996-en.htm, 20 December 2018.

[81] https://www.moh.gov.sg/ifeelyoungsg/about/what-is-the-action-plan-about, 23 February 2020.

[82] *Ibid.*

> *take charge, to drive the long-term planning, development and implementation of these schemes and policies. Private sector operators can only play a supporting role in specific verticals. The government has to do so, in order for the country to sustain its economy and maintain stability in the society. Hence, this means the tackling of not just economic issues but also social challenges associated with an ageing society. Bonding the community to ensure there is no intergenerational tension and alleviating the financial burden on the working population are just a few of the many challenges the government has to undertake. The short-termism of politics these days make for an even more difficult task against the reality of a need to persevere with a long-term solution. Otherwise, the problems associated with an ageing population will grow exponentially.*

Where does the responsibility of the government end and that of the individual begin? These demarcations can often by blurred by the politics of the day.

Resisting Pressure to Conflate Roles

There are examples aplenty where governments knowingly over-step their regulatory boundaries in order to flex their muscles over a politically sensitive development, such as in the face of a truckers' protest, disallowing the collection of tolls upon completion of a new highway constructed under a PPP arrangement. However, to be fair, it is not always the government that chooses to conflate its various roles towards a political end. Given the preponderance of populist politics these days, the public will not hesitate to lean on governments to do their bidding than have a clear separation of roles. Often, it involves a bailout or in plainspokenness, an unplanned burden to be assumed by taxpayers. This is particularly so during major financial crises affecting numerous retail investors.

The precipitous fall of a once-Singapore favourite national champion Hyflux was a particularly painful episode to witness, least of all the dismantling of the crucial strategic asset base that was painstakingly built up over the years.

Example 7.10: Problems at Hyflux — Muddying the Waters

Watching how Hyflux, a once-promising environmental solutions provider built on its successful membrane inventions, has unravelled from a misstep in financial modelling, is instructive. When insolvency becomes real, who should take leadership or responsibility in addressing the challenges? Should the state be expected to bail out the provider of a key desalination installation?

Creating a NeWater Solution

It was the stuff that entrepreneurial dreams were made of — a highly driven and self-motivated chemistry graduate founded Hyflux whose water membrane inventions enabled Singapore to enhance her own supply of water for both household and industrial purposes. Moreover, these "environmental solutions", comprising membranes and the associated operating systems to form a water value chain were scalable and portable for use in countries that were struggling to provide clean water for their citizens. Hyflux's offerings were very ably extended to include seawater reverse osmosis desalination and integrated water-and-power capabilities.

Before long, there was no shortage of capital providers. This enabled Hyflux to fulfil its ambition of meeting the needs of many communities, from China to the Middle East to North Africa. As water is a critical and strategic resource in all countries and deemed by many to be a public good, that should be made available at a low (read subsidised) cost, the water business is thus highly politicised. The huge capital expenditure (capex) outlay meant that it is incumbent on any investor to carefully assess the political and sovereign risk as the room for error really does not exist.

When it Turns Murky

Hyflux's woes unfortunately began at home in Singapore — in the form of an under-recovery bid for a desalination project, on the assumption of an ability to generate enough surplus revenues from the integrated waste-to-energy plant to cross-subsidise the shortfall. This did not come to pass; an oversupply of gas put paid to projected electricity prices. The cookie crumbled when preference shares could not be redeemed and had to be refinanced at a higher coupon rate, thereby stressing cash flows further. Before long, Hyflux simply had too much debt (S$2.95 billion as at end

March 2018) and was technically insolvent. In May 2018, Hyflux filed for court protection from creditors.

The first appearance in October 2018[83] of a possible white knight in Indonesian entity SM Investments and the ensuing proposed S$400 million restructuring plan provided some brief respite, albeit offering very little comfort as there was an extremely low recovery of investment capital even if approved. The government's regulator Public Utilities Board (PUB), following unsatisfactory performance by Hyflux in not delivering acceptable water quality, gave notice of possible exercise of their contractual rights to take over the Tuas desalination plant for zero value but without seeking compensation. On the back of an assessment of a low probability of resolution of membrane quality issues, talks with this potential white knight SM Investments fell through.[84]

In late November 2019, along came another potential white knight, Utico, a company incorporated in the United Arab Emirates.[85] Utico was prepared to inject an aggregate of S$300 million and an additional Working Capital Line of up to S$100 million. Another investor, Aqua Munda, turned up in December 2019 with a proposal to purchase the debt of specific Hyflux entities.[86]

Who Should Fix the Problem?

This case study is not meant to discuss what went wrong at Hyflux but the controversy around who should fix the wrong. Whenever options look limited, if not unfavourable, the aggrieved lay investor tends to look to the government as the "rescuer of last resort". Let's distil the challenge from the various stakeholders' perspectives.

Investors: Hyflux's creditors are numerous and apart from more than 20 banks, hundreds of noteholders, there were on record some 34,000 perpetual and preference (PnP) shareholders who were owed S$900 million and 16,000 ordinary shareholders. Many felt they had picked a low-risk,

---

[83] https://www.theedgemarkets.com/article/hyflux-rescue-bid-smi-falls-through-amid-conflicting-statements, 6 April 2019.

[84] https://www.straitstimes.com/business/companies-markets/hyflux-says-rescue-deal-with-indonesian-investor-terminated-cancels.

[85] http://investors.hyflux.com/newsroom/20191126_124613_600_DRZL2ALMJPYH XJRI.1.pdf, 26 November 2019.

[86] http://investors.hyflux.com/newsroom/20191217_203147_600_ZMK69TMIIOF3ZLA9. 1.pdf, 17 December 2019.

safe investment, the business of which they understood. After all, Hyflux was supplying water to no less than the PUB, which was most unlikely to default. Besides, the perpetuals offer was rendered readily accessible through the Automated Teller Machines, enabling wide participation by many retail investors. Another school of thought revolved around justifying governmental support for a once-successful local enterprise.

Retail investors have received much-needed support from the Securities Investors' Association (Singapore) (SIAS) who has been representing their concerns and posing probing questions on the proposed deal features.[87] In fact, as early as February 2019, SIAS had already drawn up a list of pertinent questions covering financial and corporate governance, use of funds and business development strategy.[88]

Creditors: This is understandably reduced to a financial equation ultimately. Financial institutions have limited options but to proceed with securing the collaterals whenever a loan turns bad. Other creditors likewise have no alternatives except to try and recover as much as possible, through legal means.

Company and Employees: Demand for clean water has hitherto been strong and the challenge was mainly one of picking sound government counter-parties, weighed against the availability of capital for such heavy capex projects. Operating cash flow management would or should have been top priority.

Employees have obviously been slogging hard given the brisk pace of project development across several geographies. While many shouldn't find it difficult to identify alternative careers, there is presumably pride in the company and the satisfaction of delivering something as essential as water to appreciative communities.

Government: The responses by PUB as a Partner/Client would be largely guided by Water Purchase Agreement terms. Charged with ensuring water security and where the desalination plants form an integral part of Singapore's plan, PUB has very little option but to act responsibly and in national interest. As regards rules governing retail investments, such as easy access to subscription, the Government may indeed review them if these can or should be refined. Ultimately, investor responsibility *vis-à-vis* one's own risk appetite must continue to be the operating principle. The Government should never bail out bad retail investments.

---

[87] https://www.businesstimes.com.sg/companies-markets/sias-asks-utico-hyflux-to-clarify-scheme-terms-for-pnp-investors, 4 February 2020.

[88] https://www.hyflux.com/wp-content/uploads/2019/02/SIAS-Letter-to-Hyflux-Board.pdf, 8 February 2019.

General Public: There was some polarisation between the retail investors in Hyflux and those who were not. The former felt that a government bailout was well justified, whereas the latter would be quick to question why public coffers should be accessed to bail out poor investments, should there be one.

The Hyflux saga continues as the Scheme of Arrangement and other processes would have to run their due course.

> *The state will occasionally find itself in a quandary where all options are not ideal and it remains a very interested stakeholder. Where it involves a contractual relationship with a supplier of essential services, the public may expect some forgiveness or even a bailout when the supplier fails, not owing to fraud or financial misdeeds. Any bailout will create a vicious cycle and cause the procurement system to be dysfunctional. The state, as regulator, should however explore all means of being supportive as the impact of wrong financial modelling could sometimes have a systemic effect.*

What's Considered Essential Services?

Sensitivity over seemingly mundane public amenities can occasionally generate serious, unanticipated concern. What's considered essential services that the government must provide as a "public good" can in itself result in a philosophical debate. Many will readily agree that defence is an essential service that the state must own and deliver, ditto building power plants, the national electricity grid, hospitals, roads, schools and the list goes on. What about national parks? The answer depends on where you are.

Example 7.11: Don't Go Privatising National Parks

Preserving national monuments and heritage sites is often considered to be part of the government's responsibility. In some countries, this can be a heavy recurrent burden which public coffers may not be able to sustain indefinitely. In such circumstances, the answer may be for the state to turn to public–private partnerships to preserve and upkeep these sites lest they fall into disrepair. Such projects have been proven possible in countries such as the US and Italy, but others, like India, are struggling to gain public acceptance.

The Indian government first launched the "Adopt a Heritage" scheme in 2017, an arrangement that would allow private and public corporations to adopt 93 of India's heritage sites for a start, including the iconic Red Fort and the renowned Taj Mahal. These companies would take on the responsibility of preserving property, and building, operating and maintaining amenities at these sites. In exchange, these adopters would receive brand visibility and would be "allowed to charge visitors for semi-commercial activities".[89]

Somewhat surprisingly, this well-intended move was met with significant backlash from the public, with critics fearing this was the government's way of privatising these historical sites. Detractors were vocal in questioning why public–private partnership of such heritage places was even necessary and that it was unacceptable for the government to even think of doing so. There were concerns over the content of the audio-video guides to be produced by the company managing the site, as many monuments have controversial histories, so there would be no telling which historic sources the companies would be using in their guides.[90]

The government has countered such criticisms, insisting that such companies will not be allowed to profit from management of the sites. All advertising and prices set by the company will be subject to government supervision,[91] and profits generated will have to be used for development and maintenance of the site.[92] Moreover, contracts will last for a maximum of five years and will be readily cancelled if government guidelines are not met.[93] The Indian government points out that this project will only help the tourism industry, with upgraded amenities and facilities that would

---

[89] https://thediplomat.com/2018/04/adopt-a-heritage-should-private-companies-be-care-takers-of-indian-national-monuments/, 30 April 2018.

[90] https://www.theguardian.com/world/2018/apr/30/taj-mahal-at-risk-of-being-privatised-under-new-heritage-adoption-scheme, 30 April 2018.

[91] *Ibid.*

[92] https://scroll.in/article/873416/adopt-a-heritage-should-india-let-private-companies-manage-tourism-at-top-monuments, 29 March 2018.

[93] https://www.theguardian.com/world/2018/apr/30/taj-mahal-at-risk-of-being-privatised-under-new-heritage-adoption-scheme, 30 April 2018.

otherwise not be possible with the government's limited budget allocation for heritage conservation. Hence, such an initiative would lead to a win–win situation, with companies fulfilling their corporate social responsibility (CSR) needs by helping make these heritage sites more tourist friendly and also getting to boost their brand visibility on souvenirs and signs.[94] At the same time, the government and public will benefit from improved and well-maintained heritage sites.

Less Controversy Elsewhere

The fact is many countries have already allowed private funding for national parks and monuments — the US and Italy just to name a few. In the US, since 1923, there have been many public–private partnerships with regard to national parks. Some 70 organisations have non-profit partnerships with National Park Services (NPS), and they "enhance visitor understanding, knowledge, and appreciation of the national parks through the services and products they provide" through merchandise, park-related publications and audio-visual programmes, to name a few.

NPS also partners with for-profit companies and works with the National Park Foundation to create licensing agreements for secondary logo placement to allow these corporations to carry NPS-branded items. These companies in turn donate 5% of sales to NPS charities and make grants to NPS friend groups like the Washington State National Park Fund. Such partnerships are crucial in allowing the NPS to obtain funds for the maintenance and development of national parks.[95]

Italy is another prime example of how such partnerships have flourished. The restoration of the Colosseum was the flagship of a series of restoration projects across Italy. Once a tobacco-yellow building with grime-covered surfaces that hadn't been cleaned in over 2000 years, the Colosseum is now creamy white with its intrinsic details on arches clearly visible. This was funded by Tod's, with the project costing US$27.6 million. The public initially had reservations over the private funding of the monument's restoration, which lead to adopting the company's logos crassly appearing on national monuments. Moreover, they feared that it would set a precedent that would lead Italy's heritage sites onto

[94] https://qz.com/india/1266837/red-fort-dalmia-should-private-companies-manage-indias-historic-monuments/, 2 May 2018.

[95] https://theoutline.com/post/6051/the-national-parks-are-in-a-financial-crisis-please-buy-this-sweatshirt?zd=1&zi=3p7hwaop, 27 August 2018.

privatisation. Their concerns were put to rest as the only place Tod's name was visible was in the small lettering on the legally required restoration signs.[96] The dose of subtlety helped with gaining public acceptance.

> *The US and Italy are just two examples of how such initiatives can succeed. In India's case, the problem may be more of a social one than anything else. The government will need to take steps to frame the scheme carefully and set up strict guidelines to ensure this remains a project for the benefit of the public.*
>
> *Given the large budget allocation preservation and maintenance work for national monuments and heritage sites would otherwise impose on the government, such partnerships with the private sector would be helpful, if not necessary. And as shown in the US and Italy, they can work. The Indian government would do well to continue to persevere and address any adverse public opinion.*

Action Towards Social Ill

Every nagging social ill will eventually have a tipping point which then will compel the government of the day to act. Online gambling, ranging from the age-old lotteries to football betting, has been the elephant in the room in many countries. Unlike new-fangled online financial products, online betting has been sitting around, creating discomfort for decades. Often viewed as more a nuisance than serious addiction, many governments have been lethargic towards imposing curbs or tightening regulations. The UK government decided in early 2020 that enough is enough and moved decisively to curb the use of credit cards for gambling.

Example 7.12: UK Not Taking Any More Bets on Credit Card Gambling

> *The indications are all there — gambling addiction has led many to chalk up an unsustainable mountain of personal debt which*

---

[96] https://www.cntraveler.com/story/how-italys-monuments-are-getting-a-makeover, 12 January 2017.

would take years to clear, if at all. Easy access to credit clearly needs to be nipped in the bud and the UK government did precisely that in the winter of 2019–2020.

Gambling has been a centuries' old recreational activity in the UK, including horse racing and competitive sports, notwithstanding constant opposition from religious quarters and social reformers. Over time, small scale casinos became commonplace despite the licensing requirements.

The last major revision of laws regulating gambling in the UK took place in 2005, focusing primarily on introducing a new structure of protection for children and vulnerable adults and circumscribing internet gaming, bring such activity under the purview of the Gambling Act.

Since then, trends have been worrying. The concern was not centred on gambling *per se* but over the impact of easy access to credit via credit cards which is fuelling the ballooning problem of gambling.[97] On record, some 24 million adults in Britain gamble, with a staggering 10.5 million doing so online. Online gambling generated some £5.36 billion or just under 40% of the total revenue over the period April 2018 to March 2019, well ahead of other sectors such as Betting, National Lottery, Casinos, Bingo and the rest.

Anecdotally, almost a quarter of those gambling online using credit cards, totalling around 800,000 in 2018,[98] can be considered "problem gamblers". Credit card availability has fed the addiction, with holders struggling with accumulated debts, aggravated by the compounded fees and interest charges. Essentially, they are gambling with money they do not have.

Obviously, the industry would not move to curb any incidence of addiction. As it is, under the new regulations, from 31 March 2020, all online gambling operators have to offer all customers the Gamstop self-exclusion scheme. (Those who signed up for Gamstop would be unable to use gambling websites and apps for a period of time, in a bid to break the addiction habit.)

By default, the government is ultimately the moral conscience of the society. The gnawing discomfort has given way to an almost blanket ban by the Gambling Commission, effective 14 April 2020, on the use of credit card for all online and offline gambling products, except lotteries for "good causes". As one observer pointed out, a credit card ban is not a silver bullet.

---

[97] https://www.bbc.com/news/business-51103006, 14 January 2020.

[98] https://www.cnbc.com/2020/01/14/uk-government-bans-credit-card-payments-for-gambling.html, 14 January 2020.

> *Instituting a credit card ban on gambling may seem like a harsh step. To be fair, while such a ban would indeed not eradicate gambling altogether, it would nonetheless have a material deterrent effect, increasing friction to addiction formation. It is an example of a scenario where only the state can impose a supposedly draconian but necessary measure. Obviously, the credit card companies would never do that out of the goodness of their hearts. Such a ban would pave the way for the government to adopt a comprehensive approach such as the extent to which there should be advertising over television or even online.*

Reflections

Many governments are wary about sending the wrong messages regarding foreign investments as these investors frequently bring along valuable know-how and a scale of economic activity that would otherwise not be possible. Yet, the extent to which a country should rely on foreign capital is often debatable. Where does constructive economic activity end and where does geopolitical influence begin? Consistency around which sectors might be deemed more sensitive or strategically important, or the foreign ownership limits to be imposed, or the extent of regulations to be applied or the transparency of the investment approval process would be best practices to live by.

The onus on the state to make the ultimate decision, on whether a foreign participant should be allowed into a sensitive area, can cut both ways. Too much of an intrusion on sound strategic grounds could wind up with the government carrying a much heavier financial burden than anticipated. At the opposite end, too little action over a much-needed re-visitation of social considerations to revise public policies might lead to slow burn or an accumulation of challenges or unfavourable consequences.

The Covid-19 crisis has brought all these considerations to a head. Members of the EU now religiously and stringently review all FDIs in businesses considered to be of strategic importance.[99]

---

[99] https://www.mayerbrown.com/en/perspectives-events/publications/2020/04/ger-foreign-direct-investments-into-the-eu-and-germany-in-times-of-covid19 16 April 2020.

This is repeated for traditional trading activity in many other jurisdictions as well, particularly for healthcare equipment and supplies, and food security. The demand surge in something as erstwhile boring as masks has led to the Germans' accusations of piracy on the part of the US government.[100] In short, sovereignty is now in sharper focus, as is self-resilience on all fronts — economic preservation and public well-being. Globalisation is thus given short shrift; the ongoing US–China trade war has not surprisingly taken on pessimistic tones. Collaboration between countries is forced into the back-seat even as each government is directing laser focus to domestic issues. Geopolitics will take on the form of a divided world, around major players.

---

[100] https://www.bbc.com/news/world-52161995, 4 April 2020.

Epilogue

Pre-Covid-19, conventional wisdom was that the lesser the role of the government, the better. However, as the Covid-19 pandemic evolves, public expectations of the extent of state intervention can shift dramatically in certain circumstances as the ongoing responses by various governments have demonstrated.

In peacetime, for mature economies, a light regulatory touch, allowing for free market forces to prevail as much as possible, and a well-defined set of principles for competition seem ideal. In response to the technological disruption to existing businesses and increasing convergence of domains, the government should strive to keep pace with innovation. This ideally understates the inherent difficulty of prescribing the most appropriate level of regulation or intervention, purely because of the asymmetrical distribution of talent. Add to that the misalignment between the tendency towards short-term, populist responses and the usually long-term solutions that are needed for major national challenges. Infrastructure development is one example.

Climate change is another example of this misalignment. Some governments might be overwhelmed by the breadth of what the world is collectively facing, in terms of carbon emissions or global warming, in relation to what they can conceivably do at the individual country level. How would their efforts at switching to more renewable energy move the needle of global emissions? Or if agriculture is a major component of GDP, minimising slashing and burning might help reduce pollution for the world but will bring on hardship for that economy.

Or a country could be at the receiving end of a disproportionately large impact of rising sea levels that presents real urgency to what the government must do. Regardless of circumstances, climate change challenges clearly belong in the agenda of the government, in terms of its having to define the priorities and setting the appropriate commitments. The role of the government here is that of a driver who must enlist the help of the private and public sectors as appropriate.

In wartime, there is no doubt that the government must take full control, act decisively and shepherd all sectors towards a successful outcome. This is particularly evident in the war against the new Corona Virus, tagged Covid-19, for most of 2020.

Unprecedented Corona Virus Battle

The variety of responses by governments is telling, ranging from the seemingly draconian but decisive and effective containment of the spread by the Chinese government to many governments who are struggling to flatten the curve of infection, and reacting mainly to quell the panic of their citizens.[1]

Were the expectation of government leadership of such a pandemic so clearly articulated and accepted from the beginning, that would at least have solved some of the teething problems with quarantine or social distancing impositions. It was unfortunately not so cut and dried. People in many countries understandably were loath to comply with any restrictions to their individual movements or even to the minutest detail like how to greet one another or what sort of crowds should they be a part of.

Some governments appeared to be in denial till the situation escalated, with deaths mounting and the message finally hitting home. Many are observed to be scrambling for a whole host of solutions — from securing basic medical resources like face masks, test kits, personal protection equipment, material equipment like ventilators and oxygen, to ensuring the efficacy of healthcare systems, to assembling sufficient medical personnel who are nonetheless constantly exhausted from being overworked, to invoking public trust in every communication on the pandemic, to imposing an effective travel restriction policy to minimise virus

---

[1] https://www.economist.com/leaders/2020/03/12/the-politics-of-pandemics, 12 March 2020

importation, all without choking off the economy. Once a pandemic has unfolded, regardless of how or what each government is doing, the whole responsibility for dealing with it sits squarely on the government's shoulders.

Contradictory as it might sound, draconian measures like lockdowns, which clearly have a devastating effect on the entire range of businesses, with the exception of telecommunications, have strangely a calming effect on public fear. People are resigned to the inevitable, unilateral imposition of new rules that could potentially decimate many smaller businesses. Again, strange as it may seem, terrified people want their governments to be completely transparent, communicate clearly (over-communicate if necessary), act resolutely and without delay. In short, they want the government to be in full, complete control. This includes subjecting private sector activity to state control, for example, in the production of surgical masks or vaccines, in the national interest. Or the temporary acquisition of real assets or healthcare facilities for the isolation or treatment of Covid-19 sufferers, again for national reasons. Outside of Covid-19, this will be tantamount to nationalisation, albeit temporary. Yet, there is ready acceptance of a world that is "less free, less prosperous and less open".

Hopefully, there would not be too many of such episodes, a deviation from the norm. Pandemics aside, public memory is extremely short these days, as exemplified by the high turnover of political leadership in many countries. This creates a vicious cycle where politicians are motivated to deliver quick wins and live for the here and now. No politician or political party would be foolhardy enough to plan anything beyond an electoral term. That sadly characterises the state of politics in many countries, where the country as a whole would ultimately not have the benefit of long-term planning that many sound economic or social initiatives would require.

Index

CPSIA information can be obtained
at www.ICGtesting.com
Printed in the USA
JSHW021624040321
12224JS00001B/17